Winter Bloom

A Heart Warms in San Miguel

Patricia Jean Browne

Cover design by Mary M. Meade, UpDesign

Internal design by John Edwards

To all my sisters
here now, gone before and yet to come
and
Joseph Elmer Yoakum,
for the Dream

Introduction

In the summer of 1995, my husband and I made a trip to Chicago to see a special exhibit at the Art Institute on Michigan Avenue. After we'd wound through the jammed rooms of *Claude Monet, 1840–1926*, we headed for the lower floor—in Hoosier-speak, the basement—and various lesser shows. Down a corridor, around a corner, the drawings of Joseph Elmer Yoakum grounded me like a bolt of lightning.

The poster read:

Force of a Dream: The Drawings of Joseph E. Yoakum

"… in his early teens, he ran away to join the circus. Yoakum claimed to have visited every continent except Antarctica as a handyman, a valet, a hobo, and a stowaway. He ended up on Chicago's South Side. When he was 74, a dream inspired him to begin drawing. For the ten years until his death, this untrained artist created about 2,000 drawings by the simplest means."

I was 63, had been recording dreams for ten years and writing with stops, starts and stutters forever. I was convinced I would never finish anything.

Here was a model, a model for getting the job done.

Yoakum was not a sterling character—me either. He deserted his family, lied a lot, and died in a mental hospital. I'd left bruises in my wake; more poisoned arrows were yet to fly. Yet his dream inspiration at 74 and his work—powerful, phantasmagorical, prodigious—told me I could do it. If this black, untrained, desperately poor old man could spend his final years working so productively, I could, too. Yoakum's dream inspired me to write, as it had moved him to draw.

Winter Bloom is the fruit of our dreams.

☙

Mary Carr, the accomplished memoirist, beloved by me and many, opened her fabulous memoir, *Lit* with the words: "Any way I tell this story is a lie."

Same for me. *Winter Bloom* is my perspective. What is included, what left out—all my decisions, choices meant to capture my soul's truth. I had no transcripts of the conversations I report. Except where noted, I asked none of the other participant for their memories. Some names have been changed and some events condensed or moved in time for narrative flow, but I made no compromises with emotional honesty—at least consciously.

☙

Soon after *Winter Bloom* was in final form, Mexico tied Brazil in the 2014 World Cup. I rushed to email a vacationing San Miguel attorney and friend, "A great victory for Mexico."

She shot back a quick correction: "A tie is not a victory."

She was correct: the score was Mexico 0, Brazil 0.

Nevertheless, the citizens of San Miguel ran out after the game in their Mexico World Cup shirts, faces painted their flag's red, green and white, waving banners, screaming slogans, and conga dancing around neighborhood streets.

Mexico had barely made it into the World Cup competition after a lackluster year. Brazil was a soccer power and the host of the games. To tie Brazil meant victory to my football fan neighbors.

May *Winter Bloom* match the veracity in those Mexican hearts.

1

February 2001: Albuquerque Sunport

My Southwest flight boards soon. We buy breakfast burritos at Pete's taco stand and sit facing each other across the Formica tabletop. We chew in silence, intent on keeping the beans and eggs from dripping.

Harry takes off his wedding ring. It pings as he plunks it into the ashtray next to our crumpled burrito papers.

"Our marriage is over," he proclaims. He speaks *ex cathedra*, like the pope.

I suppress a chuckle.

He must have practiced the night before. The ring has been on his finger so long only soapsuds could release it. No such problem for me; I lost my original wedding ring long ago, and two replacements after. All three slid easily off my finger; one flew across the room during a yoga class.

We part at the burrito stand, me to my gate, Harry back to the car. His voice trembles, "I don't know when I'll see you again." I feign a sad look. I see I am Hard-Hearted Hannah in this scenario. Ella Fitzgerald sings in my ear as I struggle to look sympathetic:

They call her Hard-Hearted Hannah,

The vamp of Savannah,

The meanest gal in town.

Leather is tough, but Hannah's heart is tougher,

She's a gal who loves to see men suffer!

—Jack Yellen, Bob Bigelow, Charles Bates,
"Hard Hearted Hannah," 1924

I walk away exhilarated—a champagne high, a Lake Michigan high, a *Mayim, Mayim* high-step high. I meander to Indiana by my cheap and circuitous route, on two planes with two layovers, feeling powerfully alive and grateful to be on my own.

৯৯

That morning Harry's voice had awakened me. He lay next to me, our bodies separated by a few inches. We'd agonized endlessly during our two-week babysit. Should we, could we, did we want to, stay married. Our two granddaughters were still asleep; their mother, our daughter Meta, back from California where she'd earned a yoga teacher's certification.

It is time to get up, get ready.

Harry clears his throat. "I talked to Meta last night, and it seems to me it's over. Why don't you take the big suitcase so you can fit more things into it to take to San Miguel?"

I reply, "If you really think our 48-year marriage is at an end, don't you want to talk about something other than suitcases?"

Harry frowns, gives me *the look*. A withering scowl, a flashing red light that signals the line crossed from good wife to traitor. Amazing what Harry can convey with raised eyebrows and downturned mouth.

I am making the right choice. I no longer want to be with this man.

≥●

The dramatic airport denouement is Harry's scene. My plan is a cab to the airport. I am on my way to our Lafayette apartment to pack my personal belongings and return to San Miguel de Allende, my newly chosen home. Later, Harry will fly to San Miguel, pack his gear, and return to Lafayette after I clear out—eliminating another potentially wrenching parting.

But Harry insists on driving me to the airport. He needs help with his ticket. His return ticket from Albuquerque is to Mexico City. Now that I will not be flying with him, this will not work because he does not speak Spanish.

Vintage Harry. I neither blink nor protest.

Mexico City's Benito Juarez airport is huge, crowded, noisy. Takes energy to manage, Spanish or no Spanish, an annoyance Harry is spared by the personal assistant at his side.

At the Continental counter in the Albuquerque Sunport,

the rep speaks English, but Harry's ticket is stamped "Senior Coupon." A change might take time and patience. He risks questions, papers, possible extra charges. His tone would lower; he would enunciate ever more distinctly—not one to lose his temper with a clerk, *noblesse oblige*. Then it might be too much, Harry would explode, demand a manager. The rest of his day will be ruined, given over to self-righteous rehashing of the encounter.

Madame Efficiency Personified glides through the tangled 20-minute process; Harry is squared away with a ticket to BJX in Leon for the coming week, where a van can whisk him straight to his door in San Miguel.

A flawless final performance as spousal caretaker.

৯৯

Spousal caretaker—icy, clinical.

A Good Girl from the Midwest does not leave her husband without a qualm, let alone with a song in her heart. No drama. No emotional turmoil at ending half a lifetime of marriage. No compassion for her bereft husband, no guilt at illicit sex, no mourning for a partnership tended with loving care.

Maybe I deserve the epitaph Harry emails me three times after our breakup: "You betrayed me, you abandoned me, and you broke my heart."

My eyes roll the first time I read it, still Hannah possessed. In the heady first months after Sunport, a tsunami of euphoria sweeps away all in its path.

Then, a sting: Do I feel nothing for the father of my three cherished children? Harry is a good man, as good a partner as he knows how to be. Embarrassing to admit that is not enough. Makes me a princess, a quitter. Not titles I want carved on my tombstone.

My son Tom emails after a paean about my new life in San Miguel: "Please find someone else to crow to about your glee at leaving Dad."

I recall son Ben's comments when my mother refused to go to 12-step meetings after getting sober: "She can never admit she was an alcoholic, because she would have to face the pain she caused those she loved."

Am I ashamed to own the pain I caused?

I cringe; only a monster or a sickie would betray, abandon and break the heart of a husband like Harry. His charge sounds like the script from *As the World Turns*, but the cold fact is that I left him after 48 years for no better reason than because I wanted out.

Hard-Hearted Hannah is soap opera material, too, but there is more to Harry's misery and my flippancy than mawkish melodrama. There is a story, my story.

A story I am called to write. Not that the world needs another memoir. Personal recollection is a crowded genre; the publishing business would fall even flatter on its face without it. The best-sellers are either about famous people or personal triumphs over deprivation, violence or tragic loss. Nothing resembling my life in Green Meadows, the Indiana scene of my married life, or Union, Missouri, the little town where I grew up neither famous nor tormented.

My childhood was tranquil. My mother helped me cut butter cookie dough into stars and press silver balls into the five mushy points. My father bought two horses when I was the right age, just so we could enjoy riding together. My grandmother introduced me to ice cream drumsticks. The nuns at my Catholic school were caring women, not the reincarnated mafia of *Saturday Night Live* fame.

૨ം

After I married—as we all did—more low-key scenes roll.

I pour over the *Lafayette Journal Courier*, clipping coupons for the week's groceries. I comb the A&P aisles for the bargains, and toss *Woman's* Day into my shopping cart at the checkout counter. (TV campaign: "She has to go out to get *Woman's Day*.") I serve Unstuffed Cabbage to my husband and three children from a recipe in *McCall's*—that subscription is delivered to my mailbox. When they sop up the sauce with my homemade bread, I file away the tomato sauce-stained page in my maple recipe box. We watch *Leave It to Beaver* as a family.

My quiet corner of the 20th century is more likely to incite yawns than exorcisms. It is a tale with no villains or scandalous secrets—just the day-in, day-out routines of a marriage, largely unremarked and unexamined—so mundane who would want to read it? Or write about it?

And yet.

I share those days with a generation of sisters—my State Street Gang high-school buddies, fellow members of the Green Meadows babysitting pool, and a shadowy cadre of nameless, voiceless women. We recognize "the problem that has no name," in *The Feminine Mystique*, as soon as Betty Friedan captures it in black and white. Why, when we have the good life of our aspirations?

Friedan's analysis portends the Pat who left Sunport with a spring in her step. Unclear how or why, as befits a problem with no name. The answers are buried in my history and Harry's, our origins and the 17,520 days we shared. If Pompeii was reconstructed from shards of pots, icons of goddesses, and discarded spears, I can unearth clues in our life's clutter. My dig will mine the years from the 1930s to the end of the 20th century.

Telling our story is my special mitzvah, for myself and my silent sisters.

An ancient tradition teaches that every Jew has a special mitzvah (good work) to perform, one that belongs to the unique root of that person's soul, and it is waiting for him or her to discover it.

—Arthur Green, *Ehyeh: A Kabbalah for Tomorrow*

2

St. Louis, 1935: Wives Take Care of Their Husbands

Patricia Jean Browne, born October 20, 1932

Back, further back, all the way back—to the roots of the Pat springing onto her Southwest flight to Indiana without a pang for the pain she left in her wake. To little Pat, where Wife, Mother, Grandmother, Father and Husband first transfused into her child-sized veins.

Grandmother (Gram)
Lillian Rose Hendricks Neunuebel, born September 5, 1886

Father
Andrew Barnes Browne, born May 29, 1900

Mother
Virginia Nora Neunuebel, born February 12, 1912

ð&

My mother stands over the kitchen sink, her hands plunged in the white foam on my father's head, bent over in front of her. Water and suds run down her elbows and disappear into the sink. She stands tall in her high heels. When Gram tells about a neighbor who cannot wait to kick off her shoes after work, Mother brags, "I always do housework in my heels."

ʃ✦

Mother washes my hair in the bath. It feels good. She kneels by the side of the tub and tells me to keep my eyes closed so I don't get soap in them. I obey. Bathing, shampooing are luxurious, sensual—although no one ever says so. A hot bath is still one of my life's special treats. I wondered why Dad preferred showers and was not content until we got our own house, so that he could put a showerhead in the basement next to his punching bag. He boxed as a young man and still worked out on the punching bag hung from the ceiling.

ʃ✦

In St. Louis we share the basement with three other flats. A turtle lives down there. He wobbles out when he hears Gram and me coming down the stairs. Gram comes to our house once a week to "do a wash," a far cry from loading clothes in one machine, then moving them to another in 2013 mode.

First Gram rolls out three big silver tubs from the corner, fills one with hot soapy water, another with cooler water, a third with bright blue water that I now know is bluing, a product that disappeared with the ice man and his cold shoulder. One tub is topped by the infamous wringer, which Gram repeatedly warns me about with the dramatic tale of Aunt Lillian getting her hand caught. Since I can barely reach the wringer, I enjoy her animated storytelling but never fear the wringer like I do cockroaches.

When she spills water or empties the tubs, the turtle drinks, stretching his neck with its wrinkled skin collar out of his shell and tilting his beak up to let the water flow down his throat. The turtle's job is to eat the water bugs so they don't come upstairs, where there are already roaches. Roaches are my mother's nemesis. She does battle with the sneaky creatures constantly. The ones upstairs are smaller and redder than the ones downstairs. And very, very determined. Mother prides herself on a spotless house, would never leave a dirty dish in the sink for more than the time it takes to finish a meal.

Roaches are a sign of a slovenly housekeeper, an indicator of filth to my mother. And there they are, every time she turns on the kitchen light, racing like lightning for safety, higher than she can reach, or into a crack in a cupboard door. Sometimes they freeze stock-still, hoping to disappear into the wallpaper. But Mother sees them. She screams, "Hermans!" (Their species is the German roach, which she translates into a German name common in our South St. Louis neighborhood.)

She grabs the slipper off her foot. When she squishes one, it explodes into ugly gummy gunk and shattered dark red shell on her clean wall—disgusting. I still respond to the sight of a roach like a cave woman confronted with a charging mastodon. They are the hidden evil forces that lurk in dark corners, and no amount of rationalizing and talking to myself helps.

ꝫ🙽

The basement holds many treasures besides my turtle. There is the furnace, a dark metal monster that swallows Gram's shovels of black lumps from the pile higher than my head in the corner. On the wall above the pile is the dark square metal door that swings open to let the coal truck dump coal and soot between our flat and my playmate Ronnie's building. (I get my first lesson in gender differences when Ronnie pees on the sloping door while we are playing in the passageway, and I wet my pants trying to do it, too.

ꝫ🙽

When Gram is in our house, she "fires the furnace." Mostly this is shoveling the coal into the open metal door. Unless the fire has gone out, which means someone has forgotten to add coal. All agree Gram is the best fire starter. I watch her twist newspapers, lay them in a pattern, then add kindling to the furnace's stomach.

Mother forgets to go down and add coal one cold wintry evening. Dad, then still at work, forgot to buy kindling. Mother chops up his rowing machine to start the fire, a story Dad tells later at Brusati's to every friend that comes into the bar. "Can you believe she did that?" Dad would say. The newcomer laughs and stops at our booth to schmooze.

On Friday nights, if Dad comes home early enough, we go to Brusati's for supper. I order a miniature hamburger. My bottom slides around in the polished booth as I sip root beer through a straw and listen to the grown-ups. It is our neighborhood living room; most flats are too small to hold many people, so the community gathers here at the end of the workweek to unwind. Brusati's gives me a warm feeling for taverns; our little threesome belongs to the wider world of neighbors who all seem to know us and like to be with us.

This is my introduction to my father's charm. Later, I loved hearing him recite parodies to Robert W. Service poems. My father knew many of the Scotch poet's verses by heart, and frequently wrote parodies to them for special occasions, like this one based on "The Shooting of Dan McGrew." I only remember the first lines:

> A bunch of the boys were whooping it up
> At Friese's corner saloon.
> When the boys from the cutting room walked in …

The first stanza of the original:

A bunch of the boys were whooping it up in the Malamute
saloon;

The kid that handles the music box was hitting a jag-time
tune;

Back of the bar, in a solo game, sat dangerous Dan
McGrew,

And watching his luck was his light-o'-love, the lady that's
know as Lou."

Around the dinner table, Dad's stories captivate all guests.
His mother says her son, Andy could charm the birds right
out of the trees, which I gather is an old Irish expression.

ِ

Mother is always around, but not my father. He is "at work".
Mother sighs that sometimes he does not see his Pat from
Monday through Saturday because he leaves our flat before I
am awake and comes home when I am in bed. The
arrangement seems normal to me, but Mother misses having
Dad around more.

I see where my father works on the night of the Veiled
Prophet parade (see Chapter 3A) in December. Mother, Dad,
Gram and I go downtown to the Browne-Tilt office. Other
employees and their families crowd the office and the windows
above the parade route. Mother lifts me to a windowsill and
guards me with her arms as the parade approaches. I watch the
glittery troupe in the street below—a float where the Veiled

Prophet waves to the crowd. He is surrounded by his Queen of Love and Beauty and her four debutante attendants in fluffy long dresses, carrying bouquets.

❧

Every Sunday morning my father appears and takes me to the St. Louis zoo. We tour the bird house, snake house, the sea lion tank and the monkey house, where I remember seeing the monkey's bright red bottom as he clings to the wire high up in his cage. My favorite is the hippopotamus' deep, dank-smelling tank. It stretches right up to the bars where we stand. On lucky Sundays his shiny, black leather shape rises from the water. He climbs the steps on the end, shakes his giant hippo self and showers droplets on Dad and me. He looks too top-heavy to walk, but he pads around the wet cement, each broad foot hitting the concrete with a slurp. I am told I report to my mother every week on the "hip-on-the-pot-a-muss."

Sometimes we stop on the way home. I am just big enough to swirl around on the leather barstool. Dad coaches me on our routine, when we get home:

Dad: "What did we do after the zoo, Pat?"

Pat: "Went to Brusati's."

Dad:" What did you do there?"

Pat: "I had red soda; Daddy had brown soda."

Mother manages an appreciative "Oh, Andy" on cue.

My whooping cough is a milestone; what I remember best is my Jeep.

Dad takes me every night to Dr. Vandover's office for a shot in my bottom. When the series of shots is over, I choose my reward for bravery at the Walgreen's on the corner of Kingshighway and Chippewa: a Jeep doll. The Jeep is a character in the Popeye comics Grandpa Browne reads me every Sunday; a magical animal that can go through walls and make himself invisible. He never lies.

I am disappointed when I take him out of his box; he is the same daffodil yellow as Popeye's Jeep, but different from his image in the funny papers. My Jeep has jointed arms, legs and tail; Popeye's is all smooth yellow fur and huge red nose.

I understand my Jeep can't go through walls, but I pretend that he can. I send him to listen to my parents talk in the next room. My lifelong habit of eavesdropping is launched; the Jeep made me do it.

When I cough so much I cannot keep food down, there is serious concern for my life. Overheard conversations I later piece together condemn Dr. Vandover, who refused to give me the new whooping cough vaccine earlier, saying it wasn't proven, and if I got sick, he would give me small doses so that I would have a mild case.

My father is angry. "Mild case, like hell. Damned old fogey, Pat could have died because of him." My mother just cries. Maybe that is why it is my father who takes me for my shots; I sense there is something hush-hush about it. I hear Gram repeat several times that Dr. Vandover is a good man, his son went to high school with her son, my Uncle Eddie.

When I can eat again, we celebrate at Pelican's, with its white tablecloths and huge menu with Technicolor fish and lobsters swimming around its cover. There was no fast food then; restaurant meals were rare treats. We order dishes we don't have at home, like fresh fish or handmade ravioli. Mother orders for me, the child's frog legs plate: miniature deep-fried drumsticks. I chew the woody remains down to the last bone-sucking, gristly, salty, greasy bite. Pelican's frog legs foreshadow an adult guilty pleasure—the Colonel's deep-fried chicken wings.

❧

Mine is a female adult landscape. No other little people; we soon move away from next-door Ronnie. There is Cousin Margaret Ann, but she is three years older and lives at Aunt Hattie's house, far away in my childhood geography. It is a warm world. I loll immersed in the rhythm of Mother and Gram's palaver, at their feet, in their laps, on the couch under the afghan Gram crocheted, peeking through the holes of rose, yellow, blue green and purple yarn, dozing, lulled by their buzzing voices.

Warm memories: Hand-held walks on St. Louis pavements—Lindenwood, Mardell, Watson Road; big people towering by; my white-socked black-patent-leather foot raised high over every gaping joint: "Step on a crack, break your mother's back."

Davincini's grocery, where Mother enthrones me on the counter. Mrs. D's high pitched coos as she picks the ripest berry from each wooden box to pop in my mouth.

Escalator rides, feet planted over moving ridges disappearing into the floor. Aunt Thelma takes me up all eight floors at Famous Barr, from sweet-smelling ONE (Cosmetics) to drab EIGHT (Office) and a U-turn down to THREE (Hats), where Mother asks Thelma, bow or flower? I roam the hat-filled tables. One color to a table: red, blue, purple. Back to mother at the straw-colored table, where a lady slides a daisy hat into a striped FB box. Mother holds the braided string handle high when she steps onto the streetcar home.

Visits to Gram's flat where we walk down the street to a belled door where a lumpy man's hand disappears into a case, holds up two drumsticks, crinkly paper wrappers dusted with fluffy ice crystals. Nearly back to Gram's, sated, I bite the cone bottom for its nugget of solid chocolate. White ice cream trails melt on my jacket. Gram laughs, stops, spits on her handkerchief, wipes my mouth, finishes my sagging drumstick.

New Year's Eves at Gram's. At midnight we bang pots with spoons in the street. Only us, no neighbors come. Later Gram confesses she set the clock ahead; when our closely watched clock hands were straight up, the real hour was 9 o´clock, my bedtime.

Aunt Hattie's house. My great-aunt Hattie raised Gram after their mother died. All the women of the family crowd into her South St. Louis bungalow, a streetcar ride away from our flat on Lindenwood.

Two outsized cherry trees in her backyard -yield pie cherries every spring. Margaret Ann and I scale the thick lower branches, pick what we can reach, pop the ripest into our mouths, the rest in the coffee cans hung around our necks with the soft heavy string that comes on packages in the mail. Uncle Martin picks the tops—what the birds don't get—on a creaky extension ladder.

The adults bake pies—plain cherry, cherry custard, cherry-rhubarb. The overflow goes into cherry preserves and rows of shiny square Mason jars with lids of silver lined with white ceramic, ready for winter baking. Aunt Hattie's house smells like hot cherry juice.

We feast at a table that fills the room—Mother's *mostaccioli*, Aunt Nettie's baked green peppers and tomatoes stuffed with rice and ground meat, Gram's German potato salad, Cousin Lillian's spaghetti from her Italian neighbor's secret family recipe.

The Buder School picnic in June is bigger than Christmas Eve: Margaret Ann's school's end-of-the-year picnic at the Forest Park Highlands.

We arrive early on the streetcar, Mother and Gram lugging a giant picnic basket and heavy purses. Lillian, Aunt Hattie and Aunt Nettie meet us at the park with Margaret Ann in tow. The women commandeer a massive wooden picnic table on a concrete slab in the park pavilion. They play cards all day—poker or every rummy game from gin to Liverpool. Never mahjong; the tiles are too valuable to take out of the house and risk losing.

Margaret Ann and I ride the rides. The Tilt-A-Whirl is our favorite until we are old enough to ride the monster roller coaster, The Comet. We bounce from ride to ride, cotton candy to Cracker Jack, with Margaret Ann's Buder School passes or nickels begged from the card players. At noon the picnic baskets come out from under the table. I eat Gram's coleslaw and breaded pork chop sandwiches, still the Blue Ribbon picnic fare for me.

This warm sisterhood wraps me in its embrace. I plan to bask in it forever.

Until an even warmer community bobs up to lure me away.

੧

Aunt Thelma is not with Mother and me on that momentous day. We shop, first at Stix, then Scruggs, then end at the old reliable of the triumvirate of department stores in downtown St. Louis—Famous & Barr Company. The three stores and the paths between them are as familiar to me as the rooms of our flat. Downtown St. Louis was an enchanted land: bustling, fresh, a different adventure every trip.

Mother says she is taking me to the Playroom. She says "Playroom" with a lilt; I am suspicious. She used that tone before my first visit to Dr. Vandover's office. I don't trust her smile and light patter. I tighten my grip on her hand.

A lady talks to Mother at a big door with two halves; one swings in to where the lady stands in a bright blue smock with something printed on the front. I see many people my own size inside. Some are at tables with crayons, others sit in sand in a box on the floor. When I get inside, I forget Mother. A boy takes my hand and pulls me to a dark green ... I don't know what it is, but we bounce up steps to where other children sit in the corners. It's a boat, a boat that rocks when we jump up and down or lean back and forth in the seats. We scream and laugh, all squeezed together in one corner. The boat floor goes waaaaay up. Better than eight floors of escalators, and from then on I beg to be taken to the Playroom whenever we go downtown. Mother is not always cooperative. I think she had some trepidation, maybe even guilt, about leaving her child in the care of strangers. Mothers were supposed to be on duty 24/7, after all.

Seventy years later, the boat shows up in a dream, still a symbol of delight. Some boat.

ə⁂

Gram and Mom natter on about shoes and blouses and white socks. New things show up—a book bag with leather straps and places for my new pencils and crayons and erasers.

Mother and I walk down Kingshighway, across the street from Kreigshauser Funeral Home, all the way past the Avalon Theatre. Up steps. Through a door. Down a hall. An open door. Boys and girls just a little bigger than me—many, many more than at the Famous Barr Playroom. Mothers are there, too. I get a name card with "PAT" printed in big letters. The teacher smiles as she pins it on my blouse.

After that I go to kindergarten every morning at Mary Magdalene. There are colored papers on all the walls with pictures and letters and numbers. The teacher reads to us in a big circle. Sometimes I read to other children when it is play time. Mary Magdalene does not have *Dotty Dolly's Tea Party**, which I memorized at home, but a long shelf with many other books. I tell the story about the pictures as I turn the pages, fun for me and the other kids, too.

We sit in little wooden chairs and draw or color or paint. I sit next to Eugene Bodendistl the day we make paper chains. I know his name, a real South St. Louis moniker which still makes me smile, because Eugene's father works with my father. He shows me how to hide the paste under the table and eat it when the teacher is not looking.

❧

I have a copy of *The Queen Cooks*, a collection of recipes published as a fundraiser by Mary Magdalene parish women. There is an ad for Kreigshauser Mortuaries promising "Unexcelled Parking Facilities." The Avalon Theatre, where we got free Fiestaware dishes, says, "For a pleasant evening's entertainment, visit the Avalon Theatre at Kingshighway and

Chippewa." (Today Fiestaware sells at Macy's for $27.99 for a four-piece place setting.)

ॐ

The next year I start first grade at Mallinckrodt School, in a trailer. The school is still a big hole surrounded by piles of dirt and bricks next to our playground. Emil Mallinckrodt, another South St. Louis tongue twister, founded a pharmaceutical company in 1840, now based in Dublin. He must have given the land or money for a new public school. Mother grumbles that her Pat should not have to go to school in a shack, but my cozy classroom is perfect in my eyes.

My teacher is my idol. Miss Barker can print words on the blackboard just like they look in our Dick and Jane book. She knows everything.

"Think about your summer," she says. "Now go to the board and write a sentence about what you did."

Perfect—I went north to visit my father's cousins. I rush to the closest blackboard.

"I went to Eo Claire and saw an Indian," I print.

Mrs. Barker erases "Eo Claire" and prints "O'Claire."

"That's not right," I say.

She prints "O'Clare."

"No, no," I protest again.

"Those are the only two ways, so pick one," she says, and moves on to the next student.

Shock. If she couldn't spell the most important city in Wisconsin, well ... I chose O'Clare because I did not want to hurt her feelings, but when I got home and Mother wrote *Eau Claire,* I knew Miss Barker was not infallible—which made me more skeptical of the Pope later.

❧

The community I first met in the Famous Barr playroom, Mary Magdalene's kindergarten, and first grade with Miss Barker was the breath of life. I inhaled it all and went back for more: books and paper chains, bobbing for apples on Halloween and hopscotch at recess, blackboards and composition books, fat crayons and tasty paste. I came alive as a student among students. *Dotty Dolly's Tea Party* and the funnies with Grandpa on Sunday morning paled after I discovered school, the real thing. I hoped to spend the rest of my life in this paradise.

> Sooner or later something seems to call us onto a particular path. You may remember this "something" as a signal moment in childhood when an urge out of nowhere, a fascination, a peculiar turn of events struck like an annunciation: This is what I must do, this is what I've got to have. This is who I am.
>
> —James Hillman, *The Soul's Code: In Search of Character and Calling*

3

Shadows

There was more to my early life than the Buder School picnic, idyllic rides on the Famous Barr boat, and trips to the basement to visit the turtle.

Charged voices drift from other rooms, through doors left ajar. When I move closer the talk stops or I am sent away with a book. In my books no one shouts, gets mad, or slams doors. I strain to hear the dark things that get everybody excited—the names hissed in guttural asides looking back over shoulders. "Don't let Pat hear."

વ

There is something about bars. Our Friday nights at Brusati's are respectable, but drinking causes trouble, too.

Aunt Nettie's son, known as Drunken Uncle Louie, binges his family into destitution, so a sympathetic pastor appoints him sacristan at St. Roch's. One evening Louie has a "predomination." As he climbs the church steps with his mop, St. Roch's statue glares from his perch at the top of the steps, raises his shepherd's crook, and whaps Uncle Louie on the head. Louis awakens at the bottom of the stairs and swears never to touch a drop again—a promise he keeps for 24 hours, according to the version repeated at family gatherings, to appreciative guffaws.

I know the right word for what Dad drinks after the zoo is "beer," but "brown soda" changes it to an okay story, like the priest sprinkling holy water on Gram's rosary. No holy water can excuse Uncle Harold when he spends his paycheck at the bar next to work so Aunt Nettie has no carfare to get to her sister's, nor Uncle Eddie's "night out with the boys" that makes him pee in the closet when he gets home.

è▲

Some people are shadows, off limits. Margaret Ann's father. Whispers—Was he French? Far away? Margaret never talks about him. I learn much later that Margaret's mother is pregnant again, long after the marriage breaks up. When her belly gets too large to conceal, Aunt Hattie confronts her daughter and arranges to "take care of it." I wonder if my cousin Margaret ever knew. She is dead before I hear the story.

My grandfather. Gram never mentions her husband. Only slips:

Gram to Mom: "... always taking laxatives—many's the time I got the Milk of Magnesia out for you and he drank it first."

"Too bad you and Ed got your father's slew-footed walk. Bob was lucky and escaped."

Mother to me: "When you were a baby, I took you to the hospital so my father could see his first grandchild before he died."

Ѣ❖

My mother had two brothers, Eddie, the elder, Gram's Golden Son, and Bob, the younger. When I begin this memoir, with Gram dead and my mother's brain pickled, I mail the first chapters to Uncle Eddie to read.

When I visit him in his Arkansas home, he says I got his father all wrong.

"You say your parents' marriage caused trouble between my parents?" he asks.

"Yes." I repeat the official family script, that my grandfather was a strict Catholic who could not countenance Mother's marriage to a divorced man. It would mean, in the church's eyes, living in sin with my father. Excommunication. Gram sided with Mother and the marriage. The clash was one of the reasons for my grandparents' separation.

"My parents were never divorced," Eddie huffs, as if this proves his point.

"I never heard about a divorce, but they were not living together when your father died," I said. "Right?

Eddie answers agitated, annoyed.

"My father loved Andy. He thought he was a fine husband for your mother."

"Then why did your parents break up?"

Eddie pauses, sighs, "I really have no idea."

ε.

Eddie and Uncle Bob lived in their parents' apartment at the time of the separation. Not a big space, likely. No sign of trouble visible between a couple living under the same small roof?

I would ask Bob.

ε.

Later that summer I visit Bob in Michigan, retired from his final working days in Taiwan. His third wife, Piquei, brings tea and leaves us to our talk. I report my conversation with his brother.

Bob turns away and looks out the window, where Piquei is filling the gazillion bird feeders in their spacious yard. He lights a cigarette, takes a few puffs, and turns back to me.

"Eddie threw Dad out," he says.

"We all lived in that flat on Mardell—hard times, you know—the Depression, not much work. Dad came home drunk and belligerent one night, mouthed off to Mom, and Eddie threw him out in the street. His clothes after him."

He pauses, looks at me, sees I am shaken. I suspect that is all I will hear. But after a moment, he continues, his voice darker, secretive.

Months later a message comes. His father is sick. Bob goes to the address, a tavern in a raunchy neighborhood. A woman leads Bob through the bar, not yet open for business, through a storage room piled with empty beer cases. The woman says she owns the tavern and is Ed's woman. They enter a cramped room where his father lies amid the smell of dank sheets. His father can barely speak; Bob calls a doctor from a pay phone in the darkened tavern. The doctor arrives and sends his dad to a hospital, where he dies of rectal cancer shortly thereafter.

ও

A different story is spun around the family table.

Mother needles her brother Bob about the visit to their father in the hospital. Told he would need a transfusion, both children agree to donate blood. Bob turns white at the prospect, and Mother offers to be the first donor. Bob opines it is not right to let a woman go first; he will steel himself. Their father dies before the blood is needed. Mother laughs, says Bob got off the hook.

ও

The lessons I learned at home: Husbands earn money and women maintain a welcoming home for them to come home to. The women's world of high heels, warm afghans, hot baths, breaded pork chop sandwiches and cherry pies is warm and embracing, but there are rules: Ignore unfortunate pregnancies, never mention family members' misdeeds, and transmute tragedies like Uncle Louie's alcoholism and Grandpa's death to a good story.

The Famous Barr boat, *Dotty Dolly's Tea Party*, Mary Magdalene and Mallinckrodt are all refuges from the shadows. As is my house in Mexico on Refugio Sur.

3A

The Veiled Prophet: A Detour to the Main Road

Curiosity prompted me to Google "Veiled Prophet Parade and Ball" after writing about it. I wondered when the arcane custom had ended; sure it could not have survived into the 21st century. Wrong. The 2014 Ball is scheduled for December 22; the parade has been moved to the Fourth of July—better marching weather in St. Louis. The photos of the 2013 Ball published in a St. Louis magazine include one black deb among the blond beauties. The Veiled Prophet Organization's website lauds the group's current civic-mindedness.

The more I read, the more I knew the Veiled Prophet belonged in my tale. A better representative could not be found of the sexist, racist, classist milieu into which I was born than the Veiled Prophet of Khorassan. The Prophet's events, a parade and a ball, were the brainchild of a St. Louisan who'd admired the New Orleans Mardi Gras and imagined a local version. The Veiled Prophet of Khorassan is a fictitious character in a poem by Thomas Moore.

The St. Louis knockoff followed the year after the Great Railroad Strike of 1877, a bitter dispute that included large numbers of African-American workmen, men called by an uglier name in late 19th-century Missouri. The first parade and ball were poster events for the all-white Social Register crowd. Nonetheless it caught on with rich and poor; the first parade and grand ball, on October 8, 1878, attracted over 50,000 spectators.

An incident in 1928 says it all. The official records for that 50th anniversary celebration list no queen. Mary Ambrose Smith had secretly married Dr. Thomas Birdsall days earlier, wantonly ignoring the rule that the Queen of Love and Beauty must be a "maiden" (read virgin). She wore her scarlet letter silently (would that be "W" for Wife?) for 50 years, but in a 1979 interview with the *St. Louis Times*, Smith talked. When the scandal broke, the Veiled Prophet demoted her in a huff, told her to get out of town, not to register at any large hotels or use her real name. Smith had disgraced her family. She was barred from former friends' homes, never invited to another VP ball, her picture removed from queens' portraits at the Missouri Historical Society, and her name deleted from the Social Register. Take that, ingrate non-maiden.

Voices were raised against these human rights violations over the years, among them, protests by the *St. Louis Labor*, the leading socialist and working-class newspaper. The dissenters were dismissed as Communists, the all-purpose description of protesters or, indeed, union members.

In those same years, my father recalled delightful nights spent drinking in St. Louis riverside bars with "Communists" in the days before his marriage. Maybe he took my mother, too. One of the gals always jumped up on the table to dance—in her bare feet, which Dad thought was a racy tweak. He made the people sound like great fun, Commies or no. One of the people he especially liked was an artist named Joe Jones, who I learned was a successful artist as well as a rabble-rouser. *The Encyclopedia of the Great Plains* praises his painting depicting workers' demonstrations and a lynching, and then remarks that his flight to New York to escape prosecution in St. Louis on a charge of spreading Communist propaganda was "a wise career move."

Meanwhile, the good people of St. Louis continued to wave at the Prophet and his Court every December.

In 1972 the civil rights group ACTION (Action Committee to Improve Opportunities for Negroes) held a number of demonstrations against the Veiled Prophet's human rights record. The climax was during the Ball itself, when protest journalist and activist Gena Scott slid down a power cable in Kiel Auditorium and unmasked that year's Prophet, Monsanto Company Executive Vice President Tom K. Smith.

Scott's car was later bombed, and her apartment vandalized numerous times. Her "subversive act" unveiled the prophet in more than his costume. The publicity that followed revealed that as late as the early 1960s, Jews could not attend the Veiled Prophet Ball. In 1979 the Veiled Prophet Organization admitted its first black members. Two years later, fair officials closed the Eads Bridge to pedestrian access from East St. Louis on the day of the parade, fearing for public safety from protests. East St. Louis is largely black.

Dissenters grew when it was circulated that the Veiled Prophet events, supposedly advertising a united St. Louis, used taxpayers' money to venerate rich white folks. William Maritz, an ex-Veiled Prophet, complained, "People are saying 'get that goddamned ball off of television.'"

Recent commentary is more pointed.

Angry Black Bitch Blogspot rebuked the editor of Vanity Fair for a 2010 cover picture of a bevy of Hollywood stars for its lack of diversity with the comment, "My gods, man ... that cover is a freakish look-a-like of a debutant class photo from the Veiled Prophet Ball ... Sincerely tired of this tired ass shit."

❧

Four-year-old Pat, watching the parade pass in the street below, was oblivious to all this, but in later years I was troubled by my parents' divergent views when December and Veiled Prophet time came each year. When my mother oohed and aahed over the pageantry and gorgeous gowns, my father harrumphed.

To him the whole shebang was another vulgar display of upper-class wealth. He compared the Veiled Prophet to the

British royal family, which disgusted him with their hoity-toity ways. Always a loyal Irishman, my father could not forget what his people suffered at the hands of the English.

Mother admired the rich; my father rolled his eyes. I was more sympathetic to my father's opinions, but I resented Dad's sneering at Mother's views as silly, womanish, borderline stupid. And I liked the pretty dresses, too.

It took me a long time to sort it all out.

4

1935–1953: Union

A move was in the works, a move to Franklin County, Missouri: a step closer to my husband-to-be. Thirteen years, a bat mitzvah age later, Harry and I would meet in my parents' home in Union. He lived in Washington, 10 miles distant over a two-lane road winding through rolling hills.

≈

While I was reveling in first grade, my father hatched another business. Suddenly St. Louis was history.

His first entrepreneurial venture, Browne-Tilt Pattern Company, was what had kept him so busy I rarely saw him in our Lindenwood flat. He'd quit his job at another pattern company in protest. His salary, along with everyone else's, had been cut because of the Depression, which he considered unfair since he was the company's most productive salesman. He could do better on his own—typical of the cocky Irish grit that propelled him far. It was 1935, the year the WPA (Work Projects Administration) was founded by Congress and funded with an initial $4.9 billion to give jobs to unemployed workers.

"Good thing I didn't realize that my reduced salary would buy more than the old one because of so many prices falling. If I hadn't gotten mad and quit, there'd have been no Browne-Tilt and no Bourbeuse Shoe; I might have gone to my grave working for somebody else."

His new venture was a high-fashion women's shoe factory. He and his partners zeroed in on Union, a hamlet of 2,000 souls on the banks of the Bourbeuse River. The town's biggest employer, another major shoe company, had closed its doors the year before after a prolonged strike, throwing its crew of skilled shoemakers out of work. Union was desperate, like many little towns in those dark years.

Excerpts from my father's speech urging investment in the new factory:

Members of the Chamber of Commerce of Union:

I am not going to attempt a speech, nor talk at great length; rather I will give you the facts of our venture in plain unvarnished terms.

Last Monday night at the request of Mr. Jennings, a group which included besides himself and myself, Mr. Neunuebel and a salesman who is now out on his territory, all successful men in the St. Louis shoe area, made an offer to open a shoe factory here under certain conditions. We are practically set to open in an Illinois city, but Mr. Jennings prevailed upon us to come to Union to see if something could be worked out for us here.

I could stand here all night telling you how much an additional factory would benefit this city, and I would merely be telling you something you already know, and have known for a long time. It would reduce unemployment by a considerable degree, and give many families who are perhaps now just getting by, a sufficient income to buy more and better merchandise, and in many cases replace furniture and equipment around the home, articles that people just don't replace unless there is ample money in the house.

The idea of our factory was conceived some six months ago, and has progressed to this point in an extremely orderly fashion up to even having our first shoes sold. All of the men in this group have known each other over a long period of years, and are thoroughly familiar with one another's ability. In a conversational way they discovered that all had ambitions in the same direction, namely to get into the shoe business, and felt that if they banded together they would have an extremely strong organization. Every necessary corner is filled by a man expert in his field, without any dead timber; the organization is as clean as a hound's tooth.

While these might sound like strong words, they are nonetheless true. Mr. Neunuebel is without a doubt the most able designer in the popular-priced field, and is recognized as such by many of the country's largest shoe buyers. He has styled the K.D.K. line in Washington, Missouri, for the past year and a half, and many of you are familiar with what he has done there. Shortly after he went with them they raised their grade by a dollar, and the factory has been sold solid ever since. He resigned this week, without giving any intimation of his future plans, and has already turned down an offer which would net him $15,000 per year. His salary with us will be a very small part of this amount, but he knows with the organization we have, he will be far better off in the long run working for himself. However, the present sacrifice he is making indicates what he thinks of the future of this company.

Our salesman, whose name I cannot mention at this time, can sell practically our entire output. He will work on a commission basis just as he is now, and at present his commissions are running around $20,000 a year.

He has held most of his present customers for the past 12 years, and is the type of salesman whose customers rely upon him for merchandising advice, such as what types to buy for the coming season, what colors, how many pair, how to promote them, etc. He is not leaving 12-year-old connections without being very sure of his ground, you can bet your bottom dollar on that.

Mr. Jennings is too well known for me to say much about him. We know he is the best shoemaker in our grade in the St. Louis area, which is the wide world as far as we are concerned. I want to say now that if Mr. Jennings does leave Union—and I know he has other offers pending, most of them with a damned sight less work than he will have opening a new factory—if that should come to pass, your loss would be far greater than any of you can realize.

That leaves me; I make and grade shoe patterns. Mr. Neunuebel and myself have worked as a team for a long time with great success, and know what we can do together. After calling on the trade for some 12 years, designing, selling and making shoe patterns, I helped organize the Browne-Tilt Pattern Company some three and a half years ago. The firm was successful from the start, is highly successful right now, and I am leaving it for one reason only; this looks like an opportunity of a lifetime to me.

Our plans call for getting up to 600 pair as soon as possible. That would make an annual payroll of around $100,000 per year. Know that we will be successful and that when we are, we will have an outlet for three times that amount. Getting up to that figure when we have a going business will be a very easy matter.

It will take $60,000 to supply capital for this project. We will put up the first $20,000 and have the factory going before Union puts up a dime. We are not asking this as a gift, we will pay 5½ % interest for it and carry it as preferred stock, redeeming it as soon as possible if you so desire. Your committee has a plan on the raising of this money which I will leave to them for explanation.

In most cases the trend of manufacturing is from the smaller cities to the larger ones. The Wage and Hours Bill has made manufacturing in the smaller cities much less attractive because of the increase in minimum wages, and of course, the lack of facilities in the smaller cities looms up much stronger under these conditions. I naturally feel this is a wonderful opportunity, or I wouldn't be going into it. Remember, while we are asking for help, we are not asking for one penny in donations.

It's not easy for me to stand up here and speak—speaking is a bit out of my line, but it is easy to make statements as I have tonight—however Dunn and Bradstreet as well as Bankers and Businessman will back every statement I have made. I said before we are ready to go now, in fact putting it off any longer would mean to miss out on the coming fall season, hence I say no time can be wasted. In a word, we are anxious to get started. Are we coming to Union? The answer, gentlemen, is up to you. Amen.

A historical note regarding the men my father mentioned:

Mr. Jennings was Charlie Jennings, who lived in Union and had been superintendent of the now-closed shoe factory— a crotchety old guy but "the best damned superintendent in the business," according to my father. Mr. Neunuebel was my Uncle Eddie, my mother's brother. The shoe salesman investor was Abe Gilbloom, from Chicago, a round-as-a-ball Jewish shoe salesman with a wife named Pearl and a daughter named Money. These four put up $5,000 each to invest the

43

$20,000 mentioned. They include a Freemason (Jennings), a Jew (Gilbloom), and two Catholics (my father and Uncle Eddie): a mix my father considered auspicious. The shoe salesman whose name could not be mentioned was Sam Greene, a top-notch salesperson in the Southern states. K.D.K. is Kane Dunham Kraus, a shoe factory in nearby Washington, Missouri.

৯১

For Mother, Union was bitter exile. She did not drive, then or ever, so the city she loved would be a bumpy two-hour bus ride away. Fifty miles was a long way in 1938. Leave South St. Louis, her lifelong home? Aunt Hattie's cherry trees, family mahjong games, Famous Barr, carry-in Chinese and Mavrakos' gooey butter cake? She squirmed, resisted, cried.

Couldn't Andy come home on weekends?

He could not. The town already fears the new company might abscond with their cash to another town. They demand a local name for the factory. Since Union is too common, Franklin (County) not much better, the new factory is christened Bourbeuse, for the river. Since Bourbeuse was a challenge to spell or pronounce, the partners dubbed the new line "Glamour Debs by Bourbeuse," an easier-to-market compromise.

৯১

Mother gives in. We move. Gram comes along, I suspect as my mother's consolation prize. She lives under my parents' roof and on their largesse for 40 years, until she enters a nursing home for her final years.

זא

The house on West State Street is my castle. It's a big square white frame bungalow with a porch along the entire front of the house. There is a real yard—not a narrow walkway between two flats like on Lindenwood. A gnarled wild cherry tree in front is perfect for climbing.

On summer nights we sit on the front porch and listen to the "locusts" (our family's name for cicadas). Gram never fails to say, "Listen to that. Gonna be a hot one tomorrow." Dad corrects her a few times: "The insects' song reflects a hot day today, nothing to do with tomorrow." Soon he gives up and nods when she repeats her prophecy.

When we are ready for "black cows," I bicycle to the West End grocery store, six blocks away, and pedal home fast before the ice cream melts. Our icebox melts ice cream. Mother and Gram make the root beer floats for everybody but me; I get my special pink elephant, with cream soda.

When Abe Gilbloom is with us, he adds to the evening's entertainment with his jokes and family stories. He rides the train down from Chicago and stays with us several times that year while Bourbeuse Shoe is in its embryonic stage. He calls me a pet name in Yiddish, which he translates as "Sally Off the Pickle Boat." A package of saltwater taffy arrives for me after one of his visits addressed to Sally Off the Pickle Boat. The Union postman delivers it to our house, probably rolling his eyes at another sign of our weirdness. We are considered outsiders in this close-knit little town where everybody is related to everybody else.

I discover a black widow spider in a pile of old lumber in the dilapidated garage behind the house. It looks just like its picture in my bug book, with its bright red hourglass spot. Gram is horrified when I show it to her. "You could have been killed," she gasps, covering her ears with her hands. (Did she think spiders made noise? No, she just did not want to hear any more horrors.)

Woven wooden slats enclose the space underneath the front porch: black, forbidding, full of shifting dry leaves that might harbor lizards or rats or unknown varmints. One of the sides has a hinged panel that opens wide enough for me to squeeze through, but I never get up the courage to crawl all the way in.

I commandeer the empty lot next door with its appealing weeds, buzzing insects and the smell of summer. My new friend Peggy and I stomp down paths through the waist-high weeds for an African safari. By 1942 it is an island in the Pacific, where we American GI's spy on the "dirty Japs" from behind the bushes. We learned about our monstrous enemies from Movietone News.

Movies are big in our new Union life. The Williams Theatre, owned by the family across the street, changes its program three times a week. Movies run Sunday–Monday, Tuesday through Thursday and Friday–Saturday, with special kids' matinees on Saturday afternoon. Gram, Mother and I sometimes go three times a week. Dad is busy at work, there is not much else to do, and in the summer, the Williams is the only air-conditioned building in town. The Williams' proprietors had the foresight to dig a deep well next to the building that pumps cool air into the theater.

I remember all the kids' movies: *The Jungle Book*, *Fantasia*, *Dumbo*, *Bambi*, and *Pinocchio*, which I especially liked because I owned the book, a hefty big-print volume with many illustrations, which I reread after seeing the movie. *Rebecca* and *The Maltese Falcon* were some of the grown-ups' favorites. Gram and Mother laughed so hard at *Arsenic and Old Lace*, we went back to see it again the second night. I decided to be a swimming star after seeing Esther Williams in *Thrill of a Romance*, where she gets to kiss Van Johnson.

Mother wouldn't let me go to *The Ox-Bow Incident*—too scary—but she took me to see *The Outlaw* in St. Louis one afternoon while waiting for the bus home to Union. Father Hubert had read a letter from the archbishop at Mass the Sunday before, urging all Catholics to boycott the dirty movie.

Mother scoffed at the archbishop and said I wouldn't understand what was going on anyway—I was 11 at the time. I don't remember seeing anything shocking, but I was thrilled to be considered grown-up enough to see a C movie (the Catholic rating for "very bad").

෯

A Catholic family lives across the street: the Lakebrinks. Their two daughters fascinate me as they race around their yard playing tag or swinging from a rope in the big tree.

"Can I go barefoot like the Lakebrink girls?" I ask Mother. She collapses into an armchair and holds her head in her hands.

Mrs. Lakebrink comes across the street to warn Mother.

"You know, Mrs. Browne, they'll be oiling the streets soon. You might want to get boxes from the West End and put cardboard down on your floors."

My mother smiles politely and thanks her. And raves, after Mrs. L goes home. Dirty cardboard from the grocery store on her clean floors—cardboard undoubtedly full of roach eggs? Might as well live in a tarpaper shack.

෯

I hear the Lakebrink girls squealing, and run outside. A rusty, dented pickup truck with "City of Union Street Department" written on its side is inching down West State, driven by a weathered-looking guy in a billed cap and overalls roomy enough to hide another man. A cigarette dangles out of the side of his mouth. He leans out through the open door, watching a thick black river oozing out onto our street. It shimmers in the hot sun and smells like the garage where Dad gets his car fixed.

Another truck follows. Louder, spreading the kind of gravel that fills Missouri's riverbeds: a distinctive blend of oranges, beiges and browns in so many shades it looks khaki until you get up close.

The Lakebrink girls and I follow both trucks, and another that shows up the next day. More impressive, a huge cylinder behind this driver, a cigar stub in his teeth instead of a cigarette and a huge red umbrella over his head attached to his seat. We tag along behind the roller. When we get to Linden, the cigar man, without moving his cigar, yells, "You kids stay back, now. I'm making the corner here."

Dad explains to Mother that the gravel covers the oil that seals the winter's cracks, then the roller cements it into place. But gravel piles up in some corners, spreads thin in others, and the inky resin bedevils Mother for the rest of the summer. One more reason to hate this "dinky little hick town" with no streetlights and crumbling pavements. Where people come calling when you are trying to fix dinner, because the fools think noon is dinnertime so they cook all morning. And husbands straggle in from work in the middle of the day expecting to be fed.

ع▲

Her complaints sound trivial from my vantage point 75 years later. They worried me then. I wanted to be in sync with Mother and Gram; they were my guideposts. But they were dissing things I loved: the Lakebrink girls, our new house, the funny upturned sidewalks that made roller-skating a challenge. (I always had at least one skinned knee.) Union was my Land of Oz, where Gram's welcoming lap was available always. I began censoring my comments; I wanted to be a loyal member of the team, but I could not trash my Eden. I kept my mouth shut. If Mother found going barefoot horrifying, what would she say about my liking the Union sidewalks?

5

The Lakebrinks

Mrs. Lakebrink walks across the street to tell us about school: Immaculate Conception, where all of her six children went, only two now, fifth- and sixth-grade girls. She has chucked the apron I think of as her uniform, and smoothed her graying hair into a bun behind her ears.

She and Mother and Gram sit in our front room, glasses of green Elco with real ice in their hands.

Elco is bottled syrup from the West End grocery store. It comes in purple grape, lime green, orange orange, lemon yellow, and my favorite, cherry red. The iceman delivers "real ice" (quite superior, we think, to ice made in the refrigerator) twice a week: 5-, 10-, 25-, or 50-pound blocks, depending on the number on a piece of cardboard displayed in our kitchen window. When I cut the display sign up to make flash cards, Gram wails, "It took two weeks to get that crabby iceman to leave us that card. He'll probably charge us for another one."

Her two girls can walk me to school, Mrs. L assures Mother, whose face is set in a plastic smile. "My big girls are in school right now," she says, "or I'd of brought 'em. They'll come over when they get home—more'n likely past three, and it ain't no two yet."

Polite thanks from Mother, but when Mrs. Lakebrink's backside is out of earshot, she turns to Gram.

"Can't anybody in this damned town speak English? I saw her 'big girls' coming home in their school clothes, and I will not have Pat wear those boobely uniforms and long cotton stockings. Whoever heard of stockings in May? Rumpled from the minute you put them on. It's that German priest, thinks he's still in the Old Country. And why is Andy so set on Pat going to a Catholic school?"

&

The week before, my mother and I had visited that Catholic school. My take was not like Mother's.

Sister Gabriel smiles and grasps Mother's gloved hand. Mother wears white gloves and a hat, her shopping-in-downtown-St. Louis clothes. Sister Gabriel wears a flowing ankle-length costume, black except for what look like starched white handkerchiefs buttoned around her face under a black veil. Even her shoes are black, like Gram's, but over black stockings, not nylons like Gram's. She is shaped like Gram, a nebulous oval, but with a rope around her waist rather than Gram's cloth belt that matches her housedress. She ushers Mother and I into a parlor for a talk, then down a hall into the classroom where I will start second grade in the fall.

I stop listening and devour the scene. Blackboards cover two walls, with letters, numbers and pictures in long rows above them. A is still for Apple, but is B is for Baby—a fat pink blob wrapped in a white curtain with a gold ring around his head. Baby Jesus, I learn. All these Jesus and Mary images are new. A teacher's desk in the middle of the blackboard wall faces rows of wooden desks with hinged tops, screwed to the creaky wide-board floor. Windows line another side, reaching almost to the high ceiling. I learn that the windows open with a hook on a humongous pole.

Sister Gabriel leads us down another hall and out a door overlooking a field as wide as the building. A long gentle slope ends in a border of trees—a leafy green fence. It is recess; little people run, chase each other, disappear behind trees, throw balls and shout words I cannot catch.

ॐ

Once in school, I discover the row of trees hides a meandering creek, a gold mine of possibilities: rocks, tadpoles, fish, moss. It is off-limits at recess, but accessible from my daily route to and from school. At recess, I learn Dodge Ball and Red Rover and after the first snowfall, Fox and Goose and Angels in the Snow.

ॐ

Immaculate Conception is another pearl on my string of school gems. I can't wait to start.

6

Immaculate Conception

The Lakebrink girls are at my door the next morning. Since there are only three weeks of school left, I am spared the hated uniform. Mother coos about how pretty I look in my special dress from Famous; the other children will be envious. I would prefer a uniform like the other kids. While Mother delights in my specialness, I want to blend in. Fat chance; I already talk different and know nobody, and in my dress, I will stand out more than ever. At least Mother lets me go. She said it was silly to start school for three weeks, since my old school, Mallinckrodt, has "passed" me to second grade already, but she decides it will be good for me to meet my prospective classmates.

Six, eight blocks later, up a steep hill and around a corner, we join a stream of boys and girls, four or five across, carrying book bags. All the girls wear blue flannel pleated skirts and dark blue shirts with little black ribbon ties. At the door, the L's hand me off to Sister Gabriel, who walks me to my classroom and introduces my teacher, Sister Berenice.

With barely time to arrange my pencils on my new desk, a bell rings and Sister Berenice shepherds us into two rows.

When she sees I have nothing to cover my head like the other girls, she takes an ironed white handkerchief from her desk and uses a bobby pin to attach it to my Indian straight hair. It makes a lump over the bow my mother pinned on this morning and feels funny; I worry it will fall off and make me even more conspicuous.

The church has big propped-open doors on top of wide steps. We are first in a line of three more groups of Sisters and children. Our class marches to the right side of the church and files into pews halfway back. My companions flip a wooden board up over our feet, and we kneel down on its padded frame.

I am mesmerized; I have never been in a church before. Statues—I recognize Mary on the left in flowing blue robes and golden crown holding baby Jesus, the "B" on the schoolroom chart. I figure that is Mary's husband, Joseph, on the right holding a lily. Two boys in long black dresses with white lacy blouses on top scurry in and out of the doors on either side. They use long poles with flames on the end to light the altar candles high above their heads. An organ cranks up. Sister Gabriel runs through a melody, then we stand up and everybody but me sings.

છ

When I am a seventh grader, I play the same organ for a funeral. It is summer when no Sisters are around. The funeral

Mass is filled with colored people, none of whom I ever saw before or after. The only black people I have seen are those who pay their dime at the Williams and go up the stairs to the balcony to watch the movie. After the funeral, a dark-skinned man in a seersucker suit thanks me for playing the organ and for "the little angels," my classmates, who sang next to the organ in the choir loft.

ॐ

Many years later, at an interfaith Day of the Dead ceremony in front of the San Miguel *parroquia* church, a priest chants the Dies Irae from the Mass on the Day of Burial. I sing along in Latin. Our Jewish representative leads the Kaddish. I speculate to my companion that I am the only person in the *jardín* who knows both the Dies Irae and the Kaddish.

ॐ

Peggy, the girl next to me in the pew, pokes me—time to sit down. Her dark hair is braided right onto her head. How does her mother do that? My classmates wiggle their bottoms into each other's on the polished pews; I am glued to the action in front.

When the altar boys and the priest march out to start the Mass, I see Father Hubert—that "know-nothing German," in my mother's opinion—for the first time. He is short, with barely enough white hair to pull a few strands over the top of his head. His brown Franciscan robes are covered with vestments that are new to me, too. The three stop at the bottom of the steps to the altar and take turns speaking to the big cross on top of the altar, or so it appears to me.

The pageantry continues. We kneel, sing, sit, stand and make the sign of the cross—luckily, Gram taught me how. My pew-mates know all the secrets; Peggy takes charge and clues me in. She becomes my best friend, and still is.

ક

The boys practice the Prayers at the Foot of the Altar in the classroom, mornings before catechism. Only boys; girls are not permitted on the sacred altar. Nuns and old ladies are allowed to dust the altar, arrange the flowers, and sweep the carpet: my introduction to the ironclad sexism of the church. As a seven-year-old, I notice; as a mature Catholic, I scream and stamp my feet.

Because this is the classroom and not the holy church, Sister reads the priest's part,

Et introíbo ad altáre Dei, (I will go unto the altar of God.)

The boys respond, *Ad Deum quí laetíficat Juventútem meam*: (To God, who giveth joy to my youth.)

ક

When I tell about the altar boys at home, Dad recites the chant in an exaggerated singsong. Mother says, "Oh, Andy." I am delighted; my father has a warm connection to the goings-on in the church. I am uncertain what Mother thinks. She talks about being Catholic as something wonderful, but the reality of Immaculate Conception School never seems to suit her.

Mother tells "Catholic stories" about her father's mother, Grandma Nora Brady Neunuebel. Nora emigrated from Ireland soon after the Great Famine and met my grandfather Neunuebel as a waitress in the restaurant where he was the steward. They married, an unusual match since Irish and Germans usually kept to their own. The reason rumored was that Nora was extraordinarily beautiful and swept Grandpa Neunuebel off his sturdy South German feet. They had three children together before she learned the husband she'd left in County Mayo was still alive. A friend had written that he'd died at sea, not an unlikely fate for a fisherman off the West Coast, but not former husband Coyne's destiny. Nora Brady Coyne Neunuebel was mortified; a good Catholic is not a bigamist. She was so distraught about being thrown out of the church by this error that she became bitter and super-pious.

Mother laughed that all of the grandchildren watched the clock to be sure they were elsewhere when the noon church bells rang, so they didn't have to kneel down and say the Angelus with Grandma. If she woke on a stormy night—and there are many storms in St. Louis in the spring—she would rouse all the children, sprinkle them with holy water, and lead a rosary. Mother and her cousins swear she almost drowned them in holy water during one particularly severe thunderstorm.

I'd laughed at the funny stories about Nora Brady, at how she smoked little cigars, spiking them on a hairpin when they got too short for her to hold. Now that I was saying the rosary and dipping my fingers in holy water at the door of the church, the tales of Nora's mindless piety had a different ring. She belonged to the tribe I encountered in my new school and longed to join.

꿍

Immaculate Conception is my portal to another world, another family. Attractive, puzzling, a network peopled by ghostly saints and ancient stories along with all us live Catholics. I feel embraced and cozy, like when Gram's wool afghan covers me stretched out on the sofa.

The Dick and Jane books, weekly spelling lists, times tables, penmanship paper with three lines for swirls and sticks and circles are all Mallinckrodt familiars. My new school adds Bible stories about crossing the Red Sea, holy water fonts, prayers that begin and end the day. We print "J.M.J." at the top of each page for Jesus, Mary and Joseph—the same words Mother bellows when she finds ants in the sugar bowl. There are gilt-edged holy cards: pastel saints in voluminous robes,

Jesus with long curls pointing at a bleeding heart outside His robe. I earn a Saint Veronica for 100 percent on a spelling test and a Holy Family for giving a dime to "ransom" pagan babies.

Mother is especially hard on the pagan babies. The Propagation of the Faith takes up collections for ransoming pagans, especially baby pagans.

"Where are all these babies? Why do they need ransoming? And why are the nuns always asking for extra money? Nickel and dime you to death," she says.

The case for pagan babies sounds weak to me, too. But there is more than pagan babies.

❧

There is prayer. I know prayer only as an occasional grace before dinner: "Bless us O Lord, and these Thy gifts, which we are about to receive from Thy bounty, through Christ our Lord. Amen."

If Cousin Margaret Ann is around, she says the Lutheran one: "Bless, O Lord, these gifts to our use and us to Thy service, in Jesus' name. Amen."

Neither seems to mean much; saying grace is a routine like washing your hands before dinner, only skipped oftener and with less fuss.

Dad often chimes in: "Good food, good meat, good God, let's eat!" or "Father, Son and Holy Ghost; who eats the fastest gets the most!" or "Hail Mary, full of grace, Notre Dame's in second place."

Mother chides "Oh, Andy" and smiles—like she does for "brown soda."

At Immaculate Conception the prayers touch me, especially the litanies, chanted while we march around the church, often with lighted candles:

> Mystical Rose, pray for us …
> Tower of David, pray for us …
> Morning star, pray for us …
> Mirror of justice, pray for us …
> —*Litany of the Blessed Virgin Mary*

I feel close to another world, a world as attractive as the creek at the bottom of the playground.

The nuns and priest take prayer seriously. Father Hubert, with his German accent and snuff-stained teeth, explains the Eucharist in a hushed voice. Sister Berenice testifies to God's mercy, the warmth of the Blessed Virgin, then shifts to a sad tone for sin, evil, which means losing touch with God.

❧

There is ritual. On Sundays smoke rises from a silver container on a chain, held aloft by a fellow student who strains to swing the smoking incense burner by its chain. I inhale the intoxicating smell hungrily. I recall my father's chant in pseudo Gregorian mode: "What did you do with the incense pot? Put it in the corner 'cause it's too damned hot."

I grin to recall Dad's words, but with warmth. I feel a connection to the incense swirls; all over the world Catholics like me are swinging incense pots and inhaling the comforting smell.

≥♥

May is the month of Mary, Jesus' mother. Every day during May we bring to school fresh flowers for Mary's altar. I make my own May altar at home with a statue Mother brought me from St. Louis. Every day I put flowers in front of Mary's statue, light a candle and sing her song.

> May is the month of our Mother,
> The blessed and beautiful days
> When our lips and our spirits
> Are ringing with love and with praise.

One evening Gram and Mother are off someplace, and I decide the candle is more impressive behind the statue, with a halo of light glowing behind Mary. I am on the final chapter of *Glinda of Oz* when I smell smoke. The curtains behind Mary are flaming. "Fire, fire!" I yell. Dad runs in, shouts "Jesus Christ," pulls the curtains down and stamps on them. I am embarrassed. Dad will think I am silly for having a May altar and sillier for lighting a candle under curtains. I don't know what to say. I say nothing, always a wise course in my house. Especially since Dad goes back to his paper after putting out the fire, and jokes about a candle "damned near burning down the house" to Mother and Gram when they return.

&.

"Catholic" is confusing, mysterious, another topic we must not talk about, like Grandpa Neunuebel. If the Catholic religion is the only true faith like my mother says, why does she never go to church? It seems my father is the one who wants me to go to Catholic school, but I overhear a conversation that unsettles me.

Dad and a leather salesman from St. Louis are having scotch and sodas in our living room when I burst in the door wearing my school uniform. The salesman says, "Oh, I didn't know your daughter went to Catholic school. Is your wife Catholic?"

"We are both Catholics," my father replies. "I can't say I believe in any of that stuff, but I got a good foundation in Catholic schools. Sunday Mass is a good habit; we should all think about something other than making money at least one day in the week."

That was miles from how Father Hubert or the Sisters saw it. Sunday Mass was not just a good habit. And what was this "good foundation" I was getting?

ε**&**

Sister Berenice lets me talk to her at her desk. I admire her little silver crucifix on a stand and finger it as we talk. On my birthday she gives it to me with a note: "It isn't new, but I couldn't find another one like it. You may have it for your birthday if you like." I like. It stands on my bookshelf, 73 years later, a symbol of the connection that captured my heart at Immaculate Conception School and began a quest that continues from that day to this.

7

From West to East State

While I revel in my new school, Mother gets more comfortable with Union. She begins to make friends and host poker games. She stops complaining about our house and tells upbeat stories about Union when she visits our St. Louis relatives. My favorite is Dad's furnace grate expedition.

❧

A square grate sits in the middle of our house, the whole width of the hall. The furnace grate, I am told. I lie on my belly and look down the shiny tube below, trying to figure it out. Our Lindenwood flat had radiators, nothing like this.

One summer day, with dinner keeping warm in the oven, Mother prepares to take her bath and await my father's homecoming. She pulls off her apron, a wraparound that covers her housedress, sticky with sweat (and identical to the aprons still worn by the more traditional *amas de casa* in San Miguel).

Out of her apron pocket, her engagement ring tumbles across the floor and down the grate: her diamond, a stone without flaw, my father's tribute to his pure young virgin bride. She hears its clinkity-clink on the metal duct below.

She and Gram hurry downstairs and sift through the cold furnace ashes—no ring. They mope and wring their hands until my father gets home. He has lifted a few with the boys on the way—or maybe it is his Irish talking—because he immediately assures them there is no problem. He will retrieve the ring posthaste.

Father disappears into the bedroom and comes out in his swimming trunks with a clothesline tied around his middle. He slides the heavy grate over till there is room for his body on one side of it.

He explains he will tie the rope to the grate and lower himself into the duct.

My mother is frantic. And laughing hysterically.

"Andy, Andy, you'll break your neck. No, no, don't do it. I don't care about the ring."

Soon we are all howling at the comedic scene—even my father, who puts his bathrobe on and sits down for another beer before dinner.

The next day Gram and Mother huddle on the basement steps, scrutinizing the two workers as they disassemble the ducts. They do not trust these strangers. The ring is found.

ੴ

When the factory thrives, mother exchanges her engagement ring for a cocktail ring, then all the rage, with the perfect diamond in its center. She has an amethyst, her birthstone, set in the original, old-fashioned setting, but never wears it. I take it to college, where I tell the gynecologist who fits my diaphragm it is my engagement ring.

The ring is a bauble; the Browne finances are sufficiently stable for a more important addition. My parents decide to have another child. They try for more than a year and are delighted when my mother finally conceives.

ᐥ

Toni is born in January of 1941, the sister I had longed for since I fell in love with my playmates in the Famous Barr boat.

I come home from school that afternoon with the fluffy delicious white flakes melting on my tongue that Gram calls "big flakes, little snow." I turn into a neighbor's walk, a block before Aunt Thelma's West State Street house, where her bridge club is meeting. My mother has been in St. Louis for two weeks, awaiting the birth. My father and Gram left this morning on word labor had started, leaving me to stay with Aunt Thelma. My birth took three days, so nobody thinks anything will happen soon.

Thelma is sitting at the bridge table, engaged in a hand, but when I run over to stand next to her, she puts her cards down and gives me a hug. "It's here," she says. "The baby is here."

Her hands and voice are charged with Christmas Eve/Buder picnic warmth. I am overwhelmed, tongue-tied.

"Don't you want to know what it is?" Thelma prompts.

I nod, still mute. "A girl. A little girl." Thelma is gleeful.

I smile, so glad I got the sister I was hoping for.

Alas, infant Toni was not a fun playmate for a nine-year-old. The interactions I might have had with her—carrying her around, changing diapers, cooing and oohing—don't happen. Mother is a jealous custodian. Maybe not exactly jealous, but she guards Toni as if she is the prime target for kidnapping—the Lindbergh baby, kidnapped and murdered the year I was born haunts mothers still.

Toni's shiny new maple crib, bedecked with pink blankets and stuffed animals, is tucked in a corner of a bedroom devoted to the New Baby. Gram and I double up in Gram's room.

I overhear whispers, concerns about Pat's feeling slighted because of the new baby. Mother does not want me to feel burdened having to take care of my sister. My longed-for sister is a china doll on a shelf—albeit a beautifully decorated shelf—not a living presence I can touch and talk to and get to know.

On Toni's first birthday my parents make sure I have a special gift: a Swiss music box with a painting of a family of dogs and ducks on its hinged wooden top. I watch its tiny roll of pins plink out "Three Blind Mice" and "The Parade of the Wooden Soldiers" through the glass cover over the works. When one foot breaks off, Harry replaces it with a Lego tile. It sits on my altar in Mexico.

My sister blossoms into a blond-ringleted, blue-eyed toddler. "The pretty one," my mother and Gram christen her, while Pat is "the smart one." Adult Toni shares an insight from her therapy: This implies Pat is "the ugly one" and Toni "the dumb one."

The fall after my sister's first birthday, my parents decide it is time to move out of their rented house on West State.

❦

Glamour Debs by Bourbeuse are selling well. My parents buy a house on the east end of State Street, making them the first homeowners in either of their families.

For Mother, the new house is her castle—without the moat. She welcomes guests with grace, whether beloved Aunt Hattie or a stray tradesman from the city.

Her newly well-feathered nest makes her a queen. The bill from a fine St. Louis furniture store is in her box of memorabilia when she dies 54 years later. The yellowed page is from

Craig's Furniture Co.,

4901 Washington Ave.,

St. Louis (no state necessary)

Two typewritten orders lists $1,339.01.

There are eight additions on the bottom, in Mother's neat script, the most expensive of which is "drapes, $311."

❧

Mother reigns over her new fiefdom like the Perle Mesta of Franklin County.

Bowls of meticulously prepared dishes come through the swinging kitchen door as if borne aloft by footmen. Each dish is special, whether a platter of oven-fried chicken or a cut-glass bowl of beets, home grown and pickled by Gram. Guests rate steaks or roasts, serving bowls heaped higher, an occasional dessert.

Gram says Virginia wants enough food on the table at the end of the meal to feed another shift. "That is my downfall," Gram opines, cupping her ample belly in her hands. Gone is the hourglass figure of her younger days, she sighs, even though she has given up sugar and cream in her coffee. ("And third helpings," I observe silently.) After especially bountiful meals, Gram rolls her napkin, fits it into her napkin ring, and sighs, "If I ate what I wanted, I'd weigh 300 pounds."

Guests are frequent and welcome. Many come from St. Louis, 50 miles away, to do business with Bourbeuse Shoe. Mother's cuisine is many cuts above Union's lone, pitiful café, *The Colonial Tavern*.

Conversation flows like the drinks before dinner; laughter floats over the "pass-the-salts" like a benevolent cloud. Mother sets a gracious table, and Dad loves good talk, whether gossip from the fitting room (the buzz about the new faux snakeskin iguana, with more useable skin); the good news from North Africa, where the Brits have sent the Italians and Germans in chaotic retreat across Libya; or the latest Marx Brothers movie. My father is a huge fan; Gram and Mother think the Marx Brothers are silly. A critique of Roosevelt's latest speech sits cheek by jowl with the electrical storm that woke everybody up last night.

With her pride in home accouterments, Ginny could have been a fussy hostess, demanding formality at her regal table. Rather, she is relaxed and generous, a benign despot as long as a few iron rules are observed: Dinner is at 6 o'clock, no profanity or crude language, and respect for the food and the cook.

The 6 o'clock dinner rule caused more trouble for my sister than for the adults. I remember her toddler tantrums— fits of uncontrollable yowling and banging her head on the floor. She sometimes moved from the carpet to the hardwood floor so she could bang her head harder. My mother and Gram regarded this as an innocent phase she was going through and were convinced it would pass if they ignored it. Toni doesn't remember the tantrums, but she has vivid memories of feeling famished in the late afternoon and being told she had to wait for "dinnertime, 6 o'clock." It was believed that eating a bite of food ahead of time would spoil your dinner, and the women who prepared the main meal of the day with such devotion wanted no spoiled dinners.

I absorb the culture of the gracious table and the generous hostess, and years later struggle to replicate it in my kitchen. It yields good times and good food along with guilt and burnout. In my Union days,

I go unto the altar of my mother's table,
And her table giveth joy to my youth.

My mother is a hard act to follow. An Arab at heart, she welcomes my friends into our home like family.

8

The State Street Gang

Another Union legacy is my lifelong friendship with the Union Queens, originally the State Street Gang. Peggy, my helpful pew-mate that first day in church, is the first.

At recess Peggy leads me to a venerable catalpa tree whose exposed roots are covered with powdery clay dirt, perfect for scratching roads with sticks and zooming pretend cars of rocks. We play ball in the street in front of her house after school with Fran, her neighbor. I meet Doris and Maxine down the block.

Peggy goes off to Union High. I spend my first year at St. Francis Borgia, in Washington, attracted by their school newspaper and the Catholic label. I miss my buddies, and join Peggy and Fran at Union High the next year. Paula and Wanda hang around with us; Betty moves to town. We click. Movies at the Williams, cards or croquet at each other's houses, after-school powwows at Karraker's Drug Store over fountain Cokes—cherry, chocolate, raspberry or vanilla, my favorite. We call ourselves the State Street Gang, since three of us live on a two-block stretch of East State Street, site of my mother's dream house and my home until I leave for college.

At my house we convene around the maple table in our breakfast room, next to the kitchen; a good thing, since we require constant refueling. Packaged snacks are the new hot thing. The latest, Fritos, crunchy fried corn bits, are a close cousin to *totopos*, fried tortilla chips. Was my Mexican compass being set? The shiny packages from Nabisco edge out skillet-popped popcorn, but I maintain my loyalty to popcorn burned on the stove, and still consider burned popcorn the ultimate snack.

We drink—more Cokes. We're tame revelers, although my killjoy dentist insists the gallons consumed at our orgies rot holes in my teeth.

Mother's carton of Viceroys lays seductively nearby in the bottom drawer of the buffet. Nice girls do not smoke in public. Even grown-up Princess Margaret catches hell when a photo with an ashtray at her side hits the tabloids. We puff away, bound by mild sinfulness, then raise the windows wide, whatever the weather, fan the smoke out with arithmetic assignments, and drown the room with pine-scented Air Wick from the powder room. Useless. My mother complains we smoke so many of her cigarettes we must reimburse her.

We play a form of bridge that would scandalize Culbertson or Goren; the dummy slides in and out of her chair to concentrate on hair rollers, fingernails or slapdash homework. Bridge Lite.

Opening bid: "Two hearts."

"Omigod, pass the book. That's something serious. Hmm, says we can make game without my hand. Good thing. I have absolute zero."

"Bid!" from the opponents, eager to get a losing hand over and done.

First bidder: "This hand will require another Coke."

I jump up to grab a six-ounce glass bottle from the fridge.

છ

Boys come and go. We close ranks at their departures without fanfare. I remember no serious fights among us, even over boys, although I hated Peggy for a week when I found out she was going with the boy I secretly loved. Lucky for me. She married him and discovered the brilliance that attracted us was bipolar disorder.

છ

Only Peggy and I shared Immaculate Conception School, but Fran was Catholic, too. Her mother had found the uniforms outrageous enough to get permission from the bishop (!) to send her daughter to public school, on the condition that Fran take private instructions from Father Hubert Saturday mornings.

To the State Street Gang, church membership is filed away with irrelevant data like eye color or the car your parents drive. Our spiritual track is friendship. We care about each other, commiserate over problems: "Grandpa" Grant, the geometry teacher, puts the pretty girls in front so he can look down their dresses; Mr. Craig never calls on the girls in history class.

Betty converts from her Protestant faith when she disappoints her family by marrying a Catholic. Ever after a faithful Catholic, she is the only friend bold enough to confront me with my perfidy when I turn Jewish.

And mothers, well. They balk when we want to drape our fathers' white shirts over us like shrouds, wear Levi's—then racy attire—and rub dirt into our saddle oxfords. They decry our dedication to Frankie, label the screaming fans at his concerts unladylike, and are horrified when we identify with them by wearing bobby sox. When we get our driver's licenses at 16, they treat us like we are 10 years old and can't drive to the icehouse for a cold watermelon without crashing.

છ

The driving licenses put St. Louis within range. Our parents insist we take a chaperone on our forays, a story our children now think we made up to impress them, like walking miles in the snow to deliver newspapers.

Off we go to the big city, where the Shady Oak shows foreign films like *The Red Shoes* that would never make it to the screen of the Williams. We see *A Streetcar Named Desire* at the American, St. Louis' premier live theater in those days, and current hits like *South Pacific* at the Muny Opera in Forest Park.

We get stuck in heavy traffic on the way home from The Muny one night. I may have been driving. Impatient with wrong turns and cops whistling us into lanes we don't want, we see Kingshighway, our homeward path, at the next corner, its entry blocked by a row of "Do Not Pass" sawhorses. Two of the gals jump out of the car, move the barriers, and we are on our way, singing "Ninety-nine Bottles of Beer on the Wall."

❧

Missouri summers were boiling. None of our homes had air-conditioning; swimming pools were life-saving cooler-downers. It was a major triumph when Bourbeuse Shoe bought a run-down property a few miles from town with a swimming pool. After some sprucing up, the place opened as the Bourbeuse Resort, a summer retreat for the factory employees. Our gang had a summer headquarters.

The pool was fed by springs, and the water changed every Monday, making the icy water the perfect antidote for the burning sun. We swam, dived and lounged poolside, turning brown with the help of Johnson's baby oil laced with iodine. Nobody had heard of melanoma, and we would not have paid attention if we had.

My family had a cabin backed up into the woods at the edge of the resort property. I spent more time there in the summer than at home. At first my grandmother stayed with me to insure my safety and sobriety—alcohol was now on the scene—but soon I was allowed to stay overnight on my own.

&

One State Street Gang sleepover weekend Fran brought ingredients for a taffy pull, her family's specialty. The cabin's cooking facilities were primitive, and after a few trips up the hill to throw the circuit breaker, the electric hot plate having zapped the electricity, the taffy was pronounced ready to pull. Whether it was the muggy weather or the low voltage of the hot plate, that taffy was un-pullable.

We tried, working the goo back and forth from hand to hand. After despairing of getting taffy from the sticky muck, we gave up and relaxed with a midnight dip in the pool. The moon was out, the water felt good, and we returned to the cabin with all the failed taffy rinsed off. We fell onto our army cots and went to sleep, enough beer in our bellies to put us out till morning.

Dawn arrived. We awoke to a sugary world. Our feet stuck to the wood floor. Clothes adhered to the chairs where we'd dropped them the night before. The keys of my typewriter—an antique instrument formerly used for writing—were coated with taffy.

Armies of ants were doing cartwheels and sending invitations to all their friends to join the party. I had accumulated a number of tree toads and lizards from the woods to keep me company, and the night before, someone had brought in a large frog we found poolside. He had peed in a pool of would-be taffy, leaving a foul smell that clung to the unfortunate bare foot that first encountered it. Frogs were banned from the cabin thereafter as bad-mannered; the toads and lizards must have pooped so discreetly they left no traces.

The summer after my junior year at Union High, I spent several weeks in the cabin alone, with a few State Street Gang sleepovers. Every morning I marched five minutes to the mailbox on the road, eager for replies to my inquiries to prospective colleges. The morning I found a thick packet from the University of Chicago, I tore it open and began to read walking back to the cabin. By the time I reached my screen door, Chicago was my lodestar. It must have been one hell of a brochure, and accurate as well as persuasive. The U of C and I were a solid match.

Twenty years after our Union High School graduation, the State Street Gang reunites one June weekend at Fran's condo at Lake of the Ozarks. A huge bouquet arrives at the condo addressed to the Union Queens. An old friend has decided we need a new moniker. We agree, especially since none of us lives on State Street anymore. We have been the Union Queens in the 40-plus years since the kid from the local FTD (Florists' Transworld Delivery) knocked on Fran's condo door.

With children raised and spouses settled, divorced or dead, we spend lazy days around the pool, crowd the hot tub, and drive the motorboat (erratically) to H. Toad's Grill and Marina for lunch, where we provide entertainment to the diners watching our clumsy attempt at docking.

We dive off the boat to swim, once almost abandoning one of the gang because we are laughing too hard to hoist her back into the boat. We stay up half the night to wallow in girl talk, play bridge, drink wine, exchange family snapshots, take more pictures. Even non-smokers share nostalgic puffs over late night conclaves—Camels, wine and chocolate are our generation's drugs of choice. Late suppers in Bentley's Restaurant & Pub end with double-fudge brownies à la mode or praline pie with coffee ice cream passed from Queen to Queen to meltdown.

略

We talk and talk, but not about everything. We share the code: Ignore the bad stuff and never, ever reveal any family problems outside the family. Corollary: Don't speak about these problems candidly inside the family unless or until blood is spilled, and don't rush to call the police even then.

Years pass and our talk touches dark edges left unspoken in our State Street Gang days.

Growing up, we never suspected Doris' father, the town's respected physician, was a binge drinker. He never touched a drop in Union where he might be seen. But boozed up at his farm, a weekend retreat in the country, he mutated from the mellow family man into a mean, angry tyrant. It was Doris who badgered me into going to Al-anon when my mother was driving me bonkers. Not for me, I insisted, Al-anon is for spouses of alcoholics. ("Like you," my unspoken subtext.) She was dead right, of course; 12-step programs saved my bacon many times in the years that followed.

❧

Peggy never said much about her mother, but I heard whispers when I was 9 or 10. The town gossipmongers were gleeful when a well-off family got their comeuppance; there was an unspoken prejudice against business owners or anyone who appeared to have "made it." Karl Marx would have been proud. The rumors were that Old Lady Kramolowsky had adopted Peggy to spite her son-in-law. She planned to leave her fortune to Peggy and not to her grandchildren, the widowed son-in-law's children.

Peggy tells the true, softer story.

Peggy's adopted family owned the most popular bar in town. Union was the county seat of Franklin County and therefore boasted a courthouse in the center of town, facing the plaza and surrounded by stores and businesses, including Kramolowsky's Tavern. Legend had it that Old Man Kramolowsky once called the police to evict a boisterous drunk who came back demanding another beer after Kramolowsky had twice thrown him out. When the judge asked the drunk why he perversely returned to the bar after two warnings, he bellowed, "Because Anton Kramolowsky serves the best goddamned glass of beer in Franklin County!"

Whereupon Kramolowsky jumped up from his seat at the witness table and shouted, "I'll pay his fine."

Mr. K and the tavern were history before Peggy came on the scene and the couple's children had children of their own. When one of her daughters died in childbirth, Mrs. K took the youngest of the daughter's five motherless children into her home to ease the burden on her newly widowed son-in-law. Within a year that little girl died from one of the childhood diseases that used to carry young children off in droves. Grief-stricken Mrs. K longed for another child. Her brother, a prominent doctor at a Catholic hospital in St. Louis, was sympathetic and introduced his sister to Mothers and Babies, a home run by the Sisters of Charity for unwed mothers and their offspring. When Mrs. K walked into the home's nursery, a 16-month-old lifted her arms to her. She picked Peggy up and never put her back down.

Peggy later traces her birth parents and discovers that her biological mother died in her 20s, in a car accident. Her father is still alive in southern Indiana. Peggy travels to meet him and his family, and stays connected until his death. Along the way, she fills in the Queens about her quest—braving stonewalling administrators and searching fading records. We cheer her spunk and its happy outcome.

❧

Wanda asked the adult Queens if we'd ever wondered why her mother took in sewing. "No," I say, "I just imagined she was a super seamstress who loved her work." Wanda scoffed, "Only because my father never brought home a full paycheck in his life. A stop at The Friendly Tavern, next to the shoe factory, was as far as his money got. He was hung over so often he barely managed to hold his foreman's job at Carmel Shoe. Luckily, he could run the cutting room in his sleep."

Wanda, too, married a drunk, and divorced him before he distinguished himself by shooting himself in the head in his sister's backyard.

❧

And Paula, my wonderful friend Paula. We both wore Chubbettes and swapped clothes. Her family invited me to keep her company on drives to St. Louis or away ballgames. Sometimes her brother came along, a basketball star and the star at home, too. It did not take many rides to understand that Paula was the second-class child.

The local Catholics wondered about Paula's father because he said the stations of the cross every day on his way home for lunch. I'd seen him when our class was in church practicing for some procession: a stark, sober figure with a sour puss plodding around the church perimeter, making a hiccup of a genuflection at each station. Rumor was he promised to say the stations every day if his son recovered from a dread disease, or was it a car crash? When I got up the courage to ask Paula about it, she said she had no idea.

Paula married an Air Force pilot during the Korean War. He stayed in the service, and drank himself to death long after Paula left him. She settled with their two children in Bentonville, Arkansas, where the errant husband's brother offered help. He got her a job with newly founded Walmart. Paula rose as the company grew, dated one of the Walton brothers before he left his wife for another girlfriend. She retired with a hefty stash of Walmart stock.

❧

My final vision of Paula is standing on the deck of Fran's condo, her elbow balanced on the deck railing, face turned to the sun setting over the lake. Her platinum hair moves slightly in the breeze, making her expensive cut look even more elegant. She is still in her swimsuit, a terry cover-up loosely thrown over. She flicks the ashes off her cigarette and turns to the four Queens lounging on porch chairs, wine glasses in hand.

"Stay off diets," she says. I moan a comic moan and reach for a slice of cheddar and a Triscuit.

"Seriously," Paula says.

All eyes turn to the sunset. We still have trouble with *serious*.

"I've ruined my digestion by constant dieting, and I want to tell you not to do that, ever."

Silence. Compassionate looks.

Finally Fran speaks. "I knew your mother was always worrying you would turn out like … "

Paula interrupts. "It was her obsession. Her two sisters each weighed over 300 pounds, got diabetes, and died miserable deaths. She was determined I was not going to follow in their footsteps."

"But your mother was never … " Doris begins.

"You'd better believe it," Paula says. "She measured her food like medicine. I don't think she ever enjoyed a meal in her life. When she died, I looked through her photo albums.

Lots of pictures of me, you, too, Wanda, and some of all of us, in front of the school, at the resort. I studied those pictures of me close … over and over. And I was *not* fat. She always raved about how fat I was, but I was … not … fat."

A Greek chorus: "No, Paula, you were never fat." Paula's hip bones protrude under her sleek black suit.

"It was too late by then. I spent my life going from one crash diet to another. Now I can't eat anything." Paula turns back toward the lake as the sun plops down below the horizon. A lone Seadoo noises by below. I pull my sweater around my shoulders. Time to go inside.

Chilly, chilling.

ﻉﻉ

Paula dies two years later; we never hear the exact cause. Her death pulls me back 50 years—to my rides in her family's car, our private jokes about diets, shared eye-rolling about our overly protective parents.

We are in Karraker's Drug Store on opposite sides of a teeny round table with a giant banana split between us, two spoons and the exhilaration of a shared guilty pleasure. I catch no sign of Paula's misery; we connect over what I believe are our lighthearted cravings.

ﻉﻉ

My family is vaguely, sporadically concerned about my weight. I overhear my father say to my mother, "Can't you do something about that child's weight?" They sit at the porch table finishing dinner. His harsh tone suggests my mother needs to shape up, too. I hear him from the kitchen, where I am rinsing my empty plate, late site of my second piece of Gram's pumpkin chiffon pie with whipped cream. I take the stairs to my bedroom three at a time, slam my door; throw myself on the bed and cry. Mother and Gram fuss about their weight, too, but they think I will grow out of my "baby fat."

When I was seven years old, they rejoiced when I began to eat after my bad tonsils came out. Everything tasted rotten before that. I remember marveling at my model aunt, Thelma, sitting at the dinner table, downing forkful after forkful of Gram's Spanish rice, smiling, talking between bites. She is not just being polite, which I imagine at first, she actually enjoys her food. I wonder if I ever will. Then the magic surgery, and the morning-after surprise, the deliciousness of vanilla ice cream and red Jell-O.

My pain at my father's words was real—for 20 minutes. Not like what Paula must have endured during all the years her mother tortured her, when she was not even fat.

Could I have said something to her? Why didn't she ever say anything to me? Why were all of us so bloody close-lipped? Ours was the original "Don't ask, don't tell" legion.

We were soldiers loyal to an oath we never took but respected so much we could never violate it.

9

Sister Carlene

Back at Immaculate Conception, Sister Carlene breezes into seventh grade on a cloud of gold stars and buoyant discourse. During social studies she talks about the politics Dad is full of at the dinner table, since it is a presidential election year. Dad has decided to vote for Dewey. He reasons that he voted for Norman Thomas in 1936, then Roosevelt next time, since FDR was by then Socialist enough. This time he wants a Republican business type to have a turn. Sister Carlene is a Roosevelt fan like Gram. She explains Dewey is in favor of subsidies that will make milk and bread cost more. I ask Dad about subsidies, but I can't remember his answer long enough to explain it at school the next day. Anyway I don't want to dampen Sister Carlene's enthusiasm; I am already her loyal fan.

Her bulletin boards glitter with bright colored paper letters. Her handwriting is a baroque script, the kind I imagine angels inscribe on parchment scrolls with feather pens. She concocts charts for test grades, spelling words. In the library, rows of tiny multicolored books cut from construction paper climb up each student's golden column: one for each book read, its title printed in miniscule gold letters.

In a serious talk she reveals that Jesus was a Jew, and the worst thing a Catholic can do is hate Jews, like the Nazis. It is 1944.

કેન

In addition to my usual practicing piano during arithmetic class three days a week—I am excused from arithmetic after I learn the day's lesson, like the times tables in third grade—Sister Carlene sends me to the "library" during reading. The library is an alcove at the back of the classroom with a bookcase stacked with dusty books. Now with posters and charts à la Sister Carlene. My assignment—present a book report to the class every Friday.

I find a book about astronomy. Stars are big with Sister Carlene. She checks the sky every morning as she crosses the street from the convent to the church for pre-dawn morning prayers.

I catch her fever. Mother brings me Kevin McCready's *A Beginner's Guide to the Stars* on her weekly St. Louis pilgrimage. Today I consult its yellowed pages to decipher the Mexican skies, grateful I learned the constellations from its night charts when the sky looked like the photos. My iPad's Star Walk app is set to lowest magnitude to mirror my San Miguel sky; patterns disappear in our polluted light. Only at

Ghost Ranch, where I saw the Hale-Bopp Comet streak across the sky, or camping deep in the Michigan woods, does Boötes look like the Herdsman that strode my childhood skies.

I find a neat way to memorize the planets and their order, but the book is so old that Pluto is left out, although it was discovered in 1930 and stayed on the list until 2006.

I triumphantly add a phrase and write my perfected sentence on the blackboard.

Men (Mercury)

Very (Venus)

Easily (Earth)

Make (Mars)

Jugs (Jupiter) to

Serve (Saturn)

Useful (Uranus)

Needs (Neptune).

I add "and Purposes" for Pluto.

Voilà!

❧

I am on my way out of the classroom when Sister Carlene asks if I can stay after school for a few minutes. For a little talk. The other students leave for home and Sister leads me to a table in the library at the back of the room.

She wants to know why I am so late for school that I miss Mass most mornings and never show up for Sunday afternoon devotions.

I twist my school tie around one finger and begin to sniffle. Sister pulls a big white hankie from the wide sleeve of her habit and hands it to me. I blow my nose and look down at my spelling book on the table in front of me.

I hear my mother's voice: "Ridiculous for them to think Pat should spend Sunday afternoons in church. Sunday is a family day; Gram's not dragging her back to church again. Sunday morning Mass is enough." She writes a drawerful of "excuses" for me to take to school every Monday morning.

My discomfort with the difference between my parents' and the nuns' view of religion boils up, along with my own skepticism. All is not incense and chanted litanies.

Father Hubert gives sex instruction before confirmation—boys and girls separately. When he announces that masturbation is a mortal sin, I recognize his views on sexuality as out of touch with the real world.

Mortal sin keeps you out of heaven forever. Missing Mass on Sunday is a mortal sin. My parents never go to Sunday Mass, but my parents are not going to hell.

I cling to a story from the Catholic version of the *Weekly Reader*:

A boy in medieval times is convicted of a horrific crime he did not commit. A judge reads out his death sentence. When the boy hears, "damned in this life and for all eternity," he is comforted; he knows at least he will be vindicated in the next world, because God knows the truth and does justice.

The Baltimore Catechism comes to my parents' rescue. I memorize the three kinds of baptism: baptism by water, the normal pouring-on-the-head rite; baptism by blood, earned by Roman soldiers who—in awe at the courage of the Christians on their way to the lions' den—accept the Faith and become the lions' next meal; and baptism by desire, available to any person who truly desires to follow God's will.

As Sister Carlene questions me I try to remember about baptism by desire. I manage to choke out something between sobs. Sister looks out the window to avoid my misery. She sees my parents don't have the same ideas about religion as most Catholics, she says, but I have got to start getting to school on time.

I nod my head in agreement and ask if I can go. I escape home. Better not tell. I never do.

10

December 30, 1952: Meet Harry

I am back on East State Street after a summer of living on my own in Columbia, Missouri, scheduled to study journalism at Mizzou (the University of Missouri) in the fall. A call from my father had brought me home. He asked for my help in the transition from Bourbeuse Shoe to Brown Group (BG), and I agreed to return. Bourbeuse had just been sold to Brown, one of the big boys among shoe manufacturers, in a stock transfer deal. The rest of my father's life he held a large block of Brown Group stock. In his final days he watched the financial channel daily, looking for BG to show up on the tape running along the bottom of the screen. His comments were always jovial rather than somber: "I feel terrible today; I just lost $200. No steak dinner tonight."

My two years at college had ended in June; my Bachelor of Arts degree arrived in the mail shortly thereafter. I refused to put on a cap and gown for an uncool event like a graduation ceremony. I suspect my parents were disappointed, but I figured I'd saved them the drive to and from Chicago, so they should be happy.

&❧

An Eve of New Year's Eve party, my invention. With my high-school buddies, the old State Street Gang and more.

"Best party I ever went to," Professional Partier Bob H raves. Photos show sloshed 20-somethings raising glasses to the camera, crowded around a dining room table weighed down with plates of ham, cheese, Gram's famous German potato salad and coleslaw, rye and white bread, mustard, pickles, mayonnaise, bowls of peanuts, baskets of potato chips—all crowned by Mother's sacramental Christmas cookies, 22 varieties lined up on a mammoth platter shoulder to shoulder, two or more of each kind like the animals on the Ark. A tribute to Virginia Neunuebel Browne's 11th commandment: Thou Shalt Never Leave My House Unstuffed.

Dick Herzog arrives, invited the night before at the Top Hat, in Washington.

He'd stopped at our table after one of our visitors hailed him. Meta V had asked me to round up my girlfriends to entertain three guys on leave. One of their families is the tenant on her farm in Iowa. The Gang introduces them to the Top Hat, with its tinny canned music and grungy decor, our Top Choice despite being 10 miles away on a winding road. Its curves are wired into my brain's GPS; I can negotiate them after gallons of Budweiser, or so I believe.

My first date with Dick was a non-repeater, but like Meta V's guests, he is an Army draftee on leave from basic training at infamous Fort Leonard Wood. Only an unpatriotic ogre would exclude him from my fun party.

≈

He introduces the stranger at his side as Uncle Harry.

Next morning at breakfast, my neighbor Meta V says Dick's uncle is an old man; Harry must really be Dick's older brother. Sixty years later I still don't get what was funny about Dick's pretending his brother was his uncle. A lucky if lame joke, since I ended up marrying the "uncle."

Meta V goes on. The Herzog family moved to Washington from St. Louis years ago to open a corncob pipe factory. Meta is office manager for their competitor. The two are the only corncob pipe manufacturers in the world. She launches into a history of the corncob pipe. I lose interest until I hear, "a nice Jewish family." My ears perk up like my horse Raven's at the sight of an apple. Jewish means articulate, intellectual, a kindred spirit—like a gold Caldecott medal sticker on a children's book.

11

Harry Connects

Harry phones later that day with the classic, "What are you doing New Year's Eve?" I invite him to join the State Street Gang at the Tri-S dance in the Union Auditorium: formal wear, long tables with paper tablecloths, "set-ups," BYOB, and music by our favorite band, led by musician and chiropractor Sonny Lefholz, the Glen Miller of Franklin County.

Harry likes to dance but prefers the foxtrot to the jitterbug. I like his serious demeanor, settled style. Six years older, a longer stretch between 20 and 26 than later in our lives—eminently suitable.

A Union High classmate leans across the table and whispers, "What the hell are you doing with that guy?" He sees Harry as ancient and boring. I'm ready for boring. Previous beaux have been anything but.

❧

My first *beshert*, Yiddish for a predestined perfect mate, was George, a shy guy a row over and two seats back in geometry class.

"Can I talk to you a minute?" His serious, anxious voice arouses my curiosity. "My mother says I should take a girl to the skating party tonight, and I wondered if you'd go with me?"

George had the kind of looks that would be called "interesting": a wide mouth, heavy brows, a long face and small, deep-set eyes that radiated kindness. A strong body, well-proportioned and energetic; my grandmother would say, "He carries himself well." A modest, hesitant way of speaking that belies an intelligence and a cutting-through-the-crap sensibility that endears him to me from the first.

This is a down-home guy. Nobody but George would ask for a first date and admit his mother told him to. It warmed my heart that he approached me with such candor. He must have suspected that I would say yes even if it was his mother's idea.

I did, and found skating energetic fun, the first of a slew of fortunate firsts over the next three years. Skating parties, school dances and concerts or movies in St. Louis, sometimes followed by supper at the Rose & Crown.

៖

The Rose & Crown was an elegant restaurant that felt adult and adventurous. After our second visit George confides that he feels awkward splurging on soft-shell crabs and Bacardis. His parents would die; he manages because his rich uncle slips him cash, but something in George recoils from such extravagance.

Me, too. I squirm. My starry-eyed affinity for dim lights, white tablecloths and attentive waiters had seduced me. This was way over the top for two high-school kids from the sticks. I blush. No more. What if we ran into somebody from Union?

Already the State Street Gang had been branded an exclusive, rich girls' clique. The month before, when I was changing in the girls' john after gym class, a friend asked if I was going to the skating party that night.

"Heavens, no," I rant. "Skating parties are so childish, bourgeois, noisy—wouldn't be caught dead at one, my dahlink."

What made me say it? A whim, my flair for role-play, mimicking my father's Irish blarney? Surely no one could take me seriously since I skated myself silly at every skating party Union High threw.

The next day my friend confides that the other girls jeered after I left; said I was a total snob like all those stuck-up girls I ran around with.

How ridiculous, I reason. Our fathers include three shoe factory workers and the driver of an oil truck; surely that balances the doctor and my father. My father's prominence as president of Bourbeuse Shoe was a problem, but I imagined hardly anyone knew—Miss Ostrich with her head in the sand and stoppers in her ears.

My father talks more about his early poverty than his current success. He recalls hungry days when his mother's sisters showed up at their door with a basketful of food. My grandfather was a steam fitter, a good trade, but, often, like Roger Miller sang:

> Sitting around drinking with the rest of the boys
> Six rounds bought, and I bought five.
> Spent the groceries and half the rent
> Leaves $14 and 27 cents.

My father, Andrew, was scorned at school as one of those poor Browne boys. He got a paper route—trite, but true—as soon as he could lob a paper on a porch. His earnings bought pocketsful of candy to flash at school to rile his well-heeled classmates. Boosted his self-esteem, but led to toothaches.

Later he made fun of business owners who thought themselves special. "Snobs, high and mighty on their high horses," he said. "Put their pants on one leg at a time, just like me. We are all born equal and had damned well never forget it."

That's what the nuns said, too. "You are a bright child. Work hard; your brains are a gift from God, who expects you to put them to good use." We were all beloved children of God, a God who favored the poor and the weak, if anyone.

え&

"That wasn't our mother's view," my sister Toni says. I have called my only sibling for help writing this memoir. She and her husband, Ken, are newly settled on a ranch in the Texas high chaparral where Ken raises horses and runs cattle and Toni is building a ceramics studio. The Diamond Bar-W Ranch is an hour and a half from Lubbock, their old hometown.

My sister listens sympathetically as I explain my call. I am on a quest for "Why I am who I am, and how did our upbringing contribute?" Especially, who was our mother?

"Just a minute, I am going out front for a better signal," she says.

I picture her sitting down on the roughly hewn porch swing, looking out at the driveway toward the wooden entrance poles with the Diamond Bar-W brand on the crosspiece and the cattle guard below. The area is remote enough for a killdeer to have made a nest among the driveway rocks the previous spring. She hatched three fledglings while Ken's truck carefully avoided the nest.

"Mother had a hard life," Toni begins.

A hard life? Mother? Relaxing in her antique spool bed every afternoon freshly bathed and perfumed, reading the current book club selection. She subscribed to both Book of the Month and Literary Guild, always took the monthly selection or the alternate, sometimes both.

Dinner was in the oven; the makings of their pre-dinner drinks laid out in the kitchen. "A wife should be waiting, ready to welcome her husband when he comes home," she counseled.

"You mean her childhood poverty?" I ask, trying to make sense of Toni's words. I recall Mother's complaints—a curtain in the hall around her bed in their tiny South St. Louis flat her only retreat for privacy from her two brothers, and resenting having to quit high school because her father was out of work.

"Poverty? Yes, but more than that," Toni replies. "Her shame. Her older brother was a raging alcoholic, acted out all over town, and her father was probably a drunk, too. She once confided how ashamed she was to visit him in jail."

Jail? I knew Mother's father was caught bootlegging while eking out an income during the prolonged, bitter strike at Von Hoffman Press. This was the first I'd heard of jail.

"Later," Toni continues, "both her brothers were divorced. In fact, they had three wives apiece. Divorce was a scandal then. Their first breakups were ugly, their kids left in broken homes: another disgrace."

The album. Each brother had a toddler at the time of his divorce. The two divorce-orphans and Toni were together often; Mother took care of the cousins in the messiest days of the divorces. Mother had an album filled with sunny scenes:

snapshots of the three playing in the backyard sandbox, hunting Easter eggs with colored baskets clutched in tiny hands, icing butter cookies and sprinkling colored sugar on top. Not a cloud in sight.

"You think Mother cared that much about what other people thought?" I query.

"She valued others' opinions very highly," Toni replies, "especially those with education and class. She was very sensitive to criticism and didn't have a very high opinion of herself. I saw her as dissatisfied and angry because of that."

≈

Ah. Oh. Yes. Of course.

The dollhouse and the Storybook dolls and the fur coat.

Mother commissioned a carpenter to build a huge dollhouse one Christmas—roomy enough for an English mastiff. It lurked hidden under quilts on the sleeping porch all of October and November while Gram crocheted rugs and blankets for the beds and Mother scoured the department stores for the right furniture. On Christmas Eve it had to be emptied and squeezed sideways through the door and down the stairs to the Christmas tree. It was exquisite, charming and no one ever played with it.

The Storybook dolls filled three shelves in the toy department at Famous Barr, and the minute Mother saw them she knew I would love them. The first seven showed up under the Christmas tree, each costumed to match a day of the week: "Monday's child is fair of face …" I was born on a Thursday, and "Thursday's Child Has Far to Go" had a blue silk dress with white polka dots. She looked nothing like me with her curly blond hair and toothpick arms. A Mexican folk dancer would have been perfect, but no one would have guessed I would end up living in Mexico.

My mother knew that the winter I lived in Chicago I lacked a warm coat. So a full-length sheared beaver coat was under the Christmas tree. I never told her I couldn't wear a fur coat at school. It would scandalize my animal-lover friends.

The dollhouse gathered dust; the collection of Storybook dolls snoozed happily behind the glass doors of the secretary in the living room. Mother took them out one by one and explained Pat's dolls to visitors.

ਦਾ

Until my sister spoke I had never questioned Mother's gifts. My mother gave me what she had missed: being a privileged child safe in a warm fur coat to admire her tony doll collection. Now as a gracious mother of culture and means, she could pamper her daughter.

I gulp. Is my appreciation for bone china and chic haircuts my personal taste, or am I still trying to make my mother happy? I put down the phone with my sister and resolve to look for what the real Pat wants.

Not a fancy car. My father's Cadillac embarrassed me.

He began driving luxury cars at the prodding of the Bourbeuse sales staff. They insisted the car the president drove displayed the company's success. In that case, my father said, he should drive a beat-up Chevy to prove he was a frugal manager. The salesmen groaned. President Browne caved. It was a Cadillac the rest of the Bourbeuse years. My mother loved it—more dolls and fur coat.

≈

When his mother died the first thing Harry bought with his inheritance was the car of his dreams, a Mercedes. I was uncomfortable with the new car without realizing why, until a flat tire made Harry late for our son's wedding. When he explained he'd left his metric jack at home and couldn't find another, I blurted, "It was that goddamned car, that stupid Mercedes," shocking the bride's uncle, the Methodist minister waiting to perform the wedding ceremony.

≈

My father's and the nuns' democratic spirit won my heart, but my mother's anxiety over public opinion lingers. I am sheepish about using Clinique cosmetics. I can't relax in the VIP lounge when United gives me a free pass, and I couldn't travel first class if I had a gazillion dollars. I want to be a working-class woman, descended from "hearty Irish peasant stock," as I explained my heritage. Now I recall my mother overhearing me and objecting that we were *not* peasants. A slow learner, I did not get what annoyed her. My sister was a more astute observer, or maybe I was better at ignoring whatever I did not want to hear.

Early in my childhood I began adjusting facts to make a better story. I'd heard my family polishing their history around the table; I absorbed the lessons of making stories come alive with a few omissions and dramatic details that might have occurred—or not. Now it was hard to sort the truth from the marvelous tale. A hearty dose of Irish livened up a retelling. I developed a style. At our 20th reunion my high-school classmates remembered a joke I'd told in senior year. After they reminded me, I remembered and retold it to hilarity all around.

꿎

I still polish my image, although for a different résumé. A friend at a party recently said "There goes the corporate executive again" as I was organizing the food and serving.

I paled, asked where she had gotten that idea. "It says you were vice president of a bank on your computer," she says. Ouch. I'd posted my old desk nameplate, "Vice President and Trust Officer," on my printer to remind myself how lucky I was to be out of that world, never imagining anyone else would see it in my private office. Someone did; someone clueless enough to think the printer was a computer, but observant enough to read what I thought was my private joke.

"If a vice president of a bank isn't an executive, who is?" laughed another partygoer.

"It was a very small bank," I began, then saw I was making things worse. Better just throw the telltale nameplate away when I got home.

12

Why Marry?

Marriage. 1. The act of marrying, or the state of being married; legal union of a man and a woman for life, as husband and wife; wedlock; matrimony. 4. Any intimate or close union.

—Webster's New Collegiate Dictionary

An early reader of this memoir remarks that as a young adult, I talk more about boyfriends than my future. I cringe. Was I boy crazy? Wasn't my experience typical? My high-school buddies were preoccupied with their boyfriends. Even at U of C, that bastion of freethinking, my women friends spent considerable energy finding, connecting with, and breaking up with guys.

Dating was the first round in the challenge that awaited us. Marriage was our final passage into adulthood, a milestone, like leaving home for college, learning to drive a car, or shaving our legs. We were all headed for the altar—a real altar; weddings in city parks or justice of the peace offices were as deviant as reciting vows underwater or while jumping out of an airplane.

Everybody got married, many right after high school, if not before. For those of us who went to college, engaged by graduation was the norm. I sneered at my peers' conformity. I was not going to college to get a husband, by God.

A progressive woman like me was in search of fulfillment—engaging work that would transform the world, meaningful dialog, intimate connections with my fellows. I dreamed of studying child development on a kibbutz, reporting for the *New York Times* (maybe the *Chicago Sun Times* for starters), having my short stories published in *The New Yorker*. I rallied to the cause of liberation, mouthing slogans from the security of my traditional box seat.

I need to choose a partner sooner or later. Why not now? The marriage thing keeps coming up. The guys are in a hurry. Getting married frees them to get on with their real lives, that is, their careers. The stale saw about the woman trapping the man into matrimony was for the Johnny Carson show and its ilk. Men want sex, so women trap them into marriage, flaunting their feminine wiles while demanding a ring before "putting out." In Johnny's scenario, they then withdraw their sexual favors and demand alimony.

The prevailing cliché sung by Professor Harold Hill in *The Music Man* was that innocent virginal types were out to hook men like fish. Plop! Another man in her net.

When I look back after time and reflection, I am not so sure. Was I the one in a hurry? Hardly an innocent virginal type, although I see now how innocent I was about more serious issues than virginity. Did I want to get marriage out of the way and get on with my life, whatever I envisioned it to be? Was I the one doing the fishing when Harry swam unsuspectingly into my net? Once the marriage question was settled, I could get on with my life.

Sor Juana saw the convent as the only route to an independent life. Marriage was mine.

❧

My Thinking Rock, so helpful in my summers on East State Street is now covered with January's snow, or I would go there.

My rock is behind the East State Street house, 100 yards deep in the magical, mysterious woods that soothe my soul as soon as I enter their humid warmth. I can be alone. Even in summer my mother never follows me. The buzzing insects and scratchy weeds would repel her. In better weather I sit on the rock, surrounded by woods, and share space only with a few spiders and ants. I go there to ponder, plan, review my life. I feel the heat coming up from the ground, hear the noisy bugs, and connect with the life around me. I go there to plan how to learn to play softball, whether to quit St. Francis High School, and how to dump Chicago Mike. My visits presage the quality of later meditations.

True, whether or not to marry Harry is a case for my Thinking Rock. I settle for a Friday afternoon bus ride from St. Louis to Union to spend the weekend. I have a date with Harry Saturday night.

13

Why Harry?

Bumping along in the very last seat at the back of the bus, chosen so I would not be disturbed by the stops at little towns on the way, I get serious. Harry is about to pop the question—seriously retro, but so is Harry. He later officially asks my dumbfounded father for my hand.

The Missouri landscape of red rock hills and clumps of barren oaks, arms raised to the sky, flies by the bus window, then darkens into black silhouettes as the sun sets. A Conoco station blazes up, pumps shining: Regular, 19.99 cents a gallon. We pass the giant, amazing, all-purpose Diamond's Truck Stop where I learned to swim; its twin pools are now buried under a concrete parking lot.

A husband is in order; should it be Harry?

"Uncle Harry" is a tall drink of water—six feet, taut, skinny, wound up like a watch spring. He moves quickly, chooses his words with precision. A large head for his narrow frame, full lips, china blue eyes, wavy straw-colored hair; cast in the proud Hamel mold of his mother, Delphine Hamel Herzog. The Hamels are from Darmstadt, the same German town Harry's father's Bendheim ancestors claim. Powerful genes; all three of our children inherit the Hamel "look." When Delphine's sister sees our first grandchild, she weeps with joy: "She looks just like my babies."

ॐ

Harry and I talk and talk—both the older child of entrepreneurs. I work during the week in St. Louis with my father, overseeing the endgame of Bourbeuse Shoe; Harry is a partner in the family's corncob pipe factory, Herzog & Bendheim.

Harry's father and brother are senior partners; Uncle Leo retired a while back. He'd been the salesman, spent most of his time on the road. His wife jokes that she sometimes forgot what he looked like, and maybe wouldn't let that stranger in the door at the end of the next trip. He calls on wholesale tobacco dealers scattered through the countryside, riding slow trains, slower buses, staying in shabby rooming houses when no hotel can be found. His territory sprawls from Minnesota down to Arkansas. There is an East Coast salesman—corncob pipes are most popular in the big cities of the East. In his final years on the road, Uncle Leo drives a black Lincoln tank over roads almost as slow as the trains. Eisenhower's authorization of the interstate highway system was years away.

Harry replaces Uncle Leo as traveling salesman, "calling on the trade." An awkward role for him, but not because of the difficult travel. He laughs about the time he got stuck in the Minnesota snow and a customer was shocked that he did not carry a shovel in his trunk. Asking for orders is Harry's nemesis—a role uncomfortable enough he worries he will never get the hang of it. No time for road trips since his father's heart attack two years ago. Harry now manages the factory, the office, the books, the works.

We go to St. Louis symphony concerts and movies at the Shady Oak, where Harry sleeps contentedly through the foreign films. Time to talk on the long rides back and forth. He tells his story. His mother insisted he go to college. None of the Bendheims or Herzogs had more than high school, if that—tutors at home for the girls. Delphine treasures her degree from Washington University, an uncommon feat for a woman of her time. She values education as much as my mother, who still mourns having to quit high school and go to work when her father lost his job.

Fresh from Purdue, with a B.S. in mechanical engineering in his pocket, Harry went to work at H&B. No option, he says. His family expects it.

Sad. My father's encouragement to learn the shoe business was friendly persuasion. I cannot imagine he would insist on a career I did not want.

Sad and strange. Harry recites the story of feeling chained to the family business as if he is reading the weather report. His voice is more animated when he talks about Purdue basketball or reads the daily specials from the menu at Busch's Grove, his favorite St. Louis restaurant.

I am puzzled. Are these topics too hot or too delicate for him to reveal his feelings? Maybe he has resolved to make the best of a situation and put other aspirations out of his mind. A familiar tactic in my family: Never mention Grandpa Neunuebel and the sordid truth will stay buried along with him.

Maybe Harry has no one to talk to about these things. He mentions a ban on sharing family business with outsiders. His opening up to me is a leap of faith. I feel special, warmed by Harry's telling secrets he exposes with such difficulty. Airing family flaws to outsiders is equally taboo in my family. This man sees me as a reliable friend. That much confidence in me after so short a time feels like a good fit. We will be able to resolve our differences.

ʦ

Do I love him? I recognize my warm fuzzy feelings from previous flings, but milder, calmer. After the initial hot flashes, my emotions always spin off into a script—what comes next? Romantic struggles through school (George), an exotic mission to an Israeli kibbutz (Mike). With Harry, a Happily Ever After script, a cozy, soothing prospect.

ʦ

Should I marry Harry? Today I might construct an Excel spreadsheet, assign weights to negatives and positives, and spit out a statistical solution. Then, I rummaged in my overstuffed purse and pulled out a notebook and pen. I scribble a list in favor of Harry, the husband:

✓ Grounded, a solid citizen, unlike my loopy earlier beaus, except for George
✓ Works at a real job
✓ Decent education. I poke fun at his Boilermaker mania, but a Purdue B.S. in mechanical engineering represents hard work and competence
✓ Our families live in the same county, are both business owners, similar social class
✓ We share tastes in food. Our family tables feature South German cooking, his from his parents' heritage, mine passed down from my only German ancestor, Great-Grandfather Neunuebel, a steward in a popular St. Louis restaurant
✓ We both love music, especially classical. (When wedding plans turn ugly beause I want a Catholic ceremony, I interrupt the negotiations to suggest that we give our duplicate LPs, Dvorak's *New World Symphony* and Beethoven's

Fifth, to my sister. Relieved, Harry infers this to mean I am still willing to marry him despite the wrangle.)

- ✓ Talk. Our conversations range from Eisenhower's inaugural address to Little Ricky's birth on *I Love Lucy*. I need talk. Talk breeds intimacy. Like Willy Nelson, "I just want someone... that I can talk to ..."
- ✓ Last, but weighted heaviest of all, off the scale compared to South German cooking or classical music, Harry is a believer.

He's a fake Jew it turns out, an Episcopalian like Barry Goldwater. When Meta V called the Herzogs "a nice Jewish family," she parroted the town's crude categorization. Harry was reared in his mother's Christian faith. His father had Jewish ancestors but zero interest in religion of any kind. Harry sought out St. John's Church while at Purdue, and was confirmed an Episcopalian there. His faith informs much of his life. He is a Christian who shares the "Jewishness" I find harmonious—intellectual curiosity, concern for the widow and orphan, a low macho quotient.

Harry scores high enough to be a serious candidate for a lifetime partnership.

Negatives? From a tense encounter last weekend, I suspect he wants to marry me to get out of his parents' house.

❧

We were parked in Harry's maroon Studebaker coupe on Art Hill, the grounds of the St. Louis Art Museum. With its sweeping view of the city, it's a favorite smooching spot for young lovers. Harry asks for a cigarette—a sign something important is on the agenda. He forsakes his H&B corncob pipe for a cigarette when he needs a tranquilizer.

He lights the Lucky I hand him, takes a drag, and peers out his driver's side window. An octave lower than usual, "I've been to a psychiatrist."

He turns his head my way without meeting my eyes. This is tough—something he thinks he must tell me before he asks me to marry him, a flaw in his suitor's résumé. I am touched.

He addresses the windshield. "I was called up for the Korean War. Funny, I was in the Navy for a brief few weeks in 1944, my second semester at Purdue. I reported to Navy Pier, went through a bunch of tests, was sworn in, due to leave for basic training the next day. An officer called me in and said my sight wasn't good enough for the Navy; they'd missed it in the first go-round. I got a medical discharge and went back to college. Thought that was the end of the whole thing, that I was disqualified for good.

"Then this notice from my draft board, ordering me to report to Jefferson Barracks in St. Louis. Quite a shock. I still thought they'd turn me down when they gave me the eye exam. But this time, after all the medical stuff, the checker—later found out this is Army code for psychiatrist—stamped 4F on my papers, checked 'psychological reasons,' and advised me to get psychiatric help.

"I dreaded telling my parents. Found a little neighborhood bar near the barracks and had three boilermakers—good thing I didn't get stopped on the way home.

"Mother called her sister's husband. Uncle Leo had done a residency in psychiatry at Washington U. He recommended a doctor, and I saw the guy every week for ... for a long time."

Harry pauses, glances over to me, then scrambles to neutral territory in his normal voice. "It was the first time Mother spoke to her sister in years—some family tiff."

I learned later that Delphine was often not speaking to somebody. She once cut off communications with her father for two years. Harry's mother now speaks of her father, long dead, in the hushed tones Sister Carlene reserved for Saint Therese, the Little Flower of Jesus.

"It was a tough step for Mother to call her sister, but neither she nor Dad knew where else to turn. They couldn't ask our doctor or anyone else in Washington for fear it would be all over town the next day."

Silence. Harry flips his cigarette butt out the window.

"Did the sessions help?" I ask. Harry's teeth unclench. I had not jumped out of the car.

"He kept telling me I should move out," he replies. "I never could bring myself to do it—would have caused a scandal not to live at home. Mother put her hands over her face and cried when I brought it up."

è▲

The bus turns off the highway onto Jefferson Street and chugs up the hill, headed for Pautler's Variety Store, where we will disembark. I close my notebook, heave my purse onto my lap and hug it to my chest. I mull the final score.

Children then often lived with their parents until marriage. My setting up a home of my own—a tiny efficiency in a private residence, hardly a den of iniquity—was considered daring. Harry's reluctance to leave his family home is understandable, if extreme, in the face of his psychiatrist's counsel.

If I had examined his history objectively, I would have been more concerned. Harry was 26 years old; my foray into independence was at 20. He felt bound by his parents' iron wills, both as to where he lived and what he did for a living. Taken together these should have set off caution lights at the least.

Not for romantic, all-powerful Pat. I count Harry's visits to a psychiatrist as positive. I file his family struggles in the same pigeonhole with my friends' growing pains, all part of normal young-adult angst. Most of my peers are in therapy; I am the oddball. Just across the quad from my college dorm, David Riesman lectures on the inner-directed man, soon to emerge in *The Lonely Crowd*. A gal in my Soc. 3 class works at Bruno Bettelheim's Orthogenic School for disturbed children.

Talk therapy is in. Carl Rogers hones his new client-centered therapy in the counseling center. A popular caricature:

> Client: I want to jump out of the window.
> Therapist: You want to jump out of the window?
> [Client jumps.]

Besides, I will be Queen of the Soothing Spouses. I have flagrantly ungrounded faith in the ability of a Good Wife to steer a marriage on a safe course. Together Harry and I will ford all streams, navigate all falls, weather any hurricane, our snug bark fortified with mutual trust and endless love. I had seen Rosalind Russell and Cary Grant do it many, many times. Love conquers all in the Hollywood Credo, memorized in my years spent in Union's Williams Theatre. Harry is a project crying out to be tackled. Enfolded in my loving embrace, his so-called psychological problems will melt in a puddle at our feet.

I am invincible. Admitted to the only college I apply to—how's that for hubris? Place out of so many courses I graduate in two years.

Brashness and academic skills are not strong qualifications for weaving a partnership, but I spurn realistic assessment and plunge ahead. I have 20 years of practice at denial. Differences in our upbringings that later turn toxic I view through Super Pat's Rosy Lenses. A wedding will solve everything.

Ironic—Harry marries me to get out of his parents' house; I marry Harry to get on with my life. Neither of us has a clue how shaky are our skills for the challenge we face: weaving a whole cloth from two unmatched skeins, one of dark thick wool, the other bright diaphanous cotton.

We stay together for almost 50 years, a tribute to the shared values that I weight so heavily on my checklist.

ह

The bus stops. Passengers stand up, stretch, head toward the door. I stay put for a moment to gather my thoughts.

I will say yes. Harry is a good bet.

14

The Wedding

Delphine Hamel Herzog is a flash point from the beginning.

When Harry and I announce our engagement, his mother coos. My father is president of a shoe company; I have a college degree. All goes smoothly until Delphine's Wednesday afternoon bridge club. Madame Tattletale is a woman already labeled a smart-alecky Catholic newcomer—only been in town 10 years. She casually drops her bomb as the foursome arrange their hands before the bidding begins, "I hear Harry and Pat are going to be married in Pat's church."

My mother fills me in. My parents' bridge and dinner club meets at their house. Madame Tattletale follows Mother out into the kitchen at the break between the food and the card playing. She stacks the dirty dessert plates on the sink and sidles over to Mother, busy dumping the coffee grounds into the garbage.

"Virginia, such good news about Harry and Pat. I was just wondering …will they be married in church?"

Mother lights up as she tells me, "I was so proud to be able to tell her, 'Of course. In Immaculate Conception Church, right here in Union.'"

Delphine confronts her son, who confirms not only the scandalous wedding site but that he is undergoing mandatory instructions from a priest to make it possible. Delphine blows, as in "Hell hath no fury."

With Delphine's onslaught, my previous mild preference transforms to a crusade. I will skewer the nasty bigot; the wedding will be in Immaculate Conception Church.

Harry recoils but grits his teeth and agrees after a mentor friend tells him to forget the religion, just get the girl. Harry must have known what was coming from his mother.

Catholics are ignorant, priest-ridden dullards to her. She will be uncomfortable at her son's wedding and at the later baptism of her first grandchild. She will keep up appearances by her oohs and ahs at the events, saving the true script for her Protestant confidants, who agree that the Union Brownes are basically bumpkins. All smiles for her Catholic friends; Washington is a Catholic town. Delphine sees no irony in her affection for her dear friends the Mauntels and her conviction that all Catholics are mindless puppets.

Her anti-Catholic stance puts her among the Neanderthals in my book. Later I realize that the stain rubbed off on her son. Harry goes to the polls in 1960 agonizing that a vote for Jack Kennedy will put the pope in charge. He manages to pull the Democratic lever with his fingers crossed.

Harry is loyal to his clan, Episcopalian or Jewish. Others are, well, *others.*

Our older son, Tom, believes his father looked down on me because I wasn't Jewish. His comment puzzles me, since Harry was a loyal Episcopalian until after Tom left home. Flashback: Tom and I going to Mass, Tom lighting the candles on the altar, Tom making his First Communion. Harry admits it is hard for him to enter a Catholic church, much less see his family participate, but I bury that deep until my son speaks. Tom has the label wrong. Harry looked down on me for being Catholic—even a dubious, marginal Catholic. Tough to see his smart wife in a class of uneducated, lowbrow sheep. Tom's child radar picks up what neither parent can bear to admit.

ૐ

Before Delphine plays her Bad Catholics card, I am ambivalent. An elopement would suit my modern woman persona better. A Catholic wedding is important for my mother. I want to be the daughter my mother longs for. She knows her Pat will never marry a *real* Catholic since I ignore the church's rules on premarital sex and birth control and scoff at most of the creed, with its Virgin birth and descent into hell. She yearns for a public acknowledgement of our faith. Our family is only marginally Catholic in local eyes. A church wedding will publicly validate our credentials. A wedding seems a small concession for me to make.

Now I see that I sold out to the wedding *shoulds*. Certain elements are key: the bride in a long white dress, preferably with train and veil; bridesmaids in matching dresses, matching bouquets, all in the wedding color (pastels more tasteful); a religious ceremony followed by a receiving line, with all family hands on deck; a reception with enough food and liquor to get drunk on a full stomach. Dancing optional but preferred; a cake, sinking under the weight of six tiers of inedible icing and sugar rosettes, which the couple cuts in a ritual that concludes when the bride stuffs the first piece into the groom's mouth. My wedding album holds a picture of me doing just that.

When the couple leaves for the fabled wedding night the bride tosses her bouquet over her shoulder, and whoever catches it is the next to marry. No wedding signals a problem---pregnancy, parental disapproval, unsuitable match, free thinking. The only State Street Gang member who flaunts tradition and elopes is pregnant.

Harry is the brave one on the wedding scene; he defies his mother, a first. We marry at the Communion rail; in mixed marriages, one spouse not Catholic, the couple cannot approach the altar. Two Catholics can marry at the altar, a special dispensation for a female to enter that sacred space. Hmmm. Does that mean two Catholic men can be married at the altar? Maybe not.

Delphine survives. Pictures at the reception show the mother of the groom smiling in every shot.

è▲

I withdraw from the scene after vanquishing Delphine. I refuse to pick the wedding cake. My grandmother reluctantly visits Schulte's bakery and orders one with no input from me. I buy the least formal wedding dress I can find, plain white organdy, no train. Our bouquets are daisies, a working-class flower. I decree a wedding reception at the resort, scene of our gang's orgies, a nontraditional choice.

I want my friends with me, and five loyal State Street gals rally around to be bridesmaids. My cousin Margaret Ann is my matron of honor. I was her bridesmaid when she married at 16 to a handsome Irish groom now drinking himself to death. My sister and one of the divorce-orphan cousins are junior bridesmaids: a five-year-old friend is flower girl, and my youngest cousin, Eddie, ring bearer. Quite a production for a bride who would rather elope.

With me dragging my feet, my mother is over her head with the arrangements. She needs a wedding planner 50 years before one is available. The logistics of feeding 200 people with minimal kitchen and dining facilities make the resort an impractical choice. Renting tables and chairs is not easy and finding a caterer even tougher. Some of my parents' loyal friends volunteer to set everything up, cook the food, and serve it.

There are a few glitches. The volunteer servers feed the wedding party first, while our guests mill around in the nearby dance hall, unsure what is going on. They seat only the wedding party together for our meal; the spouses of our attendants are marooned among our families, mostly strangers to them.

Mother and Harry and I begin to greet our guests when we arrive at the dance hall. I suspect Mother didn't know how to get Harry's parents on their feet as the guests started lining up, although afterwards she complains about having to receive 200 people on her own. Where was my father? Probably telling stories to the delight of his listeners.

In the official photos I look radiant waltzing with Harry and my father and jitterbugging with my sister. I remember a festive event with me a shadowy figure. My clearest memory is repeating the traditional vows in a loud, clear voice, the same tone I used to recite Edgar Allen Poe's *The Raven* in the eighth grade. I feel like a performer rather than a participant.

ða

The charade ends at our 40th anniversary party. Harry and I plan that gathering to our taste—at the YWCA, where I work out and go to League of Women Voters meetings. We choose

Judy to cater, the downhome chef with a big belly and a bigger smile who cooks for many a Lafayette political rally, wedding, birthday bash—more ham and cheese than caviar and champagne. I cajole a folk dance teacher into leading the guests in a few easy dances. I wear culottes with matching top, bright violet cotton with multicolored flowers. The invitation announces Harry will not be wearing a suit. The 40+ guests get a printed program with songs for a sing-along: *Joe Hill, Let There Be Peace on Earth, He's Got the Whole World in His Hands, Cockles and Mussels, We Shall Overcome, Amazing Grace* and *Oseh Shalom.*

Our three children and their spouses and children all show up. Three Union Queens drive over from St. Louis, Harry's brother and wife from Washington, the Gilners and Harry's cousins from St. Louis, my sister from Texas. My mother is there in a wheelchair, minimally conscious of what is going on. We plan events for the out-of-town folks; a dinner in our home the night before, a brunch the day after at our daughter Meta's house.

Grandson Andy and his father, Tom, welcome the guests. Our six grandchildren, from 2-year-old Paul to 5 1/2 year old Shona, dance and sing with the music. Elizabeth grabs the mike at one point to lead the singing. I create a children's table with a balloon cluster and carefully chosen table games.

Our favorite local trio plays. The lead singer, an African-American soul singer, leads us in *Amazing Grace* as her final number.

I follow Harry to the podium and say thank you to everyone who made this possible, then take off on an impulsive riff on why I wanted this party to replace the memories of our wedding. God knows what I said, but after, a friend comments, "You really did not like your wedding, did you?"

Her comment shocks me; I didn't hear my resentment until she played my words back to me.

I spoke truth. I demanded a ceremony my mother wanted, then felt trapped. I was stuck with 15 attendants and 200 guests when I thought a graduation ceremony was too formal. I anesthetized my feelings and then denied there was a problem for 40 years. Amazing grace that Harry and I stayed together 40 years and then some.

§

Married life begins with a honeymoon in an emergency location—Excelsior Springs, Missouri. Harry must meet H&B's principal cob grower, who is recovering from a recent heart attack. I accompany Harry to the farmer's house, chat awkwardly over coffee with the polite wife while Harry talks business in the fields. That I could stay behind to explore the town never enters my mind. Our hotel is a spa with a hot springs, probably has massage and swimming, maybe facials; I never investigate. Better to be on call should Harry need me. He never does, but I tag along anyway. I am Mrs. Harry Herzog now, loyally velcroed to my husband's side.

15

Washington

We begin married life in a new duplex a few blocks from the center of town. We furnish our love nest with care and wedding gifts—the money wedding gifts. The others run heavily to silver: platters, bowls, pitchers that we store in my parents' basement for 10 years, then sell at auction. I smoke cigarettes, as do many of our friends, so we put the silver Ronson lighter on our prize purchase, a coffee table made of natural blond wood slabs supported by black metal tubes, *muy au courant*. The silver ice cube bucket gets heavy use. I brew a pitcher of tea every morning, and a tray of cubes is essential for every glass of iced tea, according to Gram, my tea maven. Revere Ware is in vogue; we hang three skillets and four saucepans on our kitchen wall. I keep the copper bottoms shined.

We buy canvas butterfly chairs, the latest: one black and one orange. Harry builds a room divider to separate the living and dining areas, and paints it flat black. When our record collections, books, phonograph and my stash of old *New Yorkers* and *New Republics* are loaded onto its shelves, I am at home.

We paint our bed royal blue, Mexican *azul real*. The bed is a simple maple four-poster, my parents' original marriage bed, preserved by my mother's 24 years of exceptional care. She offers me anything I want from her house. I earmark the Primal Bed, now in a guestroom, my desk, my bed, a couch, miscellaneous tables, lamps and more. Lots more. When Gram sees Harry drive up in the beat-up factory pickup with a helper to load furniture she says, "I'm going upstairs to lie down in my bed so they don't take that by mistake."

I unpack my clothes, many bought for college. Bought, not worn. *Seventeen* assured me orange and black were the colors of the year, but when I get to Chicago none of my classmates read *Seventeen*. We are all Trotskyites and wear faded jeans and turtlenecks. First time I venture uptown, Washington's town center, in my orange corduroy skirt and black sweater, I turn heads. They don't read *Seventeen* in Washington either.

Not that they are Trotskyites. Dick, now my brother-in-law, warns Harry to cancel my subscription to *Dissent* when he notices the magazine on our prize coffee table. A suspicious mailman might report me. Dick is back from a tour with Army intelligence in Italy, where he identified which Italians were Communists, hence unfit to be hired by the U.S. forces for the many construction and other jobs that needed doing.

In 2013 I stop writing and search *Dissent* online. A miracle. It is still published. I subscribe.

Harry has a grungy pair of "senior cords." The Purdue tradition is for seniors to wear gold corduroy trousers emblazoned with their school, year, girlfriend's name and so on. Black and gold are Purdue's colors. Harry's pants are faded to palest yellow, with ME '47, a slide rule and his honorary society's emblem emblazoned in broad black marker. His butt is so narrow they fit me, with considerable roll up because of his 6-foot frame. Harry's mother "calls" one afternoon, finds me wearing the cords and shrieks, "Didn't your parents buy you a sufficient trousseau—you have to wear rags?" I know she believes my parents are spendthrifts, but she is usually subtler. I laugh and say the well-washed corduroy feels soft and cozy; I love wearing Harry's senior cords.

I confirm Delphine's suspicion that I am just like my extravagant parents when she finds a "good wool dress" in my wastebasket.

"That dress is 100 percent wool," she scolds. "It will be a long time before you can afford another like it."

True, but I wore it to death in the cold winters at school, and I am tired of it. I show her that my elbows are coming through the sleeves. "I will take it home and sew on elbow patches," she says. I demur and toss the dress in the garbage can as soon as her car clears the driveway.

"Calling" is a polite Washington custom I could do without. A visitor may show up anytime, expect a cup of coffee with a sweet nosh on the side, and waste an hour of both our time assuring me how lucky I am to have moved to this warm welcoming community. Delphine has been known to ring my bell at 8 a.m., the middle of the day as far she is concerned. I have not gotten my sea legs in this new pond, so I do not object. I never do.

A neighbor invites me over for the Tuesday evening rosary. I go, loyal to my tribe, but beg off when her daughter returns the next week to remind me.

Harry has lodge one night a week at the Mason's Hall. His fellow lodge members are of his parents' generation. I am told I am eligible for the Eastern Star, the women's auxiliary, where I could wear formal gowns at their rituals. I pass.

The rest of the Washington social scene is equally appealing, as alien to me as Union was to my mother 17 years earlier. There are many parties. Two varieties: large cocktail parties where everyone mingles and pops olives stuffed with cream cheese or chicken livers wrapped with bacon into their mouths; dinner parties where we sit at formal tables for 10 or 12 and discuss the seasonal variant of "Do you think the rain will hurt the rhubarb?"

The town's social elite invites the New Couple to every "do" along with Harry's mother and her cronies. Our peers desert this village as soon as the ink dries on their degrees.

Like Harry, a few lonely inheritors of family businesses are stuck, far outnumbered by their parents' generation, a new and stifling version of togetherness.

Harry and three tennis buddies play most weekends at the court his uncle has built behind his home. I do not play tennis, but I tag along and cheer everyone's good shots. I like his tennis buddies; one is a shoe designer who knows my father.

Uncle Leo comes out to watch the play, sporting his corncob pipe and a wide smile under a giant broad-brimmed straw hat. After the four come off the court hot and sweaty, Aunt Louise ushers us onto the screened porch where cold beers and a pitcher of iced tea await. She brings us each a huge slab of watermelon on a dinner plate. The shoe guy eats his down to the rind and leaves the plate looking like it came out of the dishwasher. All the rest of us have a lake of red juice and seeds slopping over our plates. My most entertaining social event to date.

I escape every week to Union. My friends are largely off someplace following their drafted husbands and having babies, but my family is around. East State Street never looked so good. I overhear that Harry's family considers my trips to Union a waste of gas. Am I overly dependent on my family? My husband is supposed to come first.

A month later Harry takes off on his first road trip. Dick is back from the Army and Harry can leave the factory in his brother's charge. While he is in Wisconsin their father succumbs to his second heart attack. Life changes for everyone.

During the wedding infighting Harry's father sat on the sideline with a twinkle in his eye. When asked if Harry was at his lodge meeting one night, he quipped, "Yes, he is, but you should ask which one. He's now eligible for the Knights of Columbus as well as the Masons, you know."

Harry senior's death liberates his wife. His first heart attack had severely restricted him. In those days heart patients moved like turtles—no stairs, no driving, naps every afternoon—constantly on guard against the dreaded second attack. Delphine confides to me a week before her husband's death how miserable she is with her confined life; she must drive her husband around, take care of him, cook special foods, and give up many social engagements. Not what I expect from a Model Matriarch about her lawfully wedded spouse, and it is what I remember when I hear the fatal news. After DHH's open distaste for the burden of a sick husband, I expect minimal mourning. Instead, she is a Tragically Bereaved Widow. Her complaints were private; the widow role is public, and a proper face to the world is essential Delphine dogma.

ع▲

When Harry's parents invited mine to dinner to seal our engagement before the wedding ruckus, Harry senior served Manhattans before dinner. My parents are scotch drinkers but lift their crystal stemware and toast the union with grace. Delphine passes a silver tray with fancy morsels tastefully arranged. She gives us each a linen cocktail napkin, an H embroidered on one corner. When my parents accept the third Manhattan, Harry's parents are scandalized.

Harry's father has a talk with him the next day. He warns his son of the perils of alcohol. "Shicker is a goy," he says, a Yiddish expression meaning Jews aren't drunks. Which they weren't in his generation. It is the only time I hear his father mention being Jewish.

Harry tells me the story. I am amused; the hint that Irish Catholic genes have anything to do with alcohol abuse is so medieval. He never brings it up again, even after my drunken wedding episode.

る

A month after our own wedding we attend the wedding of a prominent Washington family. The only thing I remember is slowly tearing the paper tablecloth in front of me into tiny strips. I lingered too long at the champagne fountain. Harry gets me back to our apartment and pours me into bed, then drives into the countryside, rents a boat and rows into the middle of a fishing pond. I learn about his boat trip years later in a joint therapy session. The psychiatrist labels it a stellar example of avoidance. I suspect Harry wondered what he has gotten himself into with this marriage. His father warned him.

The morning after my champagne debacle we drive to Union for brunch at my parents'. I can barely keep my head up; the smell of food nauseates me. Gram pats my hand. Everyone at the table smiles at my fun-loving overindulgence. My mother commiserates that champagne is treacherous—can keep you drunk for two days.

ë❧

Maybe if I'd installed a champagne fountain in my kitchen Harry and I would have had serious conversations about addiction. Or maybe I would have died of alcoholism like my mother while everyone looked the other way. The sad, unacknowledged reality is that addiction haunts our marriage, even though neither Harry nor I are alcoholics. Good food is our addiction.

16

Shorty's

My early days in our dollhouse duplex revolve around cookbooks, menus, shopping, chopping, cooking and serving exceptional meals. Food and the ritual around it play a big role in both our lives. I am critical of Mother and Gram, who define themselves too narrowly as Chief Cooks and Bottle Washers. I vow to liberate myself from this humdrum role. Reality intrudes.

A bride is responsible for filling the communal table with good food, in my case, in the South German style enshrined in Irma Rombauer's *The Joy of Cooking*, revered as the Bible in both our parents' kitchens. My wedding present edition included a recipe of Harry's Aunt Paula's, purged from later editions. That recipe is lost to me now, since my original cookbook collapsed long ago under a coat of spilled cake batter and badly burned corners.

High standards I take on with gusto. The wife cooks; the husband feasts. I study *The Joy of Cooking* like I am cramming for a comprehensive exam. I tackle Konigsberger Klopse, Liver Dumplings, Poppy Seed Cake with Custard Filling. The hardest thing is getting everything on the table at the same time. Why didn't I serve in courses? I must have thought everything had to be done just like at home on East State Street.

ॐ

Breakfast, that most intimate of meals, is a snap.

During our courtship Harry says he eats scrambled eggs and biscuits for breakfast every morning. I file that away and when we return from our honeymoon, bake six buttermilk biscuits as the coffee brews. Uncomplicated and ready in 15 minutes, along with the eggs and my toast.

"Wow, biscuits for breakfast," Harry burbles, the first time he raises the napkin keeping the basket of biscuits warm. After two weeks, he sheepishly admits that he is tired of biscuits; the biscuits were a joke.

It seems Uncle Ike once scorned an acquaintance as "the kind of woman who would bake biscuits for breakfast." Harry's mother latches onto that; a man who demands biscuits for breakfast becomes her equivalent of a chauvinist pig. She scoffs, "What do you want, biscuits for breakfast?" to requests she considers over the top. Since my mother and grandmother consider biscuits for breakfast no big deal, I don't get it. When Harry confesses, I preen. I am confirmed as a gracious wife, giving Harry "good measure, pressed down, and shaken together, and running over," Luke 6:38. Not a Scrooge like his mother.

I expected the rest of the Bible verse to follow: "Give, and it shall be given unto you ... For with the same measure that ye mete withal it shall be measured to you again."

A dangerous assumption.

I am a star cheerleader. Harry blossoms. His painfully skinny frame fills out, his chronic back pain improves, and friends comment that he seems happier than they have ever seen him. I am proud. Everything is under my competent control.

I blossom, too. Being a wife is one of life's major assignments, and I am on it.

❧

One night soon after our marriage we head to Shorty's Diner, the homegrown precursor of Denny's—without the "Welcome to Denny's, I'll be your server." A waitress would never get to "and my name is Brenda" before Shorty would be at the pay phone on the wall, dialing the sheriff, suspecting a zombie took her place. Not exactly a greasy spoon; the spoons are clean, but nobody's heard of Irma Rombauer. All heads turn as we enter. A couple of the town's good old boys are perched at the counter, dragging on their cigarettes between bites of apple pie. One greets Harry with a grunt, a smirk and, "What's the matter? Can't she cook?"

My eyes smart. I am mortified but manage a good-natured half smile as we pass the jerks.

I mutter my complaints to Harry as we slide into the booth farthest from the counter. He assures me they are harmless old farts without much to do but trade insults at Shorty's. But the old goat's jibe drives a dagger through my heart. My biscuits, the liver and onions that are the best Harry's ever eaten, the cream puffs his mother never made, all for nothing. I am exposed to the whole town as a slug.

17

Sporlan

Slug. A small gastropod mollusk having a slow-moving body and no shell. Informal meaning: A sluggard. A slothful person, an idler.

—American Heritage College Dictionary

Money is tight at H&B; we draw only food and rent money every month. Since there are no profits, Harry's share of the partnership steadily reduces in value.

I look for a job.

Sporlan Valve, a local producer of refrigeration valves, is hiring. I go to work in the factory. I think of it as an adventure. Super Pat waves her cape, able to work long hours in factories and leap socio-economic borders in a single bound.

Learning the job is not easy. I pack pushrods, a novice's assembly line task, but not for a novice with four thumbs. Each valve comes to my station with two pushrods—metal cylinders loosely fitted into two holes bored into the top of the valve. My task is to squirt a black, greasy blob of packing into both holes, then work the pushrods up and down with pliers until they are solid but still moveable. I master this, eventually;

145

unlike the first job I am asked to do, where I remove a nut with a power un-winder. I make so much noise the foreman moves me to rescue my coworkers from the din.

The social life of the factory fascinates me. Since the tasks themselves are repetitive and boring, people chat constantly. The topics are the various couplings and uncouplings of the workers, who is pregnant and by whom, and who was pulled over drunk last Saturday night—livelier stuff than the cocktail party patter where Harry's mother hangs out.

Jokes make the rounds. Homer, on the line behind me, walks over to tell me the latest. After delivering the punch line he hustles back to his station, leery of what innocent Pat, the new rich kid, will say.

A stewardess offers refreshments to a man on a plane. "We have many delicious choices," she says, "all TWA specialties. I have TWA cola, TWA milk and TWA coffee." "Okay, the man replies, I'll take some of your TWA tea."

As he walks away, I panic. I have no clue what TWA tea means, and I imagine everyone in the factory is watching to see if I laugh or sniff prudishly. I laugh to be a regular fellow, but my curiosity gets the best of me, and I quiz the worker next to me. She explains that "twat" is a dirty word for a woman's private parts. Since I haven't heard it before or since, even in movies that wallow in foul language, it must be a local invention. Nope, twat is in the *American Heritage College Dictionary*, "vulgar slang for the vulva." So much for my college degree and sophistication.

 و

My job ignites a fire under Queen Delphine: "Look at the damage this does to the family reputation." A Herzog working in a factory is humiliating. People might think H&B cannot support her. (The fact that it can't is a fanatically guarded secret.)

She goes to my mother for help. "I can't understand these young people," she sniffs. "Your daughter seems to think she has to work. Is there anything you could say to stop her?" My mother replies that Pat likes to eat.

Delphine pales. I must have dared to hint that the fabled family pipe factory is not making money. After his father has cautioned Harry not to tell Pat about H&B business.

و

Was part of taking a factory job another dig at my mother-in-law? Was my life as controlled by her as her son's was, since I reacted to her jibes rather than plotting my own course? It sounds trite and whiny in retrospect, a bad joke on a sitcom, where the mother-in-law is always the villain.

Then I take the first step toward becoming a mother-in-law myself.

18

Motherhood

Something in me cries out for a child. Six months into the marriage I play Russian roulette with my diaphragm. There is dreamy talk with Harry about parenthood, intermittent primal urges to hold a baby in my arms. I support our sober, sensible plan of waiting ... sometimes.

Did the specter of Catholic guilt haunt me? I trumpet my sophistication loud and proud. I brag that my square parents practice birth control, which my mother daintily refers to as "Andy's taking care of all that."

Harry is aware of my oblique hints, but neither of us starts a serious discussion. Why talk about a life-changing decision when you can wait for the baby to show up on your doorstep? Cartoons still feature storks flying over houses and dropping baby-filled blankets from their beaks. Maybe I had seen too many movies, where a new mother and father do nothing but cradle the baby and coo.

❧

A month of ever more urgent examination of the toilet paper after a pee for a trace of red.

I visit Dr. Herman Meshuga, MD. He saved Harry Herzog senior from stomach cancer; the family awards him their lifelong patronage. His office is a pigsty; he frequently lowers the filthy venetian blinds to screw his mistress between patients. Unnecessary. The dust-encrusted windows are as good as shades.

Once in his consulting room, I simper on about upset stomach and dizziness. I am afraid I am pregnant, but play coy. I can't come right out and ask the question. Is it the weird doctor or my weird qualms?

ਃ

Dr. M examines me and pronounces me pregnant, the fault of my old-fashioned diaphragm, which he denounces as worthless, not to be mentioned in the same breath as the cervical cap he will install after I give birth. His miracle device will result in Meta's birth: a priceless if unintended gift from Doctor Crazy.

I meekly comply with family convention and allow this madman to deliver my first child. Why not? I plan natural childbirth, studied in Grantly Dick-Read's *Childbirth Without Fear*, a current best-seller although first published the year after I was born. If it shuts Harry's mother up to have Dr.

Meshuga attend me, no biggie. He insists I stay in bed for a week after childbirth, and I rue my cowardice. All the State Street Gang are out of bed in one day and the hospital in three. Why did I put up with this?

><

My nausea gets serious. Gram invites us to Union for dinner. My parents are away and she has found a veal breast at Frick's. Gram's stuffed veal breast is worthy of Michelin's coveted five stars. I push the dressing around on my plate, manage to down a few bites of meat. Gram guesses. When I go public she and the rest of my family cheer the pregnancy as if a new heir to the royal throne is on the way.

I am laid off from Sporlan along with two other pregnant women. I ask the manager timidly how he knew I was pregnant. He grins, says a little bird told him. This is 10 years before Title VII, before anyone dreams that hiring and firing women is anybody's business but Sporlan's. Washington is not a union town; the boss is the boss in the eyes of this conservative community. Workers, pregnant or not, have only "the right to a Christian burial," an oft quoted Missouri axiom.

I am ambivalent about staying home. I am proud to pack pushrods with the precision and speed required to keep the job. But now I tire more easily, and the last weeks of standing on the line eight hours a day, my legs swell.

ða

Harry's mother lobbies for a house as soon as she hears the news. She will give us the down payment. A rented apartment is not appropriate for a family, i.e., the Herzog image. Already my scandalous employment raises doubts about H&B; a new house is a counter tactic.

We comply. We will bring our newborn Tom home from St. Francis Hospital to a built-on-spec two-bedroom on newly paved East Eighth St: a beige shingle story-and-a-half that costs $4,500. The half is an unfinished attic.

ða

The impact of a child coming into my life overwhelms me one afternoon in the final month of my pregnancy—a foretaste of how my father's mortality flattens me later. Like the day when I know my father is dying, the scene is permanently archived. I can run the tape at will; sometimes it spins on autopilot.

Harry is away on a sales trip. I am alone in the house. It is a hot day in a miserably hot summer. I open all the windows to get a through draft, but the blowtorch breezes make the house hotter than before. I open the door to the basement and quickly close the door behind me to enjoy the welcome cool damp air that greets me. I sit down on the top step. The stairs are unfinished wood risers with no backs, leading to a full basement; Missouri is tornado territory. I lean against the doorframe, arms folded around my bent knees, and hug my big belly.

Here I am, all by myself, my final days on my own. I'd better enjoy it. After the baby is born I will never have this freedom again, or not for, maybe, 20 years. Another person will depend on me. I will not be free to decide what to do, where to go, or when. I am taking on years of responsibility and there is no way out. Meanwhile, I huddle on the basement steps, on the way to a major life transition.

Why did I make this huge decision with so little deliberation? Did I really trust this hazy urge to see me through 20 years of guiding another human? I read *Ideal Marriage* for sex, Dick-Read on how to give birth.

There must be reliable books about child rearing. Really? My real Self recoils. Learn from a book how to do the most important work I will ever do---mothering, with its years and years of complexities and nuances? Not likely. Everything in me screams that I must get this right. To fail as a mother is unthinkable.

And I am scared. The baby is now a real person, ready to take his place in my life—a major, unavoidable place—with no time off, no resignations, no second chances.

When I saw missteps in the families I observed, I assured myself that I could do better, correct those mistakes. Never buy unwanted gifts for my daughter, over-indulge my son like Gram does Eddie, or be rigid like Delphine. But where is my model for the Good Mother I must be? What book can I read, what wise woman consult? This is serious stuff.

ॐ

Meta and Ben follow Tom's birth, and it will be 33 years before they leave our house and my on-site mothering. Turns out I had good reason to worry about my shaky preparation.

Meanwhile, I still have to deal with Delphine.

19

Lunch at Mother Herzog's

Harry not only praises my cooking, he goes from 130 to 180 pounds in the first year of our marriage. I gain 50 pounds, too, soon lost after giving birth to Tom, our first child. Harry's mother interprets his weight gain as a reflection on her cooking, a personal affront from her elder son, somehow engineered by his difficult wife. No food fight, this is a call to arms, a laser of disapproval aimed at the new cook in the family.

The battle heats up. I am home, laid off from Sporlan Valve. Our first child is due in a month.

Harry drives our aging maroon Studebaker to the pipe factory six days a week. Monday through Friday he keeps the H&B books and a watchful eye on the factory floor. On Saturdays the factory closes at noon.

This Saturday the heat and boredom lure me out of the house. I ride with Harry into town, determined to find something interesting for our lunch. Harry double-parks on Front Street, with the Missouri River on one side and the factory on the other. He stands at the open car window as I slide over to the driver's seat, and leans over for a parting peck on the cheek.

"I'm headed for Frick's," I say. "I'll pick up something for a decent lunch. I need to talk." I plan to review plans for the baby's room, my ideas about my new life, more baby names.

"Pick me up at Mother's in an hour or so," he says as he swings away. I nod and do not add, "After your mandatory Saturday check-in with Mama?" Better not to part on a sour note.

There is a Frick's in my hometown, too—the family raises prize beef and horses. I once came in second to Denny Frick in musical chairs on horseback, the high point of my equestrian career. Gram said she never saw me move so fast in my life.

Frick's is higher quality and higher price, more Whole Foods than Kroger's.

I luck out. A fresh shipment of Harry's favorite Usinger's sausage is behind the meat counter. I splurge—on Harry's favorite sausage, the liverwurst I prefer, Swiss cheese from Switzerland, a passable Washington substitute for pumpernickel, fresh homemade mustard, a jar of kosher dill pickles and a six-pack of Heinekens.

I swish out of the store triumphant. A blast of Death Valley air hits me when I push open the doors of the air-conditioned store. Time for home, lunch, conversation and a Saturday afternoon nap.

Harry's mother's front door is open. I hear voices as I lumber up the concrete steps to her front stoop. Harry must already be here.

"Come in," rings out. I walk through the front hall and into the kitchen. Harry, his brother and mother sit around the square kitchen table with full plates and glasses in front of them. Drat.

Dick pushes his chair back and jumps up with his signature grin. "Well, what do you know, now the gang's all here." He often rushes to fill awkward conversational spaces—the family lightener-upper.

I smile and nod at Dick's greeting.

I seek Harry's eyes. Harry studies the sandwich on his plate.

A premonition chills me. My throat tightens. I am an amateur at this hand-to-hand combat. A Delphine had never showed up in my life before. Harry, my wimpy ally, hovers on the edge of the battlefield with a white band on his arm.

I try a diversionary tactic. "Oh, Harry, I found something really special for lunch," I begin.

I stop; all eyes are on me. The ranks close. Can't this intruder see a meal is in progress?

"We've already started," Harry mumbles.

Delphine takes command. She pull out the fourth chair at the table, motions me towards it. "You don't want to go home and have to make lunch in this heat. Everything is on the table, and I'm sure you're … "

"I don't want to eat here. I want to go home," I interrupt. I hear my puny pout rather than the brave counterattack I had planned.

"I, I have food to put in the fridge." Open another front.

Lame. Delphine glances at my big stomach and immediately diverts her eyes. In her day women did not parade in public at this stage.

"You're just tired and hot, dear, sit down and I will pour you a nice cold iced tea. Harry, go bring in the groceries and put them in the refrigerator."

I've lost the round. I decide to retreat with as much grace as possible.

"I'll wait upstairs," I say. I vacate the kitchen fast, holding back tears as I pound up the front stairs to throw myself down on a bed.

Sounds of conversation drift up to me, unintelligible. Bland, polite words, my guess, avoiding mention of my childish retreat or the hysterical, hormone-ravaged woman upstairs.

I wished they would choke on their damned sandwiches.

Sixty years later, I wonder why it was such a big deal. Why did I not just excuse myself, drive home and open a Heineken in peace?

My rage was not about liverwurst. The hurt was Harry's passivity; I felt unconnected, not valued. Delphine was controlling my life as she had Harry's. The pregnancy, the town, the heat, the loss of rapport with my husband—all converged to make me feel helpless and abandoned.

20

Decoding DHH

After so many years that lunch still gives me indigestion.

Delphine Hamel Herzog controlled her sons as she could not control her husband or many other things in her life, and she intended to keep it that way. We clashed over who was in charge many times in the years that followed.

ã

After our move to Indiana we visit Missouri every Christmas, dividing our time between my parents' suburban St. Louis home and DHH's in Washington. The two homes are less than an hour apart in driving time but light years apart in mood. We pull into Florissant, a St. Louis suburb just off I-270, to hugs from my parents, a basement filled with toys, and a fridge bulging with each person's favorite treats.

Grandma Herzog runs a tighter ship. Beds are assigned after the perfunctory welcome, clean towels laid out, and the schedule for the visit reviewed.

ã

One December we drive to Washington to spend a few days, including Christmas Eve. Grandma Herzog wants us at her traditional Christmas Eve open house, a formal, adults only party that I endured when we lived in Washington and have avoided since. This year she wants her family around her, she says. To be seen and admired by all, I think.

Shortly after we are in the door, Delphine informs us that we are all going to a gala holiday party at her dear friends the Babbits the next night, and she has engaged a babysitter for Tom and Meta. As soon as Harry and I are alone, I object. The children are not at home in this house; Meta is a toddler. Rather than leave them with someone they do not know while we all disappear, I will stay home from the party with the children.

"Absolutely not," Delphine says when we spring this on her. We must all go to the party together; the Babbits are dying to see both of us.

She is seated in her throne—a high-backed, upholstered chair in a corner of the living room, where her gaze commands the room and everyone in it.

"Well, since this is two adult parties in a row on the final two days of our visit," I suggest, "we could drive the kids back to Florissant the afternoon of the first party, then Harry and I come back for both events. It's not a long drive …"

Delphine explodes.

She lowers her head with a look that could blast rock and says in a steely voice, "If you take the children back to St. Louis, you can all stay there. I know your parents lavish more gifts on your children than I can afford, but I am their grandmother, too, and I will not have you taking them out of my house."

"I am not leaving them with a stranger tomorrow night," I say, "The party would be no fun for me." Seeing the storm clouds darken on Delphine's face, I add, "I'm just being honest."

She tilts her head until her eyes skewer mine above her glasses. In a voice several registers below her usual feminine soprano, every word in bold and underlined: "Honesty is all I have ever gotten from you, from the very first."

Her toxic tone alerts me that this is an insult.

That ends our audience. Delphine gets up and stomps into the kitchen, followed by an eruption of pot slamming. Later that day she announces that she and Harry's brother, Dick, will stay with the children during the Babbit's party, and Harry and I will attend alone.

ૐ

I tell the story to my mother and grandmother in my parents' rathskeller after suffering through the Christmas Eve Eggnog Open House. Before I finish my hands begin shaking, then my whole body. I can't stop. It takes another bottle of Budweiser before the shaking subsides.

ॐ

Delphine clearly got to me. There was the obvious power struggle: Who was to be Queen of the Walk? The script sounds trite, made-for-cable-TV; a mean mother-in-law bests the new daughter-in-law. Who will wear the crown? I sense more subtle conflicts.

There was how she treated my husband. I tried to be the understanding clinician, realizing we all parent as best we can, but Delphine treating Harry as a child maddened me. After we'd lived in Indiana for 20 years she sent Harry a blistering letter when he failed to send her a Valentine's Day card. I was in charge of birthdays, anniversaries and other command performances, but had no clue Valentine's Day called for a card to a mother, Harry's or mine. Whether he usually called his mother or sent a card himself other years, I never learned. Maybe she was just in a foul mood that particular February 14.

Her visits to our home were ordeals. She demanded I find tasks to keep her busy "helping" me 12 hours a day. As she darned socks and cut up cabbage, she ticked off what I needed to correct in the children and Harry. She kept her mouth shut about me, but exuded displeasure at my housekeeping and extravagant ways.

The children did not come up to standard, a standard so backward I found no common ground for discussion. She once insisted Tom and Meta should be spanked for taking off their clothes and running around the house naked when they were four and two: licentiousness should be dealt with sternly.

Harry worked late whenever she was in the house. They went to church together on Sunday, but his church, St. John's, was "too high." Harry explained to me this meant too "Roman," in other words, too Catholic. I gasped. Her son chose the Episcopalian faith of her dear father, but alas, it was not the "right" Episcopalian.

ès

Delphine lived by rules. Many. Non-negotiable. Dividing the sheep from the goats.

Conserving a good wool dress was good. Throwing it away before its time, profligate.

Accepting dinner invitations was proper. Not returning the invitation, dishonorable. She showed me a notebook she kept with the history of their dinners as guests in others' homes. A check mark and date noted when she entertained the hosts in her house for dinner. Woe betides the ungrateful guest who did not reciprocate in good time. No more roast lamb with new potatoes and mint gravy.

Not answering letters promptly was slovenly. Her standard comment when she did not get a reply promptly, "I might as well have thrown my letter over a cliff."

Poor woman was trapped by her own rules.

After a fall that broke her wrist, Delphine's arm is encased in a cast that leaves her the use of only one arm. Harry and I arrive to make supper and find her sitting at the kitchen table with an apple in front of her.

"I have been dying to eat this apple all afternoon," she sighs.

I don't get it. "So, what's the problem?" I ask.

Delphine looks up. "How can I eat an apple with one hand?" she fires back.

It takes a minute for me to comprehend that this 62-year-old woman has never picked up an apple in her hand and bitten into it. Apples are for slicing or apple pies.

I dutifully pare the apple and cut it into neat sections, which I arrange on a plate in front of my hidebound mother-in-law. She savors every bite.

My heart melts for a woman so convention-bound she cannot eat an apple.

৵

My distaste for the matriarch's iron hand was all I saw in those years. With perspective I see that Delphine carved out a relatively independent life at a time when women were firmly kept in their place. Hers was a milder case of the dreaded "Curse of the Mummyji," in India.

The mother-in-law syndrome reflects the skewed power relations between the sexes, as well as strife between the generations. The imbalance begins at (or before) birth. Even today, girls are likelier than boys to die in childhood; they often receive less food, schooling or medical care, or are simply abandoned. This is largely because males still wield economic power. Boys generally inherit land and other assets, and are far likelier to bring home wages. Girls are passed to other families as wives and domestic labour.

Since men control a family's dealings with the outside world, running the farm or a business, women are left to oversee the home. The legendary ferocity of the *saas* can be seen as an effort to monopolise the little power that is available to her sex. Rekha Nigam, a screenplay writer and television boss in Mumbai, suggests that enforcing order in the family is a mother-in-law's way of aligning herself "on the side of patriarchy." That often meant, and means, older women tormenting younger ones.

—*The Economist,* December 21, 2013

Born with a double clubfoot to a doctor's family in a rural Missouri town, Delphine had her feet partially corrected with early surgery. She was determined to be physically active and succeeded almost until her dying days.

The Episcopal Church was the rock of her youth, yet she consented to marry a non-practicing Jew, who, she complained, promised to convert but never did. Harry's father, like my own, was 12 years older than his bride, and in their later years both women nursed dying husbands, something they may not have bargained for.

Delphine graduated from St. Louis' Washington University at a time when many women were denied a university education; she clung to that achievement proudly throughout her life.

The senior Harry Herzog brought his bride to Washington, where his life was the family business, H&B. Delphine made a place for herself, not easy for a stranger in an ingrown small town. She founded a chapter of the AAUW (American Association of University Women) in Washington. She volunteered for her church, garden club, bridge club; in all the roles available to her, she rose to the top. Wife, hostess, superb cook, and eventually mother. The couple was childless for eight years and had given up hope when Harry was conceived.

There were limits. Her husband handled the money and doled it out. When he died, she had no idea about their finances or how to write a check.

When I came into the family, her throne was teetering. Her sons were obedient, respectful, but edging toward the door and freedom.

Harry's fall from grace with our Catholic wedding was followed closely by his younger brother Dick's taking up with a girl even more unsuitable in DHH's eyes. Rosemary was not Catholic, but her family was not well off and she was engaged to another man when Dick met her. Delphine labeled Rosemary a loose woman, hinting obliquely she was not much better than a harlot.

A tip off: Our sin was neither religion nor promiscuity; our sin was shaking the Queen's throne. While I *was* a Catholic, Rosemary was about as close to harlotry as Shirley Temple. She taught music in public school and played the organ in church. Music was her connection to Dick, an accomplished amateur cellist.

At Rosemary and Dick's wedding I overhear DHH warn her son, "Whatever you do, stand up straight at the altar. Don't slump."

As he stands at the altar watching his bride walk down the aisle, I see Dick look over at his mother in the front pew, throw his shoulders back and smile.

She smiles back.

¿&

We moved two states away from Washington and the Kingdom of Delphine.

None too soon. Neither of us knew how much family baggage moved along with us.

That camel's nose was already under the tent.

21

Escape to Eden

Early in my second pregnancy I start an ambitious vegetable garden. I study the Burpee catalog and have a wide swath of our backyard rototilled. Harry orders a load of sheep manure, reputed to grow county-fair-worthy vegetables.

I babble on about my new interest to Margaret B, the only congenial person at one of Delphine's tedious coffee klatches. Midway through my passionate précis on growing Brussels sprouts, Margaret interrupts: "I knew you would have to find a project to keep yourself busy. There is not much here to hold your interest."

Oops. I thought I presented a model of domestic contentment to Washington's social muckety-mucks.

Margaret is right on; I hoe the broccoli in desperation. My vegetables begin as a refuge but my gardening fervor sours to duty. I put on my happy face, but Margaret recognizes the mask. I must not have played my role as well as I imagined.

The *senfgurkens* blow my cover.

We return from a week at my parents, now in Carlinville, Illinois. I am three and a half months pregnant with Meta.

Half the garden is a sea of ripened cucumbers. Their withering vines expose an army of swollen phallic forms lying in wait. There are a few the right size for eating, many more fat yellow cukes just right for *senfgurkens*—mustard pickles, a delicacy and Aunt Louise's specialty—and tons and tons perfect for ordinary dills.

It is hot, August in Missouri hot. Waves of steamy air rise from the ground and envelop my sweaty body as I bend over the rows. Grasshoppers spring up as if shot from guns, manned missiles aimed at my face, buzzing ominously as they fly.

The entire kitchen is overrun with buckets full of cucumbers. I peel, slice, boil syrup, sterilize and fill jars for what seems like weeks. Nausea comes and goes, sometimes overwhelming me enough to crawl into bed with a fan turned on full force and a sheet over my head. A nightmare memory.

இ

The nightmare as I write is that I never considered letting all the damned cucumbers rot. If I couldn't stand to waste vegetables, I could have used them for compost. Might have worked; too bad I did not think of that before the pickles did me in.

As uncomfortable as I was in Washington, why did I never complain to Harry, tell off Delphine, or rebel openly rather than cultivate Better Boy tomatoes? Did I think I had no control over where I lived or how I spent my time? Looking back 60 years, I seem such a willing wimp. I saw myself as a second Eleanor Roosevelt. Two years of Kant, Plato and John Dewey prepared me to rule the world. I would have scoffed at the truth: that men and money dominated my world, that my family believed a woman's place was in the home, and that mentioning discomfort was considered unseemly.

I was a cipher in training. Wearing a mask of a progressive woman in charge of her life. Long on talk, puny on walk.

❧

It was time.

A few months after Meta's birth, Harry goes to California to scout potential business on the West Coast. He returns discouraged, surer than ever H&B cannot support our growing family. With the Queen Bee buzzing around our heads, Washington has lost any charm it had. We decide to strike out on our own. Harry's brother, Dick, is willing to take command at Herzog & Bendheim, so Harry gives him his share of the business. Dick succeeds smashingly, and sells the pipe business as a going concern some years later to a tobacco conglomerate, a testament to his hard work and business skills.

Harry finds a job at Purdue. We trade in the Studebaker and use the last of our wedding present money and a loan from my parents to buy a used Chevy station wagon. We load our modern Conestoga and set out in the fall of 1956. It's an easier, if more dangerous, trip (before seat belts and car seats for two-year-old Tom and six-month-old Meta), and we arrive eager to explore our new home—in a rental for new staff set on the Purdue golf course.

West Lafayette is the New World, and our family thrives. The freshness papers over the cracks in our partnership. When the newness wears off, I am busy with two, then three young children; not quite the barefoot and pregnant stereotype, but close. Harry titles our first annual holiday newsletter, *The Hoosier Herzogs' Holiday Hello*. We remain Hoosiers for the remainder of our lives together.

22

Home in Indiana

Our little band pulls up to the Purdue golf course with the light fading. We wind through a forest of towering oaks; their drying leaves high above us rustle in welcome. Harry turns the wagon up a drive that circles 20 or so square prefabs, searching for Number 3. He stops the car and I run to a house where we see a light. "Must be the big one at the bottom of the hill," says the woman who comes to the door with a baby on her hip. Her tie-dyed T-shirt assures me that we are not in Indiana any more.

We find our rental, settle in for the night, and awaken to a world of sky and leaves and green. Tom runs out into the yard as soon as he is dressed and heads toward the sound of children's voices up the lane. I follow with Meta wrapped in a blanket against the freshness of the morning. Doors open, I meet neighbors. We are home.

The prefabricated houses are set around a circle drive in the middle of the Purdue golf course. Meant to be temporary housing for new Purdue staff, they are replaced with fraternity and sorority houses soon after we leave. Newbies like us can rent them for a year. When our time is up we find another prefab—Lafayette is headquarters for National Homes, the first and largest manufacturer of prefabricated housing. Our Vinton subdivision was planned and built by National; hundreds of houses set on winding streets (to discourage through traffic), with a school in the center and commercial space on the perimeters.

The houses are boxy, serviceable and cheap. Our three-bedroom costs $10,000, more than twice the price of our Washington home, but this is Lafayette. Tom can walk to the tiny store a few blocks away to buy a pushup—not a bra, vanilla ice cream coated with orange sherbet on a stick. He starts kindergarten at the school two blocks from our house. He and his friends gather on the corner opposite the school every morning, watching for the doors to open. Every morning he wants to leave the house earlier. Vinton School is a hit.

ᢧ

The *Lafayette Journal & Courier* announces a meeting of the League of Women Voters. On the women's page; the newspaper then still has a women's page. I go. I join. I find my tribe. Soon I pore over position papers on reapportionment of the state legislature and the importance of free trade. I chair a committee, which means I sift through reports, summarize positions, and write resolutions, then lead discussions about the issues designed to reach *consensus*, the League's state of enlightenment.

I learn to reduce complicated issues to clear prose, a skill that transfers well to graduate school and financial planning. I testify for the League at public meetings, moderate roundtables, chair a candidates' debate. Most members shrink from public speaking. I love it. The challenge of capturing a group's attention, then moving them along with me is a high like performing *The Cat in the Hat* for Tom and his buddies. The butterflies in the stomach before a speech are a shot of adrenalin. I feel more alive in front of an audience.

ন্ত

My family made a shameless ham of me, their only child for eight years, raving over my readings of *Dotty Dolly's Tea Party*. By school age I am ripe to be Class Presenter, ready to recite on call.

At my eighth-grade graduation party we eat egg salad sandwiches on bread from which the crust has been carefully trimmed and dyed our class colors—top slice lavender, bottom, yellow. Good old Schulte's bakery dyes bread to order. As the parents' and graduates' sandwiches are down to yellow and lavender crumbs, Sister Carlene asks me to recite the poem I memorized over the Easter break. When I get to the second "Quoth the Raven, Nevermore," she tiptoes to the back of the room and switches off the lights. She must want "scary," I think, and raise the dramatic pitch.

ॐ

After Ben's birth we move to a larger house across the Wabash River in Green Meadows, a subdivision under construction just west of West Lafayette.

Green Meadows is like the Purdue golf course community, only more so. The short commute to the university fills the houses with Purdue staff. Many of us had lived in temporary Purdue housing, and we reinstitute the babysitting pool we had there. Hours are recorded: pluses for sitter, minuses for "sit-ee"; members can exchange hours and run deficits. Books pass from house to house every month. A breakdown occurs when one of our pool members moves to Massachusetts owing 30 hours. Bankruptcy; the losers never collect.

I join the Green Meadows bridge club. Kindergarten moms share a car pool. I am now surrounded by congenial peers—mothers home with young children. We shuttle between houses for morning coffees and get together as couples on weekends for backyard barbeques and pre-game football parties.

Bernie and Donna Liska live on the street behind us. We share backyards and a friendship that lasts til death do us part. Their Julie is a year older than Ben; Cheryl is Meta's age.

Ben and Julie bond like brother and sister. When Bernie builds a barn nearby and buys Julie a horse, Ben has to have a horse, too. Cheryl and Meta are squabbling sibs—best friends or fierce rivals in turns.

We share backyard cookouts and entertain each other's parents on their regular visits. Our friendship survives our beagle's eating Cheryl's kitten.

Donna and I relish our lengthy dialogs over coffee. Mostly chitchat, but we commiserate about our stay-at-home lives, husbandly foibles and child-rearing crises. Donna is one of two friends I tell when Harry threatens to leave me for another woman.

When Betty Friedan publishes *The Feminine Mystique,* we suspect she has bugged our coffee klatches. We know her "problem with no name" as the Green Meadows Wife Syndrome. We see our husbands' world as the serious path; we are just moms, extolled on Mother's Day and in the Bible, but largely ignored by the bustling world of commerce that rules. Donna is a teacher, taught high school while her husband, Bernie, was overseas during the Korean War.

I am still flailing about, unsure what I want to do when the children are all in school. That's a prerequisite. Only heartless mothers abandon their children in daycare; they are putting themselves ahead of the children. It never occurs to us that men do not have to choose between parenthood and a career.

The world is just like that.

23

How Green Were My Meadows

Donna and I read *The Feminine Mystique* and looked forward to a wider world, but our Green Meadows world was bright, too. We knew we were privileged in many ways. And we had the children.

Much of child rearing lights up my life. The feeling of a warm baby curled up against me, nursing, clinging, sleeping; playing games from *Peek-a-Boo* to *Go Fish*; overplaying a monster in *Where the Wild Things Are*.

My later study of child development and job as a preschool teacher were fed by my attraction to small children. I love their freshness and curiosity, how every bug or rock in their path captivates them.

I invent The Big Lump to amuse preschoolers Ben and Julie. They are often underfoot after the big kids go off to school. I call out in a sonorous League Chair of the Meeting voice, "I am going to make the bed now," as I finish sliding the breakfast dishes into the dishwasher. Ben and Julie scurry to my bed and pull the bedclothes over their heads.

I follow after an appropriate interval and hum as I smooth the bedspread over their little bodies. I feign alarm, "Oh, no, it's The Big Lump. Whatever will I do now?" Giggles from underneath the covers. "I will just have to squish that Big Lump," as I push a pillow down over the "lumps." Noisier giggles. At a climactic moment I throw back the covers and cry out in relief, "Oh, it's only Ben and Julie. You two sneaky kids fooled me again!"

Books compete with The Big Lump in popularity. Gram gets laryngitis on a visit when Ben is three; she cannot resist his pleas for "just one more book." Favorites are enshrined in the family repertoire. When milk spills or a chair tips over, the family chorus chants, "That is what the cat said … then he fell on his head!" These are the Cat in the Hat's words after his triumphant boast,

> Look at me!
> Look at me!
> Look at me now!
> It is fun to have fun
> But you have to know how.
> … I can fan with the fan
> As I hop on the ball!
> But that is not all.
> Oh, no.
> That is not all … "
> —Dr. Seuss, *The Cat in the Hat*

All is not *Green Eggs and Ham*, however. Crying babies and cranky toddlers overwhelm me on long days. I would have frowned on a nanny. Or someone to cook dinner. Or do the wash. The babysitting pool is okay; we share as equals. Hired help, no way—Earth Mother can do it all. Something tells me that anyone who does not do her own housework is spoiled, lazy or both.

After I "go to work" (meaning I begin earning money; mothers at home with children are not considered to be working.) I hire Merry Maids to show up every two weeks and clean the house. They come while I am at work; I leave their check on the kitchen counter. Efficient and anonymous, therefore not publicizing the fact that I am too lazy to mop my own floor.

Thanks to the babysitting pool, I expand my LWV activities. A county planning board is being formed, and the League asks me to deliver our recommendations to the Tippecanoe County commissioners: the three elected officials who govern the county. One commissioner agrees to meet me.

His bulky persona reminds me of the farmer who leans on the fence chewing a wheat sprout in *Oklahoma*. I wait for him to start singing "The Farmer and the Cowman Should Be Friends."

Instead he motions me to a seat across from him, rolls his chair forward so that his desk dents his stomach, and looks sideways at me. I am a forbidding presence—a woman come lookin' for trouble. He welcomes me with oily politeness, plants his elbows on his desk, and asks why I am there. I make my pitch; he relaxes. He looks down at his desk blotter and mumbles, "Oh, oh, yes, … I see what you mean, very qualified candidates you name, but, we have already, … the fact is, just a few days ago, …we get together for coffee you know …"

He looks up, sees I am trying to follow.

"We have already decided to appoint one of you."

I hand the League's letter of recommendations across to him. Mission accomplished. He thanks me without glancing at the letter, stands up, shakes my hand, and the interview is over. When the appointment is made public, none of the League's recommendations is named. I realize the "one of you" Farmer Friendly meant is a woman, not a LWV recommendation. One of us annoying outsiders. And of course one woman on a 12-person board is plenty. Never has there been a female county commissioner; the women in the courthouse fill clerical, not managerial roles.

❧

I discover Blessed Sacrament when the Liskas tell me about the new parish that meets for Sunday Mass in a rented space one flight up over a bookstore. It is as alien to Washington's St. Francis Church as our Green Meadows home is to Grandma Herzog's fortress. The priest is eager to form a community from the gaggle of Profs and locals that show up on Sunday. He succeeds so well we soon outgrow our rented hall. A church is planned and built. A group of monks from a Benedictine abbey in southern Indiana install the mosaic they designed on the wall around the baptismal font. The font sits in the middle of the entrance foyer, an architectural detail to symbolize entry to the Church through baptism. A flashback to my favorite lesson on the three kinds of baptism. The font's soulful metaphor makes me happy that I had water poured over my infant head.

I volunteer to teach Sunday school. The materials we use are modern and thoughtful, words I do not associate with "Catholic." Soon I am director of the religious school and teaching the recalcitrant eighth graders: just my cup of tea.

I reconnect with the Spirit I first met at Immaculate Conception, now embodied in an adult tradition.

ॐ

When my youngest, Ben, starts kindergarten, I am ready. I did my duty, kept the home fires burning. Enough already. Grad school beckons. My brush with academia at Chicago whetted my appetite, and Purdue is three miles down the road. On to the temples of learning and a life of scholarship.

I review my choices: What does a Renaissance woman take on as her life's work? I cannot choose among my enthusiasms, so I apply for admission to three departments; Psychology, Child Development and English.

My bachelor's degree was granted under the Chicago Plan, an innovation of Robert Maynard Hutchins, the maverick rock star of higher education. Students enter after two years of high school—the last two years of American secondary education being a monumental waste of time in Hutchins' opinion. The Bachelor of Arts is awarded for competence in 15 three-quarter-long courses, mastery demonstrated by end-of-the-year comprehensive exams. The wide-ranging liberal arts education is designed to turn out citizens of the world. I enter after high-school graduation, earn credit for half the courses through placement exams, and spend only two years in the classroom. I envision this as impressing everyone. Instead, this unorthodox record is not Purdue-friendly.

ॐ

The next step is an interview with each department's director of admissions. English calls first.

I placed out of English and Humanities 1 and 2, so my coursework is skimpy. The Serious Scholar across the desk from me notes this tersely as he scans my transcript.

I explain about the Chicago Plan; he interrupts my rhapsody with a stern peer over his glasses.

"And since then—what kind of jobs have you held?" he queries.

I think it best not to mention packing pushrods.

"I have been at home with my children," I say.

"So you have been at home, doing nothing?" he prompts.

I find this a humorous take on raising three children, but he is not smiling, so I try again. "I ... I read ... a lot," I say, "and work in the League of Women Voters; last year I chaired the state study on school reorganization in Indiana, which ..."

I stop. The director of admissions is looking out the window. Is he plotting his escape?

I sit up straighter, smile, take a deep breath, and move into a sales pitch.

"I understand mine is not a typical record," I begin, "but my education was first rate. It covered a lot of ground and generated broad interests. Truth is, that is what inspired me to apply to three Purdue departments."

Professor English gasps, horrified.

He fires both barrels of Basic Respect for Procedure 101, ending with, "You can't just apply scattershot to graduate school. You must decide what you are qualified to study."

Which, I see he believes, is none of the above.

I retrieve my papers in as business-like a manner as I can manage and leave, determined not to give this jerk the satisfaction of bawling in his presence.

Once home, I reconnoiter. To hell with this crabby old schoolmarm in a tweed jacket. If my degree is questionable, I will get a normal one from Purdue. My application, complete with transcripts and references, is in the mail as soon as I can pull it together.

ह

Three weeks later Harry comes home with my application in his briefcase. His buddy in the admissions department called him to pick it up, explaining, "Harry, your wife has a bachelor's degree; she can't be admitted as an undergraduate."

The shock of being labeled somebody's wife rather than an applicant for admission deflates me. I thought I was an anonymous scholar represented only by my GRE's and admission essay. To be handed off summarily to my husband is harsher than Professor English's lecture.

Worse, Harry is baffled by my humiliation. "Honey, Bert has known me forever. He was trying to be helpful in getting the message to you as expeditiously as possible," he insists. Which makes me turn redder, and sends Harry scurrying to his desk—urgent work he has suddenly remembered.

I am back in the county commissioner's office: a non-person, a nuisance petitioner. Now I am someone's nameless wife.

ह

I sit across from the director of admissions for child development, apprehensive as he reads my transcript. "I see you graduated from The College," he says.

I manage to keep my seat rather than leaping up and cheering. No one except a U. of C. grad would call it, "The College."

"Ah, you placed out of Soc. 2," he notes approvingly.

I am in: an official graduate student in Purdue's Department Of Child Development.

One more hurdle. Harry makes two "suggestions," his conditions for my going back to school. Take only one class the first semester and don't enroll until Ben starts first grade. His reasons are thoughtful, intended to guide me to success, but I feel put down. But Harry knows best; he has a job and he plays in the same sandbox with the Purdue administration. I sulk, but I follow his advice.

My first semester I take a required course in statistics. The last math I had was high school geometry; I need more. Statistics is a new world, challenging but fascinating. I am thrilled to get an A- on the first exam. At the dinner table that night, I jabber away about how helpful the teacher is; he goes over every wrong answer, points out the correct method. I illustrate with a couple of examples; I must have thought statistics fascinated everybody. Meta looks up from her plate, "How many questions did you miss, anyway?"

"Ummm, six—there was the one about … "

"Out of how many?" Tom asks.

"Thirty problems," I respond. What does this have to do with standard deviation?

"What? You got an A with, let's see, that's 80 percent? That's a high C at Klondike."

The kids cannot wait to get to grad school—what a snap.

∾

Four packed years later, a doctorate is within sight. With my goal so close, my ardor cools. The atmosphere is not the community of scholars I'd envisioned. My major professor specializes in learning theory, a dry field. I chose Dr. B because I respect her as a scholar and an effective mentor. My thesis analyzes children's responses to operant conditioning. Publishable, she assures me with pride. But boring as hell.

In the four years we work together, I observe her days—rancorous committee meetings, scrambling for tenure, colleagues carping about everything from the dumb Hoosier undergrads to the size of their offices.

I learn I could not get a job at Purdue if I wanted to; departments don't hire their own students. I see I am like Ben, who complains about the rotten cafeteria food in one breath, then adds, "And they never let you have seconds."

Where but Purdue could I go? Even a job at a nearby college would leave Harry and the children on their own. Out of the question.

è♠

Opportunity knocks.

Dr. B wants to run a study at Wabash Center for the Retarded during the summer session. She asks me to apply to teach the preschool class, where I can collaborate on her investigations. I jump at it.

Working with children at Wabash Center turns me on. More fun than encoding subjects' responses and combing journals in the psych library for papers on learning theory. Before the summer ends I apply for the full-time teaching job and quit grad school. My M.S. from Purdue is the only credential I need. My friend and neighbor, Donna Liska, is program director and will be my supervisor. The road ahead looks rosy.

Surely I talked with Harry. Maybe. The subject—my feelings about work, children, what to do with my life—were murky enough for me. Sharing them with Harry was tedious and frustrating for us both. So much was assumed but never mentioned. I was touchy about what I considered My Life. Harry wanted to help, but could not see what I was agonizing over.

190

Leaving grad school is one more impulsive decision, made with scant counsel, like where to go to college, when to begin having sex, whether to marry Harry, or when to get pregnant.

24

The Vacation

Looking back, grad school was a good time in many ways.

Child development is a small department, homey. I make friends, one still a long-distance good buddy. Judy now lives in Israel, but we keep in touch, even manage to see each other off and on. She was way ahead of me when we entered the program; already had a master's from the prestigious Merrill Palmer Institute.

Judy marries a fellow student. Aaron is a carbon copy of the East Coast Jewish students I liked least at Chicago—bright, verbal, sees himself as the center of the universe.

After they divorce, Judy recounts an incident typical of what led to their split. At a birthday party for one of their kids, Judy sends Aaron out for ice cream while she organizes games. He returns four hours later to tell her about the philosophical discussions he had on his way. The ice cream is melted; the little guests have gone home after birthday cake without ice cream.

Poor Judy, I think. Thank God Harry is so responsible. The right flavor of ice cream would have been on the table before I cut the cake; he might even have scooped it up for the kids.

I picture Harry as a jovial father, willing to build great swing sets and scoop up ice cream. My children are a happy-go-lucky Brady Bunch. Any minor woes can be solved by their understanding mother with a snack or a song, just like on the sitcoms. The whole family gathers on Friday nights for Maverick and sings along to the theme song at the opening of every episode.

> Who is the tall dark stranger there?
> Maverick is his name.
> Riding the trail from who knows where
> Luck is his companion, gambling is his game.

We are smooth sailors. Our seas never rage. The waves behave themselves. It is a wonder we did not drown while ignoring the storms sweeping over our little craft.

ॐ

Our first vacation rocks the boat.

Up til now, we have filled time off from work and school with family visits.

This will be different.

I fund the trip with my $3,000 inheritance from Meta V, our Union neighbor who let me borrow her car as soon as I got my driver's license. We named our daughter for her.

This is *my* money. Harry is the chief wage earner; our money is *his* in some sinister recess of my brain. I would have chortled had anyone confronted me with this; we were a modern couple, equal in every way. We build budgets together, and Harry's stock comment is, "Pat's caring for the children is more valuable than making money."

True, but when that $3,000 check is in my hands I am empowered. We will take a real vacation. Expo '67 is running in Montreal, the last of the big World Fairs. Harry is enthusiastic; the Chicago World's Fair with his parents was a childhood highlight for him at eight.

We think big: a grand road trip in a rented station wagon, with stops at Cleveland and Toronto to visit friends, then on to Montreal for Expo, a week on the ocean for R&R, then a flight home for five rejuvenated Herzogs.

In Cleveland we visit an old college friend of Harry's. Then on to Toronto, where my grad school cohorts Judy and Aaron are living. They make room for all of us in their small apartment. The children line up their sleeping bags on the floor in our room, but when I wake, they have disappeared. All three are on the kitchen floor, where they dragged their sleeping bags to escape Harry's snores—a creative solution, all agree. Aaron prepares omelet after omelet, each more perfect than the last, sharp cheese melting into perfectly cooked eggs flipped onto our waiting plates. I take notes; Aaron's omelets become a staple on the Herzog menu.

The Vietnam War is raging. Aaron tells us he has discovered that if an American is outside the USA on his 18th birthday—the day the law requires all male citizens to register for the draft—his name goes into a special pool, a list from which no one has ever been drafted. He takes 14-year-old Tom aside and urges him to be in Israel on his 18th birthday so that he can take advantage of this fluke.

Well before Tom turns 18, we learn that the special pool exists only in Aaron's head. Meanwhile, Tom has been mulling the kibbutz idea ever since Toronto. He spends the summer after high school graduation working on Floyd Fithian's campaign for the U.S. Senate. Fithian is a Purdue prof, a liberal Democrat, and the father of one of Tom's classmates at Harrison High. After the election, which Fithian loses, Tom is on a plane to an Israeli kibbutz the next month, a journey that changes his life.

❧

Our trip has other long-term consequences.

The children are delighted and delightful on the way to Expo. Tom is pumped; in Cleveland the son of a Browns football star comes out to play catch. When we get to Toronto the children learn to stop cars by holding a hand up to cross the street. (This works in San Miguel, too.)

In Montreal we face cramped quarters and long waits at the fair. It is hectic, as we suspected it would be. Our last stop will refresh us for the trip home: a cottage on the ocean on Mount Desert Isle.

It is neither as peaceful nor refreshing as planned. Tom and his father wrangle. Their clashes escalate as we drive east. Harry's oldest child often irritates him. I see it as a common problem between father and oldest son, well documented in the literature. I play peacemaker or sometimes just get out of their way.

The climactic incident comes on a bridge crossing into Canada. Tom tells the Canadian customs official he hopes he won't find the marijuana we have hidden in our suitcase. Tom thinks this is a hilarious joke since our family is so square. Harry turns white. Luckily the inspector shrugs Tom off as a smart aleck teenager as Harry apologizes between clenched lips. This is a just cause, which gives Harry permission to go into orbit. With minor irritations he has struggled to control his anger.

After we are safely off the bridge, Harry declares Tom's behavior outrageous, totally unacceptable. He swears he will never go on another trip with Tom.

Here he goes again, I sigh, remembering.

We cross the Mississippi River and merge into heavy traffic on the Missouri side. It is August and our aging sedan has only "470 AC": roll down all four windows and go 70 miles an hour. Unfortunately we can't go 70 in the St. Louis suburban traffic, and temperatures rise.

I pour drinks from the cooler to placate: "Almost there, kids. Less than two hours to Grandma Herzog's."

Meta spills Orange Crush on Ben's foot—squeals, complaints.

Tom yells at them both to shut up; he wants to sleep.

The whining begins:

"Do we *have* to sleep at Grandma Herzog's?"

"Can we stop at McDonald's before we get there? She'll probably have liver dumplings."

"And prunes," Meta adds in disgust.

A yowl as Tom punches Ben, who is wiping his foot on Tom's shirt.

Harry pulls over on the shoulder and gets out of the car. "I'm never taking another trip with these kids," he bellows. "This is it. Never. It is too hot."

I herd the kids out of the backseat. We hold hands and run down the slope next to the car to the only tree in sight. Ben immediately slumps down with his back against the tree.

"Good idea, Ben. Let's all lie down in the grass," in my best *Cat in the Hat* voice.

That's popular; we flop down on the prickly grass around the tree. A slight breeze floats over us.

After a few minutes, I jump up. "C'mon, troop. Time to march."

"Here we come to save the day. It seems like Mighty Mouse is on the way!" I sing.

I march around the trunk, lifting my knees like a drum major.

Tom rolls his eyes.

"Oh, Mom, Dad's right. It's too hot."

I glance up the slope and see Harry is back in the driver's seat.

The rest of us file back to the car and slide into place in silence.

I say nothing. Harry will forget all about it before we are ready to go home. He does.

෨

There are other angry exchanges between Harry and the children, most often between Tom and his dad. Maybe it is a good idea to stop traveling together. We get on each other's nerves. We will all be happier taking separate vacations.

෨

I can't wait to tell Donna about our trip when we get back to Green Meadows. She and Bernie and their two girls camp for a month every summer, pulling a little trailer Bernie built and equipped. They have been to most of the western national parks. She has urged me to try camping with the kids, and applauded my spending my windfall on a family vacation. We sit around her dining room table, where we can keep an eye on our joint backyards and the kids at play.

I lay out my packets in order—one set for each stop—3½" × 5" photographs printed on shiny photo paper that we pass from hand to hand, and which I will later paste into albums and reprint for friends. Dinosaurs now after digital.

When I get to the "pot on the bridge" episode, Donna laughs, "Typical 14-year-old smarty pants," she says. "I'll bet Harry damn near died."

"You got it," I laugh, and go on to say that he and Tom were at odds so often that we've decided not to take any more trips together.

Her smile fades. There is an awkward pause. I shuffle my pictures back into their Kodak envelopes. Finally, in a voice I have heard only once before, on the day Kennedy was shot, she says, "But that's so sad, Pat. So sad."

25

The Trouble with Harry

Donna's reaction to my glib report on separate vacations shakes me. Why didn't I confront Harry about his vendetta with Tom? Do I think I have to make nice all the time, even with my own husband? That a jingle from a Mighty Mouse cartoon will sing away all problems?

Harry turns red on prompts that amaze me. He can work himself into a lather at a misplaced magazine. "Where is yesterday's *Journal Courier*? Who tore the page out of *The New Yorker*?" I dismiss his rages as the product of his childhood traumas. In his biography, *Harry's Story*, he reports, "While Dad and Mother had their differences on many subjects, they agreed on one thing: 'Spare the rod and spoil the child' was *the rule* for raising boys. They were determined not to spoil me.

"My blackest memories of Dad's discipline are his returning from work, walking through the front door of our house, and being greeted by Mother with a report on my misdeeds. In the vestibule was a large crockery umbrella stand holding the cane he had used when recovering from his broken hip. As Mother talked, Dad would grab the cane, reach over to pick me up, turn my bottom over his knee, and hit me with the cane.

"I remember the pain of being hit, but the most frightening memory is my father's face when telling me, 'Don't you talk back to me.' Afterwards I would be sent to bed without supper, which I found a merciful withdrawal from a hellish episode."

I sympathize with his awful memories, especially since Angelo Patri, my parents' guiding light, had such strong words for this brand of parenting. In a 1926 column about fathers, he railed against mothers who tried to get their children to obey them by threatening, "You wait until your father comes home."

"That's about the worst failure a mother can make of child rearing," Patri writes. "The moment she says it, she's through as a power in that child's life. Besides all that, father is coming home. Home. That ought to mean something to the waiting mother and children. Something joyful. And a whole lot of joy should be on father's side."

Patri's syndicated column appeared in the *St. Louis Post Dispatch*. My father read every one, and quoted Patri like Billy Graham quoted Scripture. A teacher influenced greatly by John Dewey, Patri was the first Italian immigrant to lead the New York City public schools. His work, writings and lectures were influential in changing how Americans thought about parenthood.

Harry's parents were not Angelo Patri fans.

ટ&

Truth was, Harry's emotional deafness infuriated me, and my anger at his disability shamed me. Since Harry's emotional obtuseness was a hangover from his miserable childhood, I felt guilty not being able to accept it. But I didn't and couldn't, in the end. Every time he forgot who a friend was, couldn't recall something important that I'd shared, all the moments of not "getting it" with the children, drove me further and further away from him emotionally.

I wanted someone to share my most private, tender feelings. Blank looks hurt. Bland "ummms" did not satisfy. When I opened up about some of this, Harry was angry. "I can't live always watching every word I say," was his response.

ટ&

Eleven-year-old Shona, our oldest granddaughter, visited our Lafayette home in June of 1998. Two days into her visit I found her sad-faced and silent in her bedroom. She refused to tell me what was wrong.

I called her mother. "Didn't Dad tell you?" Meta asked. "Shona called me last night to say she felt blue—nobody was paying attention to her. I thought you would figure out what was wrong."

Harry had not mentioned the call. When I confronted him, at first he could not remember. Then,

"Oh, oh, oh, that's right," he said. "I remember now—Meta did call. She said Shona wasn't happy, but when I asked Shona if she was okay, she said yes, so I forgot all about it."

ॐ

Unpleasantness, especially anger, was hard for Harry to acknowledge. There was the infamous rock episode. The broad front of our ranch house in Green Meadows was landscaped with low shrubs, their roots surrounded by hard-packed dirt. Harry decided that a mulch of rocks would discourage weeds and give a neat, well-groomed look. He had a quarter truckload of the right color and size dumped in the turnaround in our drive. Tom and he would distribute them around the shrubs, he said.

It is the hottest month of a hot summer. Saturday after an early breakfast, Harry and Tom march tight-mouthed into the front yard, shovels on their shoulders.

I can hear sharp words exchanged. They are back in the kitchen in an hour, sweaty and glowering. Tom clumps down the hall to the bathroom without looking up.

"We are taking a water break," Harry says.

"Maybe you should take a break, period," I reply.

203

A dark look over his shoulder as Harry cracks the ice cubes loose from their tray.

"Harry, what's with the rocks? Is this some kind of macho challenge? You looked angry when you left the house, and you're about to boil over now."

"What are you talking about? I am *not* angry," he spits out. "Tom has been sloughing off all summer; it's about time he did some real work around here. You always … " he pauses to stuff ice cubes into his glass.

"Oh, for God's sake, Harry, lighten up … it's too hot to shovel rocks for you, too. You look exhausted. Why don't you … "

Harry turns on his heel, storms down the hall and slams the bedroom door behind him.

The rock detail continues.

ᔬ

I give Harry more love and try to ignore his angry outbursts so they will dwindle and eventually stop. "Extinguishing the behavior," is the correct professional term. I advise the children to do the same. When he screams that a pen is missing from his desk, my response is, "Oh, come on, Harry," if I respond at all.

I do not see how his anger affects the children. They must have given signals, but they were lost on this psychologizing

Mama. Only after they leave home do they speak of Harry "terrorizing them." I am blind to their pain; never imagine they are taking Harry's anger so seriously. I don't see that their father is a formidable figure for them. They can't ignore his anger or try psychological tactics to calm him.

಄

We disagree often about the kids. I am Permissive Pat; Harry is the Enforcer. Everybody knows this but me. A next door neighbor, undoubtedly having heard some of Harry's rants, sees a new title on our bookshelf and smiles, "Hey, I didn't know they had written a book about Harry." He holds up *The Authoritarian Personality*.

I think we are a well-balanced team. I skirt what I consider Harry's idiosyncrasies.

Twice, the children and I gang up on Harry; his anger sputters out, and peace reigns. Both take place around the family dinner table.

Former Green Meadows neighbors, now living in Urbana, Illinois, are coming for a weekend visit. Tom and Meta are eager to see their old pals. I suggest the way to house everyone is to buy a large tent; our visitors have four children. The kids can camp out in the backyard, and we can later use the tent for family camping, which we have never done but are definitely going to try next summer. Harry points out that my creative solutions always involve buying something. I grin.

The kids are now on to what they need for the night—flashlights, candy bars, pillows.

"A tent is out of the question," Harry says. "Just another thing to gather dust in the garage." The kids rattle on. Harry interrupts an animated debate about how to divide up the tent space with an angry, "There will be no tents in this house." He punctuates each word with a bang on the table with the handle of his table knife. Everyone stops talking and looks at Harry.

After an embarrassed pause, one of the children begins to chant, "No tents in this house." Another picks up the beat; soon all but Harry are keeping time with a knife or fork to "No tents in this house." There is an instant when Harry looks as if he might explode, then he softens, mutters, "You are all behaving like children," throws his napkin on the table, and retreats to the living room and his evening newspaper.

æ

And the French clarinet.

Meta takes clarinet lessons. The high school band is a social must; Tom plays the trumpet, and we own two, forgotten in a closet when football replaces band as Tom's passion. Meta has a student clarinet. She is on her way to France with her high school French class for six weeks of study and travel. Her music teacher says higher-quality clarinets are less expensive in France. Meta plots to avoid the duty cost by hiding the clarinet in her suitcase. I veto this, always the straight arrow.

Harry clears his throat; his face turns pink. "There will be no more musical instruments in this house," he says, definitively, but with no table banging. I change the subject. Meta returns from her French adventure with a new clarinet wrapped in her dirty T-shirts. And now, so many years later, she still enjoys playing, and I enjoy listening, even on a smuggled clarinet.

❧

I am in control of tents and clarinets. The children are raised my way. This mother knows best, with her degree in child development. Or so I fantasize as I bake birthday cakes and play Big Lump. The children do not remember it that way. They perceive that I treat their father as an annoying and incompetent appendage rather than an equal partner. Harry's and my intimate relationship is the worm in the core of a beautifully polished apple. It distorts our own and our children's lives in ways that I do not see for many years.

Harry is a model husband in all the obvious ways, a reliable breadwinner moving up through the Purdue ranks through his willingness to learn and work hard. I excel at leading impromptu Shift-the-Situation dances. I keep everyone humming along, and make sure the static is tuned out. If that means pacifying Harry or cajoling him out of his bad humor, I perform.

Ironic that while I was getting A's in child psychology, my own children suffered with their father's rage and their mother's emotional distance. Ironic, tragic and damnably hard to acknowledge. Only dozens of 12-step meetings, therapy sessions and meditation retreats later could I risk hearing their voices.

I knew something was wrong with our marriage well before I left, but I was blind to the toll it took on Tom, Meta and Ben. The Herzog children did not roam the streets dumpster diving, but their hunger for compassion drove them to seek nourishment from equally questionable sources.

As for Harry, my zealous caretaking smothers him. My good intentions create a monster; a well-cared-for pet, longing for a mate to love him as another human.

He finds one.

But not before I loose the reins.

26

Agnes

It begins quietly at my mother's Thanksgiving table.

On Thanksgiving, Christmas, Easter and some birthdays, the Hoosier Herzogs head for Missouri. We try variations on the 300-mile trip—over rolling Indiana countryside, shorter distance, less boring—or all Interstate. With three small children we squeeze into a Volkswagen beetle, Harry's Royal Roman chariot. On trips, I schmush myself into "the box," the tiny storage space behind the back seat, which entertains the kids.

This trip we luxuriate in the ample space of a boxy pastel blue Chevy wagon. First stop: my parents' home, with beds for all, a basketball hoop in the driveway and a miniature pool table next to my father's standard pool table in the basement. Mother and Gram cook each visitor's favorite dish and my father takes the children to his Ben Franklin store to pick out welcome gifts. Ben, the youngest, writes as an adult that he still remembers the feelings of love he felt in Florissant.

"Mommo and Gram really listened to me," he said. "I felt ten feet tall."

On this Thanksgiving Day we are in Florissant. The maple dining room table is set for 12. Mother's prized Waterford water goblets shine under the antique lighting fixture inherited when Meta V died two years before. My parents brought four goblets home from their trip to Ireland, the rest are birthday and Christmas gifts to Mother.

Since we are almost 20, a second table is set up in the TV room.

Bowls, platters and two gravy boats crowd the kitchen table. The bright red tablecloth is invisible except where it hangs over the sides. The windows over the sink are steamed in the late November cold. The scent of roast turkey fills the room, from a turkey cooked all night in the Nesco oven, Mother's swear-by method. There's baked ham, too, in case the turkey is not big enough or a guest does not like turkey.

No worry about vegetarians or, God forbid, vegans. It will be years before they emerge from their lettuce beds to challenge hostesses with their missionary zeal.

Agnes, the former fiery ruler of the Bourbeuse fitting room and an old friend, is next to me in the food line curling around the room. Still a spitfire, on her third husband, her hair a show-stopping orange.

"Come sit next to me, honey," she says, turning to me as she spoons gravy over pork sausage dressing. "We haven't talked in years."

"Oh, Agnes, I'd love to," I say, "but Harry is already sitting in the dining room and saving me a place."

Our eyes meet over our loaded plates; I catch Agnes' look—just a flicker, then a rare Agnes silence.

My cheeks glow; I hear myself. Married 16 years, and still has to sit next to her husband?

I always sit next to Harry: to make sure he finds "his" gravy, dipped from the pot before Mother adds the giblets; to insert an upbeat Harry anecdote into the conversation to polish his already shining image. I sit loyally by his side to leave no doubt as to our perfect melding.

Really?

Shock mingled with shame churns within me. I concentrate on fitting a blob of cranberry sauce onto my plate before I sit down—next to Agnes.

Our talk is mundane. "Does Tom still play football? Are you still in grad school?"

"How thoughtful of you to bring your special sauerkraut," as I raise a forkful to my mouth.

"Yep, left Czechoslovakia at 16, but still cook *bohunk*," she laughs. "Nobody makes it like we do—brown sugar, caraway seeds. A dinner of pork or chicken or turkey—with duck, no question, can't eat duck without it—you got to have sauerkraut. It cuts the grease."

No mention of my remark, no hint of my epiphany.

But the Pat who sits next to her husband in the passenger seat on the ride back to Indiana is not the same woman who came to dinner. A covert Observation Center is on alert.

The next day at the A&P, as I sling the Harry-preferred large-curd cottage cheese into my shopping cart, I wonder if I still like small-curd better. Would I remember the difference? Does Harry still prefer large curd?

The next Saturday I drive Harry through the jammed crowd to the Purdue stadium where he ushers the football game. Instead of driving home to undone domestic chores, I park in the nearly empty Purdue library lot and spend the afternoon reading the current press from around the world and nursing a cappuccino and oatmeal cookie in the Student Union.

In Cold Blood comes to town. The story ran serially in *The New Yorker*, and I watched impatiently for the mailman on the days the magazine was due. I call Judy, my fellow grad student, and we go to see *In Cold Blood*. I don't mention it to Harry; the film would depress him. Afterwards Judy and I go to a bar to listen to jazz.

❧

My Observer fades after a while, but not before I notice all my tiny adjustments designed to keep Harry happy. I always told myself these were too minor to notice. Don't be petty. If it is so important to Harry that his pen is put back in the same place on his desk, why not humor him?

The flame from Agnes' firebomb smolders like turf in an Irish hearth, waxing, waning, but never guttering into ash.

₰

A month later I drive the children to Missouri to visit my parents, something I had never done before. While we are in Florissant, Harry, now treasurer of Good Shepherd Episcopal Church, begins an affair with Mary Lou, the church secretary. They must have fallen in love as they counted the collection together every Monday morning.

27

Mary Lou

"I didn't want to tell you just yet."

Harry's voice lowers, softens. He turns his head away from me toward the curb, where a two-wheeler with training wheels grinds past us. We are passing the Purdue fire station on a therapeutic walk, a "get serious and come to grips with our problems" ramble. Harry is seeing a psychiatrist to "look at some things in our marriage."

Our children are driving him crazy, he says.

No surprise. He and Tom have always been at sword point, and lately Meta has been having parties that disturb the peace. Ben has trouble at school and— well below the radar of his self-absorbed parents—is using and selling drugs.

Harry does not mention me, but I am engrossed in my work at Wabash Center—customized plans for each child: toilet training, fine and gross motor training, language development. Smoothing over rough spots for Harry is no longer Priority Numero Uno.

He wants to start fresh, he says. Put these difficult times behind him.

Why is he suddenly so overwhelmed by the family annoyances he has been putting up with for years? Something's up.

He keeps talking as we walk, but I go back over the past weeks, trawling for clues.

❧

His at-home time has dwindled. Late meetings, trips to the gym. He comes home at 11 from a committee meeting. My movie buddy, Ruthanna, and I go to see John Cassavetes' *Faces* the next night. We agree both Harry and Jon would have hated it. On the way home I ask, "What was the big deal that kept our husbands so late last night?" Jon is on the same committee.

"Jon was home at 8 o'clock," she says.

"Hmm, I say, funny." No light bulb. Whatever Harry was doing, it must be important; he is so responsible.

After the annual dinner meeting at Good Shepherd, I volunteer for dishwashing. I glance up from a soapy sink as a flash goes off in the dining room; photos of the vestry and staff are in progress. The church secretary stands behind Harry's chair with her arms around his neck. When she sees me, she starts, stands up straight. How insulting, does she think I am the "jealous wife" type?

❧

I miss a step, kick a stone ahead of me: a calming technique from third grade. I hurry to catch up with Harry and the stone. Can it be? Harry, as above suspicion as Caesar's wife? Married to Patricia the Gullible?

I swallow hard, awareness weighing in my gut like biscuits and gravy.

"Harry, is there somebody else?"

He admits he has a girlfriend; he is thinking of leaving our marriage to marry her.

Tears roll down my face in silence. Harry tries to pull me into an embrace but I shove him away. I run back to the car and get into the passenger's seat. If I'd brought my keys I'd drive away and leave him stranded.

We drive home in silence. I move to a cot in the laundry room. I shun Harry's embrace. An immediate effect of his disclosure is heightened sexual desire, and I dare not lose my cool.

❧

The next day dawns after little sleep. I need to take action, do something. Harry can't get off scot-free with this "the children get on my nerves" shit.

I'll kill myself. That will do it. I know the guy next door has a gun, but finding and using it would be tricky. I haven't fired a gun since Uncle Eddie taught me how to use his wife's

.22 when I was 14. I have Lysol and bug killer, but what if they just make me sick and miserable?

Cutting my wrists sounds painful. Putting my head in the electric oven won't work. Sitting in the bathtub and throwing in a lamp? An effective method on the last Colombo episode. Will the lamp's cord reach from the wall socket to the tub? Would the lamp fit in the tub with me?

I move from consideration of method to gloat over the scene when Harry finds my body. I lie lifeless on the living room floor, my blue and white embroidered sundress spread out around my lifeless body, my perfect shoulders exposed. He comes home and sees me, beautiful but dead, done in by his betrayal. He cries piteously and feels terribly, terribly guilty. He realizes too late what a blameless wife he tossed in the ashcan.

I relish the scene and run it over and over. I rearrange details, imagine myself watching Harry's grief and after he is sufficiently chastened, deigning to offer my love again: forgiving, generous me.

But wait, I am dead. Unable to witness Harry's misery. Or our romantic embrace after his desperate pleas for forgiveness.

So end my suicidal thoughts. I don't want to miss anything.

ॐ

I fight like a tigress to save the marriage.

If Harry leaves me I will no longer be his true love. Thrown over for another woman like a used bath towel, how could I keep my vision of our perfect partnership? Do I cling to marriage as a badge of respectability? Public acknowledgement of failure would be hard to take. I cannot fail. I can fix it. I've put 16 years of hard labor into this partnership already. Any relationship can be healed if you just work hard enough.

And there is so much to save. We have braved a move, career changes for both of us, three children. Made a home in close collaboration, planning everything from bedside reading lights to a vegetable garden exactly to our tastes. Trips to the beach at Lake Michigan, to see *La Bohème* in Wash U Park in St. Louis and *Auntie Mame* at the Purdue Convos. Our favorite restaurants, with our time-tested marital tactic of ordering two entrées, each of us choosing one and splitting both.

Is Harry really saying there is nothing here for him? Our 16 years together have been nothing more than annoying kids and my bossiness?

This hurts so much I decide to hell with him. I'm through.

But the children, we should stay together for the children. There are not so many divorces then as there are now. Wouldn't they be disadvantaged being raised by me as a single parent? The idea that Harry might want custody never occurs to me. I think like Tom, who said at one point in those turbulent days, "One thing we know, Mom would never leave us. We're stuck with her." He thought he was being funny, but we both knew it was true.

Maybe the children would have been better off with an honest break then, 33 years before our final parting.

↋

A friend questions why I voice no anger at Harry, even though I am deeply wounded. I promptly make a date to meet with Mary Lou. That hypocritical upstart: She is also Meta's piano teacher. Now I know why Harry always volunteers to take Meta back and forth to lessons and ferry our daughters to confirmation classes. That prissy little kid of hers isn't a spitfire like Meta. And she's an only child. I've been in Mary Lou's house. I've seen the white couch, the white carpet, the no-tchotchke-out-of-place living room. Could Harry prefer that sterile showroom to our family room with its dog hair and spilled Cokes, practical tweed rug covered with homework papers and Meta's hair rollers? She must have bewitched him.

Mary Lou agrees to meet me on her way to work.

I park in the alley next to my favorite Chinese restaurant, within sight of the Church of the Good Shepherd, scene of the crime. Mary Lou gets into the passenger seat. I am disappointed at how she looks: tasteful makeup, casual skirt and full blouse that camouflages her big boobs. She clutches a notebook and purse to her chest and turns her head toward me. Looks scared. Good. I tell her I want to kill her and the only thing that keeps me from it is that I don't want to go to jail and let her and Harry raise my children.

She looks straight ahead, starts to reply, and I mimic what Harry tells me she says during sex. Ashen faced, she gasps, "Harry said I said that?" I recognize honest shock and pain; Harry lied.

Uh oh, Harry is sicker than I thought. This is not going according to script.

My righteous indignation voice comes back. I tell Mary Lou to get the hell out of the car quickly before I smash her jaw.

I drive home shaken, shocked at myself.

I'd hoped to blast Bad Mary Lou, a safe target for my anger. She flunks as villain.

She must be concealing her sordid wicked side.

Never mind. After all, Harry is the victim, both of that witch and his miserable early life, a *poor thing* to be protected and cared for rather than blamed.

Once again, I draw the drapes. The sun outside my bubble is too bright and too hot.

ॐ

Harry decides to stay. There is endless therapy for Harry, for me, and for the family as a group. Harry sees his psychiatrist for years, soothing proof to me that the problem is all his. He needs help and more TLC. Harry's infidelity is not his fault, and certainly not mine. It is all due to his early childhood. Says so in the literature. I am the wronged wife, innocent bystander, who has to take even better care of my husband from now on.

Another golden moment for self-reflection and change slips by.

Didn't I learn anything from the Agnes episode?

28

The New Jews

After the Mary Lou incident Harry leaves Good Shepherd church and we search for a faith we can share.

ॐ

Maxine and Frank Gilner become fast friends in their years at Purdue, where Frank is a doctoral candidate in clinical psychology. They invite us to their Seder, a special meal to celebrate the Jewish feast of Passover. Tom drinks too much wine and Frank knows exactly how to help.

They urge Harry and I to try camping now that our children are grown; we catch the fever. Some of Harry and my best times together follow: Warren Dunes, Muskegon, Silver Lake, Luddington, Sleeping Bear Dunes—Michigan state parks that fill our souls and warm our hearts. Lake Michigan was our ocean. I miss it still.

Maxine is a force, a powerful woman. Sometimes overwhelming.

She is the consummate Good Wife. Her oft-repeated mantra is that she cannot imagine a smarter man or better husband than Frank. She knits through League of Women Voter meetings and deep conversation, cooks endless meals for frequent guests, remembers every birthday, anniversary, even St. Pat's for me, her "favorite Irish person."

When illness cancels a Gilner visit to our Green Meadows home, I cry as I put away the special tablecloth I've sewn for our meals together.

Their oldest child, Hannah, is in and out of our house from the first. There is an age gap between her and her three sibs; Maxine explains that Frank's low sperm count made it difficult for her to conceive. She is the only person I know who includes her husband's sperm count in casual conversation.

ॐ

By the time Hannah is 13, Frank is a professor at St. Louis University, making continued connection easy, since my parents live in the suburbs.

Harry and I go to the bat mitzvah. It is in Shaare Emeth, a venerable reform synagogue. Harry remembers vaguely the name mentioned in his grandmother's home; Maxine finds his grandfather, Solomon Herzog, listed as a member in the archives.

The ceremony pulls me in, with wave after wave of emotion. The Torah, a huge scroll with sacred scripture inscribed by hand onto its parchment, is passed from grandparents to parents to Hannah.

The prayer book is a newly adopted version. Its words resonate with my highest ideals; my heart pulses to the spirit pervading the ritual.

> From Egypt, the house of bondage, we were delivered; on Sinai, amid peals of thunder, we bound ourselves to your purpose. Inspired by prophets and instructed by sages, we survived oppression and exile, time and again overcoming the forces that would have destroyed us. ... Our failings are many, our faults are great, yet it has been our glory to bear witness to our God, and to keep alive in dark ages the vision of a world redeemed. ...
>
> We give thanks for the freedom that is ours and we pray for those in other lands who are persecuted and oppressed. Help them to bear their burdens and keep alive in them the love of freedom and the hope of deliverance. ...
>
> We pray that the day may come when corruption and evil shall give way to integrity and goodness, when superstition shall no longer enslave the mind nor idolatry blind the eye, when all created in your image become one in spirit and one in friendship.
>
> — Central Conference of American Rabbis,
> *Gates of Prayer for Shabbat*

I cry through it all.

At the reception afterwards in the Gilners' garden, I approach Maxine as soon as the stream of well-wishers thins.

"Maxine," I say, after a long, warm hug (a real Mexican *abrazo*, although I didn't know it then).

"Maxine, you don't realize how lucky you are. Harry and I have been traipsing from church to church, trying to decide what to do about religion. You have this gift of faith passed down to you from your family, and now you are able to give it to Hannah 'from generation to generation,' as the liturgy put it."

I brush away yet another tear. "And it is so attractive, so … so heartfelt."

Maxine smiles, hesitates, then motions to an empty table. She brushes the cake crumbs onto the grass and asks her son to bring us both punch.

"Thank you, Pat. I am so glad it was a good experience for you. I could see you were crying through the whole service, and was hoping it was tears of joy."

I laugh, "No way I could hide how affecting it was. When Hannah chanted in Hebrew, it was like a voice piercing the veil dividing heaven from earth."

A bit over the top; we both roll our eyes and grin.

"She worked hard," her proud mother says. "And actually, just so you know, you could have this, too, you know."

"Have what?" I ask, after the punch arrives and we both take a sip.

Maxine continues, "There are regular classes for converts at Shaare Emeth, and I am sure somebody in Lafayette could …"

"Could what?" She is speaking a foreign language. "I don't quite get it. You mean there is a way to be Jewish without being born Jewish?"

"Of course," Maxine says.

She goes on for a minute or two before jumping up to say good-bye to another guest. I hear no more in my shell-shocked state. Jewish? I could be Jewish.

I want it.

&

On our drive back to Indiana we talk, and Harry agrees to call the rabbi the next week to investigate.

I hesitate to take the final step of conversion, regretting the loss of a tradition inherited from my family and nurtured at Immaculate Conception, where I was married and baptized our oldest child, Tom. I spoke to Tom, now a sociology professor at Cornell, saying I hated to desert a faith that needed so much help. Catholic teachings on sexuality and women were woefully in need of change, which comes best from within.

"Mom," Tom said, "you are living in Lafayette, Indiana. You have to do what's best for you here and now. If you are more comfortable in the Jewish community, do it. Let the Catholic Church take care of itself." Sounded sensible.

A year later, the Gilners drive from St. Louis to witness our conversion.

29

Leaving Green Meadows

Ben starts Purdue in 1975, and Harry wants to move. With Ben gone the house on Road 26 West has too much grass to cut and snow to plow. Harry can no longer manage either, with his perennially bad back, which means depending on iffy hired help or me. Seeing me working outside gives him a bad conscience: Shoveling snow is the man's job.

Harry prefers West Lafayette: home of the Boilermakers, a better address than Green Meadows, and a more congenial atmosphere. We converted to Judaism three years earlier, and West Lafayette is the site of Temple Israel and many of its members.

I drag my feet. Green Meadows has an emotional pull— it's the scene of so many dramas in our family's life. We moved there on Ben's first birthday. He and Meta boarded the school bus on the road in front for their first day of Klondike Kindergarten.

Three remodels made the place ours. The house starts as a built-on-spec box: "Three-bedroom, two-bath red brick ranch with attached one-car garage" the ad would have said. We transform it into a home.

First, the garage becomes a living room and the old living room, a dining room. Many a cake is borne triumphantly from the kitchen, candles blazing, Happy Birthdays ringing. Poppy seed for Harry and Meta, baked Alaska for Tom, lemon pudding cake for Ben—the only cake Ben likes. I scour *Family Circle* and *Woman's Day* and find a castle cake for Meta's children's party with the four turrets baked in juice cans. At that table we make our first Seder.

The fireplace hearth is the podium for Meta and Cheryl's *Wizard of Oz* production.

The kids hang their stockings there on Christmas Eve. It bears the scars from our first and last Twelfth Night celebration. Meta lobbies for this tradition when she hears about it at Good Shepherd Sunday school. The dry pine needles of the Christmas tree catch fire with a roar, crackle like fireworks and soar out of the firebox to burn a permanent scorch on the wood mantel.

We screen in the concrete patio off the kitchen and eat there til the snow flies. On its floor we will be abandoning another treasure, our family map. A big crack in the concrete floor reminds me of the Mississippi River. I outline it in heavy black marker and sketch the USA around its meandering path. Places where we have family, I daub crude stars. Two are clustered near the Mississippi in Missouri: one for Florissant, my parents; and one for Harry's mother and brother in Washington. There is Lubbock, Texas for my sister; Jekyll

Island, Georgia, for Aunt Thelma; and Mountain Home, Arkansas for Uncle Eddie and Aunt Faye. When friends Judy and Aaron take jobs in Toronto, we paint their star just above Lake Ontario.

Outside the porch, Harry's tomato garden lies fallow in the late fall chill. There he grew the biggest, juiciest tomatoes in Tippecanoe County—enough for our summer table from six plants. He pounds in sturdy wooden stakes to tie up the vines as they grow. He needs a stepladder to pick the tomatoes on top. He guards and dusts them jealously from threatening tomato worms and leaf rot.

For the final and most ambitious remodel, we post a drawing on the laundry room door. Each family member adds, redraws, changes. The addition is an amalgam of our work.

A new bedroom goes in. Tom gets it first. When he leaves for Israel, Meta moves in, and she and Harry paint a rainbow over her bed with a giant protractor. A picture of the two of them holding the contraption against the wall appears in a psychology text a friend publishes, exemplifying father and daughter cooperation on a project. The author also uses one of Ben and Louis, Ben's African-American friend; she needs black/white balance in her book, hard to find in white Tippecanoe County.

Louis lives in the bedroom one summer, a summer the two boys split, spending the first half together at our house, the second at Louis' in Virginia, where he and his mother moved when she began teaching at Virginia Tech. The two boys are inseparable from first grade through high school.

I look out the front door at my babies, the Russian olives. A pamphlet on gardening from the Klondike book fair convinces me that Russian olives form sturdy windbreaks. The plants arrive in the mail as dry twigs no bigger around than chopsticks. I plant them to the hoots of my children. Now they are twenty feet tall, and make me feel even taller.

In the backyard, the play equipment installed by the neighborhood guys remains. Harry, the engineer, designs it using sturdy telephone poles and strong ropes after checking prices on the flimsy playground equipment for sale. The teens still climb and swing from time to time.

The chalkboard on the kitchen wall is our family communication center. A photo records a memorable message from Ben, meant to worm his way of out of unloading the dishwasher: "The 3/5 Compromise: I do 3/5 of the work." He's studying that historic agreement in American history. When I point out his doing nothing isn't exactly a compromise, he rolls his eyes and throws himself on my mercy. Meta and Tom never have to do as much work as I pile on him, he complains.

The television in the new family room. Only one in the house; these are the Dark Ages. Every day when I came home from teaching summer school at Wabash Center, I sit transfixed by the Watergate hearings. I can see the young military aide as he testified quietly, concisely.

Yes, he had installed a recording system in the Oval Office. Yes, it had been activated in 1971 and to his knowledge, has been functioning ever since. He gives me cold chills. Politics, religion, social problems—all can move me to tears, tears unshed for the family problems buried all around the yard. I leave their unmarked graves behind—no mourning, no mention, no awareness.

Even the bathroom becomes special when Harry transforms it into a darkroom for a photography course. Artsy photos of our family slide out of those smelly chemical baths. We also use it as a tornado shelter occasionally, since it is the only windowless room in the house.

The dog pen, where our adored Angie awaits our return from work or school, will sit empty. Angie guarded Ben's marijuana plants until the afternoon I turn them into a colossal bonfire. Ben is horrified when he gets home. I thought his pot plot was a harmless juvenile diversion until I heard that if the police find the plants, we, the owners of the house, are liable, not only Farmer Ben.

All the house ghosts are not friendly.

The double garage door bears the marks of my backing my little apple-green Renault halfway through it, oblivious, splitting several boards and smashing the back of my car. I was on my way to the office, my head full of a client's pension plan. Was it the gas passer for whom I quadrupled his pension contribution so he could retire early? Or the sleep doctor whose nest egg I squandered in a failed tax shelter? Not the first time my brain on autopilot left my body behind.

The basketball hoop, indispensable in a proper Indiana driveway, whose sturdy steel pole crumpled the fender of Harry's prized VW Beetle, with Meta at the wheel.

Those damnable rocks are still around the shrubs.

I won't miss the concrete front stoop where I sat, hugging my knees, trying to figure out a way to kill myself when I found out about Mary Lou.

ঽঌ

I choose a split-level on Blackhawk Lane; the ravine in the backyard enchants me. I insist we sleep on the lower level so that our bedroom looks out on its woody descent to the Wabash River.

The day we move is moving day for Bernie and Donna Liska, too, also to West Lafayette. At sunset they show up with a bottle of champagne and four glasses, and we toast a new chapter in our lives sitting on the floor of our empty Green Meadows home.

30

A Visit to Donna

Donna's daughter Cheryl meets me at George Bush Intercontinental Airport, in Houston. Her station wagon is cluttered with her four children's gear.

The last time I saw Cheryl was 15 years earlier in her home in Princeton, New Jersey. Donna was visiting her daughter. Harry and I were at the Jersey Shore babysitting for Shona, our first grandchild, while her parents attended a wedding in the nearby dunes.

ॐ

When we walk in the front door an excited toddler tackles us singing something close to "Happy Birthday" at screech pitch. Cheryl has pulled together an impromptu birthday party for Shona, who turns one that day. Streamers and balloons are strung in the dining room. Our little greeter takes my hand. She pulls us—Shona in my arms—into the kitchen, and points to a lopsided cake with "Happy Birthday SHONA" in squiggles that start on top and trail down one side.

ॐ

I smile at the memory and wish this visit were as upbeat.

Cheryl tosses my copious luggage into the back of her wagon and insists it's no trouble at all. I know she has been diagnosed with breast cancer, and am glad to see she looks so healthy. She probably considers herself too heavy, but her curvy physique looks just right to me. She has the same glowing complexion as in her Dorothy days, still a potential model for a Swedish travel poster.

She and Meta produced *The Wizard of Oz* in front of our Green Meadows fireplace when they were kindergarteners. Cheryl aced the part of Dorothy, while Meta terrified the little kids as the Wicked Witch of the West. Their 3-year-old siblings, Ben and Julie, were the Munchkins, singing the one song they knew well enough to perform: "Jingle Bells."

Cheryl married a career Amoco man who spends most of his time in the Middle East or on an oilrig off the Texas shore. Early in their marriage, Cheryl accompanied him to Saudi Arabia while Ben was on a kibbutz in Israel. Donna and I put a map of the Middle East up on her kitchen wall and located our children with pins, embarrassed at our sketchy geography.

The husband works in the Houston office now, the better to help manage their four children and his wife's disease. And a mother-in-law with Alzheimer's: my friend Donna.

ک

"You look great, honey. How are you?" I ask Cheryl.

"Finished my chemo last month. Now I get to have a mastectomy, lucky me," she says, smiling sideways at me.

As we drive to her suburban home the conversation rambles on: our shared Green Meadows lives, questions about Meta, how eager Donna is to see me.

The wagon has barely stopped rolling when Donna is out the door, charging to the car. I jump out. When we pull away from our long hug, our eyes meet and I see Donna's are the same Alice blue that drew the guys to her side at our neighborhood parties. She is thinner than when I saw her two summers ago. Her graying blond hair frames her face in the same waves she has worn since I've known her. And her voice: I could pick her husky alto out of a crowd in the Purdue football stadium.

"Mother likes to visit the mall," Cheryl says, "so you two take my car and go over there." She gives me some cash, in case Donna wants anything. I am embarrassed; shouldn't she be giving it to her mother?

❧

The mall is the familiar conglomeration of nondescript little shops and a couple of anchor stores. Donna and I stroll up one wide aisle and down the next, window-shopping, talking nonstop.

A sign catches her eye and her step quickens.

"Let's go in here. They have super cherry pie," she says, pointing to Jenny's Kitchen.

We enter another bland space. We slide into the puffy fake-leather upholstery of a booth against the windows. The standard configuration: metal napkin holder, salt and pepper, and a tray full of pink Sweet and Low and blue Equal packets lined up on the window end of the table. Nobody but me uses sugar anymore.

"Donna, I hope you remember that cherry pie is poisonous without ice cream," I say.

She looks at me a beat too long before a flat, "I don't want ice cream."

After the waitress takes our order, Donna leans her head back on the plastic and sighs.

"Oh, Pat. He left me, he left me." Her eyes fill. "I can't believe he would do that to me. I can't believe Bernie would ever leave me like this."

Bernie died from cancer earlier in the year. He was a *mensch*: a man I would have married in a whipstitch. He was born on a Wisconsin dairy farm; his father died when he was in grade school. He helped his family run the farm, put himself through college with a roofing job, and earned a Ph.D. on the GI Bill while Donna taught school. He came to Purdue on the animal sciences faculty, went on to become dean of agriculture, and was on Gerald Ford's short list for secretary of agriculture. All overshadowed in my eyes by his humanity. He was the warmest father and husband I ever saw in action.

"Donna, Bernie didn't want to leave you. He would have given anything to stay with you."

She turns away and looks down at her hands, twisting and untwisting the stiff paper napkin in front of her. She wipes away a tear in silence.

"It is so good to see you," she says. "The old days. Remember when Ben and Julie climbed up the TV antenna to your roof?"

I smile. Donna seems rejuvenated, lively now.

"Of course I remember," I say. "You and I were having coffee at your dining room table when you looked out the window and saw them running along the peak of our roof. Who could forget the look on your face; I thought you'd seen an armed gunman in our backyard."

Donna smiles. "Little snots. And they were wearing yellow life preservers."

"Of course," I laugh. "Ben had convinced Julie, always the more cautious one ... "

"You mean the one with more sense," Donna breaks in.

"... that it would not hurt them to fall off the roof if they wore life jackets," I finish. Now we are both laughing through tears.

The waitress hovers next to our booth, unsure whether to interrupt with our pie. I motion for her to unload her tray.

When she walks away, Donna reaches across the table and grabs my hand.

"Don't go, Pat. Stay with me. Don't leave. There is plenty of room. You can sleep in Alan's room. He's at college. Stay here. With me."

I pat her hand, say I must get home tomorrow, but I will come back soon.

ॐ

I catch my flight back to Mexico the next day. I leave behind a hand-woven belt I treasure, and tell Cheryl to keep it for me; I will pick it up on my next visit.

I never return. Cheryl succumbs to breast cancer after two years of treatments.

Donna goes to a nursing home in St. Paul to be near her other daughter, Julie. She dies of Alzheimer's a few years later.

I love my friend and confidant, one of very few I told about Harry and Mary Lou, the one who shined the light on the seriousness of Harry and Tom's conflicts. The neighbor I'd coffee-ed with, worked with, cried with and laughed with over dozens of crises, real and imagined. A part of me was angry, as she had been with Bernie: How could she leave me like this? It was so unfair. The Buddha advises not to be greedy, to detach. I want to cling.

The Buddha is right; everything changes. Donna is gone, but her model as an openhearted mother inspires me still. I mourn a lost comrade; I miss her grace and compassion.

31

Mortality Intrudes

By the time of my visit to Donna, Gram, my emotional refuge, had left me, too. She and my parents had moved to Indiana in the final years of her life. Instead of Green Meadows, where my friendship with Donna took root, my family was in Wabash Shores, a subdivision in the heart of West Lafayette, in the house chosen for the ravine in its backyard.

Mother, Dad and Gram rented a house there, too, on Delaware Drive, close to Harry and me on Blackhawk Lane: the developer hoped Indian names would make the flat treeless lots feel like the forest primeval.

My epiphany on Delaware Lane happened after Gram died in a nearby nursing home, and my parents were alone together for the first time since Union, 44 years earlier.

❧

I'm back in my parents' house on Delaware. My father and I sit in front of the TV in his bedroom. Dad's voice is calm.

"I think I'll ask Tom and Ben if they will join me for a week of golf on the Mississippi Gulf Coast," he muses. Tom and Ben are college age; the three are golf buddies. "Before winter sets in." He pauses, winks, "While I can still beat those two guys to the green and putt out ahead of them."

I smile and retreat down the hall, unable to match his light tone.

"Need a cup of tea," I call over my back. "Want anything?"

I hear what my father is *not* saying: "Time is ticking down for me; time to plan the road from here to there."

ই

I have to get out of there. I hope my hurried good-byes mask my emotion as I close the door and run down the grassy slope to my parked car, tears welling.

Just three blocks to my house on Blackhawk Lane.

Keep vision clear. Clutch the wheel. Straight down Delaware, right onto Indian Trail, full stop, look both ways, hug the center with the left wheel, swing round the curve, brake gently, left into the Blackhawk Lane cul-de-sac, down to a crawl at number 106, up driveway, into the carport, pull to the right, leave room for Harry's car. Made it, kept control.

I hurry downstairs to the bedroom and stand looking out the triple window next to our bed.

I leave the lights off. The scene outside my window will heal me.

The huge hawthorn sways in the stiffening autumn breeze. A few dry leaves swirl in the firepit, our stab at recreating state park campfires. The ravine is a black gash—no sign of the trail along the storm sewer "creek."

I sometimes awaken to dawn and step out the door to the smell of fresh rain.

Once a row of possums trudged close to our window along a wind-cleared path through the snow. One spring a confused deer wandered up from the ravine.

No animals now. Not even a squirrel to distract me.

I am tired and confused and in pain. I want Gram's cool hand on my feverish 8-year-old head, her hot toddy and the feel of my hand closing around the warm glass: a "cheese glass," with tulips in primary colors painted on it, that came filled with Kraft's pimiento cheese and just fit my child-sized hand. I inhale the smell of whiskey in her proprietary formula.

Gram is dead, and my palliative backyard dissolves into darkness.

I throw myself face down on our king-size bed and pull a pillow over my head.

My father's days are numbered, but that was clear a week ago in St. Elizabeth's hospital. What was different today?

❧

Andrew Barnes Browne was a fitness buff before fitness was cool. Golf most days, gym workouts, a diet healthier than most people's in those meat-and-potatoes times. Three years before, on his 80th birthday, he could still spring from the deep upholstery of our living room couch like a kangaroo. He had a boxer's wiry 5'6" frame: He'd fought amateur bouts in his youth. Black Irish, he called himself. When shorts expose his scrawny legs with their bulging calf muscles, his skin is white as a Southern belle's protected from the sun. Thin lips, full only of his Irish gift of gab.

His shoe-polish black hair had been blond ringlets in babyhood, like my sister's. For both of them age darkened and straightened the ringlets. Dad now has distinguished white sideburns. He models the vigorous, fully lived life, poised to live past the 90+ years of his parents.

Before the cancer diagnosis.

At his age prostate cancer grows slowly, the doctor assures us; Dad would likely die from another cause. Hormone therapy is so successful the first two years, my mother swears the doctors made a mistake.

He loses the crapshoot. The tumor begins to grow rapidly. At his request I scour journals in Purdue's Veterinary Medical Library, then the St. Elizabeth Hospital library after a tussle with the hospital administrator. Ironic that my abandoned graduate studies give me the necessary library research tools, now grown obsolete with the Internet. In 1983, one could not Google prostate cancer.

Dad reviews my findings and chooses a middle course—a radioactive implant. Not so aggressive as surgical removal or as passive as doing nothing. The implant would bombard the cancer with tumor-killing radioactive cells. He instructs the surgeon not to go ahead if the biopsy during surgery finds cancer elsewhere. All studies agree that if cancer cells have spilled over from the prostate, an iodine implant is useless.

ه‌

St. Elizabeth's Hospital was the scene of my youngest child's birth. As I pull into the parking lot on Dad's surgery day, the warmth of that stay floods back: the easy birth, my genial roommate, the ice cream in our favorite flavors our husbands bring us from Frozen Custard every night. The Custard is a Lafayette landmark, dating from before I was born. Their soft serve ice cream is not to be mentioned in the same breath as Dairy Queen's.

ه‌

Today the staid old red brick reminds me of a prison. Mother and I trudge from the parking lot to the surgery waiting room, with its bad coffee and anxious families.

It is over. The surgeon ushers Mother and me into a tiny barren consultation room. Cancer cells have invaded the lymph nodes, he reports. No implant attempted.

Mother and I ride the elevator to Dad's assigned room to await his return from the ICU. She sinks into the brown plastic upholstered chair by the bed and lights a cigarette. After a few puffs she says, "Let's not tell your father just yet— no need to upset him right after his operation."

I nod and walk to the window. The parking lot is beginning to fill for visiting hours.

An hour later wheels rattle in the hall. Two orderlies transfer Dad to his bed, with "1-2-3 ups" and cheerful banter. Dad groggily returns a few words before they clear out, pushing their noisy gurney.

Mother and I post ourselves sentinel-like on either side of the bed.

Mother takes Dad's hand.

"How about the implant?" he asks.

Mother pats his hand. He turns his head to me.

"The doctor says the surgery went smoothly, and your recuperation ..." My voice trails off.

Mother picks up with how glad she is it is all over and he is back with us.

He turns toward her voice and closes his eyes.

Maybe he will drift off into sleep.

Dad turns to me again, eyes wide now.

"The implant?"

I stutter, stumble, "They didn't do it. They found cancer cells in the lymph nodes."

Before he drifts out of consciousness, I see disappointment, then acceptance flicker in his eyes. He knows he will die of prostate cancer.

ॐ

No flickers between hope and despair this afternoon. Dad is resigned, planning the last act.

I'd left my office early to stop by their house on my way home. They are at their usual stations: Mother in front of *As the World Turns* in the living room, a glass and an ashtray at her side.

Not a dirty dish or an unwashed pan in the pristine kitchen. No sign of dinner preparation; Mother is later and later with their meals, meals they eat on TV trays in separate rooms.

The St. Louis Cardinals are in extra innings on Dad's bedroom TV. He comments, between innings, on what a perfect day for golf this is. Wait two weeks after surgery, the doctor decreed. Five more days. Since he and Mother moved to Indiana, he's played the Purdue North Course almost every day that no snow is on the ground.

By next year he would switch to a cart. When he can no longer swing a club he rides a cart around the course with his golf buddies. They are pallbearers at his funeral.

The latest *Sports Illustrated* lies open on the lamp table next to his recliner. I see a stack of earlier issues on the shelf below. Good sign. Mother often pitches Dad's magazines before he finishes them. Magazines older than the current issue betray a poor housekeeper.

There the two of them are, stuck in this grim pattern, cruising down their well-worn tracks, ignoring the warning lights flashing: This lane ends soon. In these last days of their 53 years together they hide behind invisible partitions. Mother in her kitchen fiefdom or ensconced in her maple captain's chair in the living room, scotch and Viceroys at her side, watching soaps and Johnny Carson; Dad in his bedroom recliner, nibbling at the plates of food Mother delivers, watching sports and the ticker tape underneath for a Brown Group stock quote.

Death will end any possibility of change. For them. As it will for me.

I get it—in a vivid flash, like the one that knocked Paul off his horse on the road to Damascus. Unlike Paul, my eyes are opened, not blinded.

My mourning is not for Andrew Barnes Browne. The bell tolls for me.

I have never recognized limits: on my ability, my capacity, my time. Like the reluctant virgin in Andrew Marvell's poem, I think I have "world enough and time."

I sit here just like my mother, watching my life go by as I drug myself with busyness.

I keep a stock of "errands" on the backseat of my car. These are non-urgent missions: a book promised to a friend, a picture to be framed, a coffeemaker in need of new glass pot. With these on the ready I can squeeze in one more task when an unexpected half hour opens up.

Wise financial planner, kugel baker for the Temple Sisterhood sale, regular at Jackie Sorenson's aerobic dance classes, convivial wife and gracious hostess for a Purdue administrator—I harmonize my roles with near perfect pitch.

But I have not solved the "Problem with No Name" that Donna and I recognized as our own in *The Feminine Mystique*. Where was *I* in all this make-work? Was this all there was? Now that I know I am going to die, is this how I want to spend the rest of my days?

The rest of that wretched poem pounds on. Why can't I erase what I don't want to hear, like an unwanted track on a CD?

> ... then worms shall try
> That long-preserved virginity,
> And your quaint honour turn to dust,

And into ashes all my lust;

The grave's a fine and private place,

But none, I think, do there embrace.

> —Andrew Marvell, *To His Coy Mistress*

Here come the worms, crawling all over me; there goes my lust, turning to dust in front of my eyes. Before I even know what I lust for.

Ridiculous. Overdramatic. Stop carrying on like Madame Butterfly in the third act. So I am going to die. Big surprise. All this hand wringing while holed up in my private personal refuge—staring at the ravine I bought the house for?

Look around. Our Jacuzzi tub big enough for Harry and me, or four grandchildren. Maybe a hot bath—a good soak can clear away any dreary mood. Or go upstairs and open a Miller Lite.

Upstairs a door slams. Footsteps echo on the hardwood floor above me. Harry is home. Time for dinner.

&

The sound of Harry's footsteps jerks me back to the present in a panic. Whatever is wrong, I do not want to talk to my husband about it. With a night's sleep, the sun will come out tomorrow, just like in *Annie*.

My bare feet hit the cold tile, and I hurry to the mirror in our dressing room. A quick comb-through and I will be presentable; glasses on—oh no, my face cannot be disguised in time.

ॐ

"What's wrong, honey?" Harry says as he strides around the corner of the Jacuzzi. He drops his jacket before taking me in his arms.

"Dad," I manage, tearing up again. "He's so ... so weak, it is so ... hard." A daughter's grief at her father's disintegration: normal, natural, understandable.

"Oh, oh, Pat, I'm sorry." I press my damp face into his white-shirted chest. After minutes of comforting pats on my back, his back straightens.

"Why don't I run over to Lin's Wok so you don't have to think about dinner?"

I nod, leaning away from his embrace.

He empties his pockets of keys, calendar and calculator— his office implements. He checks his money clip for the price of two take-outs, and halfway out the bedroom door, calls back over his shoulder, "The usual okay?"

I nod again, wary of what sounds might come from my choked throat.

As soon as I hear the door slam I pad up the stairs to put the water on for a pot of Darjeeling, better tea than beer with Chinese. I arrange placemats, plates and napkins on the table. The dining room is right above the bedroom, and the bare, floor-to-ceiling window frames my recent path from my parents' house. The ravine is black and forbidding in the failing light. I wish there were drapes to draw.

Harry returns in record time to set the familiar white cartons in their steamed up plastic bags in the middle of the table. He tells about his meeting with the VP for regional campuses that afternoon. I spear broccoli with garlic sauce with my chopstick in grateful silence.

ঽ

Why silence? Why couldn't I talk to Harry? My husband is a sympathetic ear, not a curmudgeon. With all the counseling after our almost break-up over Mary Lou, we have grown closer. My partner should be the first to comfort me. What was keeping me from talking about my dread at my father's approaching death?

Ah, of course. Our focus in therapy was to strengthen our marriage. The only time our staying together was seriously threatened was by Harry, not me, and he'd stayed. Which affirmed our rock-solid marriage.

Something about this crisis uncovers an edginess that threatens everything I thought was solid. My father is mortal; so am I. The Grim Reaper I'd pooh-poohed is creeping up behind me. I am really, really scared.

32

The Morning After

Next morning, I gun my little green Renault out of the driveway before dawn. No need to leave so early—no appointments until 1 p.m., but I want to be out of the house before Harry comes upstairs for breakfast. I drive mechanically through the town, across the bridge, to Herzog Financial Services.

I swing my car snugly into its skimpy space in the bank building's garage with the ease born of daily practice. As I ride to the 10th floor ticking off the day's tasks, I'm still rattled. I struggle to review the spreadsheets for my 1 p.m. client.

It does not help that the desk at which I work was once our dining room table. Its sturdy oak is a Pandora's box of memories. Meals with Harry and our three children, but also, with my parents. Their wraiths sit across the table from me now, beaming at their grandchildren between forkfuls of somebody's birthday cake.

Heartbreaking that they now eat separately. My memories of meals in their homes are all bright spaces, smiling people, everyone's favorite food prepared with love and care, mellow talk, stories spun like sugar into cotton candy.

How had their *gemutlich* dinner table degraded into TV trays in separate rooms?

In Union, I caught my first inkling. I was on vacation from college. I came in from a night on the town, I found my mother asleep on the toilet. Funny, must have had a long day. But it happens again. More than once. Enough that I face what I don't want to admit; my mother is passing out drunk.

Later when I take infant Tom for a two-week visit while Harry is on the road, I notice that after the usual before-dinner drinks, Mother brings her scotch and soda to the table. She has coffee, clears the table, then settles in the living room with another drink, and falls asleep in front of the TV before staggering off to bed in the early hours.

We drive to Florissant for visits with our three children after my parents move there to open a Ben Franklin store, my father's "retirement" business. When our boisterous crew visits, all seems smoother, but disturbing clues pop up. One ferociously hot afternoon, I work up a thirst refilling the holes Angie, our dog, dug in Mother's rose bushes. I grab a chilled glass I think is mine as I walk in the door and down a slug, expecting iced tea. I choke; pure alcohol with a shot of tea for color. Feeling guilty for being suspicious, I check closets and find bottles stashed.

The story is clearer from Gram. She visits us in Indiana a couple of times a year. We plan family outings around her trips: once, to the Lake Michigan beach at Warren Dunes State Park, where she sits in a beach chair watching us frolic in the sand and waves, virtually purring with pleasure.

On this particular visit, the kids have football practice, movies to see, pizza parlors to visit, and on and on. Nobody but me wants to go to Happy Hollow, the park down the ravine from our house. Gram and I set out by ourselves, picking up KFC on the way.

We choose a rustic picnic table under the shade of the huge oaks that surround the picnic-playground. After our stomachs are full, we clear up and throw the chicken bones, plastic trays and greasy napkins in the black metal barrel with West Lafayette Parks stenciled on its side. I've brought a thermos with our favorite tea, and we take our cups to a bench facing the playground. We watch kids jump on and off the foot-powered merry-go-round, pump the swings high, and climb on the World War II fighter plane set up for their exploration.

Our easy chat slows. I gather my courage. "Mother seemed to be drinking more when we were there for Dad's birthday."

Gram turns her face away. Is she going to stonewall me again?

Without looking me full in the face, she replies with a catch in her voice: "It's been coming on a long time. I worry about her ... she's burned two holes in the carpet next to her chair from cigarettes. She stays up so late. Won't let me help with the dishes. Says she likes to do them by herself later on. I try to get her to go to bed when I do. But ..."

I pour the last drops of tea into Gram's cup.

"She probably doesn't like you telling her what to do. I noticed the two of you going at it about how to cook the bacon in the morning."

Gram's head sinks; she squeezes the linen handkerchief wadded in her hand.

"It has gotten ... awful. I've done everything I know how.

"Last summer she began saying she never had any time with Andy alone. I made up my mind to go to my room when he came home from the store and stay until she called me for dinner. I said I needed to lie down before the meal. I read and rest and it's fine, but that doesn't seem to help."

Smart solution. Like Mother, Gram is an avid reader.

"She doesn't want me to do anything anymore, says I am too slow and mess everything up."

"Oh, Gram." This is worse than I thought.

"I think it is the drink, but I don't know. She ..."

I move closer and give her a hug. I can feel her heart beat; her breath comes in sighs. This is no way for an 85-year-old to live.

❧

On our next visit, after serious spine stiffening, I tell Dad I am concerned about Mother's drinking.

His face tenses. Anger flashes from his eyes.

"Can you imagine what it would be like to have your mother live with you for 30 years?" he shoots back. "That would drive any woman to drink. She needs a bit of bottle courage, never having her home to herself, having to take care of her mother her whole life."

❧

If getting Gram out of the house will solve the problem, I can fix it.

I speak to Harry. He agrees; Gram can live with us.

When she visits again, I will speak to her. She arrives. She no longer rides the bus; we meet halfway between houses to shuttle her back and forth. A few days before we are to meet my parents to take Gram back home, I choose a quiet moment after dinner.

"Gram, we have room here for you—you know the children are gone now, and Harry and I would be honored to have you come to live with us."

She is visibly shaken, says she will think about it.

Nothing changes. I couldn't fix it. Mother and Gram continue to spar, and Dad now complains of Mother's testiness with him.

33

Addiction

> **Addict:** to cause or become physiologically or psychologically dependent on a habit-forming substance. **Addiction:** the quality or condition of being addicted, especially to a habit-forming substance.
>
> —*The American Heritage College Dictionary*

Precise, sterile definitions, far from my murky life experience.

Memories tumble out like dirty clothes from a crammed laundry chute.

Uncle Eddie. Center stage. Larger than life. A presence. When Nancy M talks about her father at Al-anon, she could be describing my Uncle Eddie. Her father's drinking and manic states messed up her life, but she's never met another man who could hold a candle to him.

He bought me my first tricycle and my first horse. My uncle is super-sized in my childlike eyes. I come home from second grade to find a fish swimming in the bathtub; a catch so large, Eddie kept it alive to impress his home fans.

His body swells to mammoth girth as he indulges his taste for fine food and lots of it, washed down with equally mammoth amounts of beer, scotch or anything alcoholic within reach. If he had been a woman, a strict diet would have been in order. In the 1940s a well-heeled, well-padded man had a tailor hide his belly.

When the booze runs out one afternoon, Eddie and a drinking partner drain dozens of miniature liquor bottles. Thelma collected them over years of airplane rides and displayed them on a long shelf around three dining room walls. I'm surprised she did not know better.

The meals at Eddie and Thelma's are orgies. Often, wild game—squirrels, rabbit, quail—with special dressings and side dishes chosen to complement the meat. My uncle is evidently a good shot; he comes back from North Dakota with his limit in pheasants.

A ritual glass of water sits before him, next to his wine glass. His custom is to drink four or five glasses of water at dinner, each glass refilled by his wife or another peon as he takes the final swig. Fine service is the hunter's just due.

Eddie is a talker and a verbal bully. He delivers bombastic monologues on topics from the New Deal to the correct way to fillet a fish, flattening opposing ideas with his sarcastic wit. With his tongue loosened by alcohol, nothing is off limits. We once went home early from Christmas dinner when he began a rant against scholarship because it did not lead to more fun in bed. He was too prudish to be sexually explicit, but Mother had had enough.

My mother disowns her brother in the early 1950s and refuses to communicate with him for 10 years. He is between wives, down on his luck after blowing the proceeds from his Bourbeuse Shoe stock. He'd demanded the buyout: Ayn Rand's novels convinced him to strike out on his own, like the Gary Cooper character in *The Fountainhead*. I suspect he knew that his drunken antics at shoe shows offended customers, and his design work suffered from binges and hangovers. Cashing Eddie out was a strain for the young shoe-manufacturing firm he and my father had built from a shoestring.

Eddie buys a bar in South St. Louis and drinks up its puny profits.

He drops in to my parents' household for prolonged visits. His mother, Gram, welcomes him, makes excuses for him, and pampers him shamelessly. At first he behaves. Then his drinking day lengthens until he is downing a few beers with the lunch his mother fixes him and closing down the bars around the courthouse every night.

One night he barely makes it to our front yard before passing out. It is mid-summer, so by morning Eddie has shed his clothes and lies naked, a beached white whale on our front lawn, which faces busy East State Street.

That's it for my mother.

Gram cries and pleads, gets Eddie to apologize and swear off the sauce forever, but my mother has had it. Out, out, damned spot, and never more darken my door. A melodrama I relish from my front-row seat, except for Gram's tears.

Eddie "hits bottom" (AA-speak) in Arkansas a few years later. He sobers up without a program or medical help and ekes out a living as a fishing guide on Bull Shoals, Lake Norfolk and the White River. He marries Faye, a good woman of infinite patience. She takes Gram's place as the long-suffering custodian of Eddie's outsize ego. He stays sober the rest of his life, but nothing else changes. After several years of his good behavior, Mother relents. Visits between the two families resume; Gram visits their home in Mountain Home, Arkansas every year.

Eddie introduced Dad to his sister, Virginia, thereby staking a lifelong claim on my father's loyalty. They were business partners, too, and Eddie's design talent launched the Glamour Debs label and contributed to Bourbeuse Shoe's success.

I hear my father's voice from his hospital bed in his final days, charging me with my uncle's care.

"Eddie's got a rough life," he says. "I know he brought most of his troubles on himself; he could have owned the same shares of Brown stock as me if he hadn't gone off on a tangent. But he's your mother's brother, and Faye is a saint to put up with him. I want you to see they don't end up destitute."

Faye is years younger than my uncle, and the two of them barely scratch by on my uncle's guiding work, meager Social Security checks and the vegetables they raise, eat and sell at a roadside stand. Saint Faye dies of cancer before my uncle, and Uncle Eddie becomes my responsibility after my parents' death.

In my father's last months of life, Eddie writes he is selling his boat to pay for Faye's medical expenses. Since his boat is a major source of income, my father sends the $9,000 owed the doctor, although he is preoccupied with his own medical and final expenses. I help with the transaction, angry that Eddie would lean on my dying father and wishing Dad would tell him to jump into Lake Norfolk. It bugs me that my uncle trades shamelessly on my father's generous spirit. And turns me into his accomplice.

ॐ

Harry and I drive to Mountain Home several times, bearing gifts, including money, from my parents, even before my parents' deaths. We find a charming local motel, the Carriage Inn, with extensive gardens, paths filled with flowers, fountains, corny statues, even a fishpond with a tiny bridge over it—an oasis in the bleak Arkansas landscape. In my uncle's final days, I fly from Mexico and check in alone. Sparing Harry, I say, but actually cherishing time on my own.

Faye was still alive on the last trip Harry and I took together. Eddie steers us every evening to a favorite restaurant. He knows my parents have given us money to pick up the checks.

His running commentary sounds like a AAA guidebook—which restaurant is best for which food, levels of service, ambiance, comfortable seating. Service earns the most stars. Instant refill of his coffee cup is a key meter. Coffee must be hot, black, and always at the ready, like his glass of water at an earlier table.

He saves the highest-rated spot for our last evening. The waitress takes our drink orders and returns with a carafe of hot coffee. She places it in front of Eddie with a flourish. He is the only coffee drinker at the table.

"Uncle Eddie, you are finally going to have your coffee just when you want it," I chirp.

A sour look and an icy reply: "I don't like to pour my own coffee."

What? This guy has whined his way into a lifetime of butler service. His mother, sister, and three wives have created a 200-pound infant who never has to do more than whimper to get his way.

And here I was catering to this outsize three-year-old. I was warned. By Uncle Bobby. Eddie's brother has his number. I had been describing Eddie's money problems over the phone, looking for advice—and sympathy.

"Don't worry about Eddie," Bob says. "He will always find some woman to con into taking care of him."

Now I was one of the women.

❧

Toward the end of Eddie's life, my trips to Arkansas are duty trips. I do my best not to humor Eddie, but he wheedles more attention out of me every time. I find myself shopping for a wheelchair. The nursing home can't get one for him, he insists; besides, they are so dumb they would buy the wrong kind. When I jockey my purchase out of the rental car's trunk and into his room, he sits in it and finds it wanting.

I go the desk, where I am informed that the nursing home supplies wheelchairs through Medicare. Why didn't I ask before?

I deal with his late-life girlfriends. Imogene warns me that Ethyl is jealous and will try to get me not to let her sing at Eddie's funeral, even though Eddie *loves* Imogene's voice. When Imogene is called away to a sick relative and it looks like Eddie will die before she gets back, she entrusts me with a recording to be played at the funeral. I comply, over the raised eyebrows of the officiating minister.

Both he and the Presbyterian minister visited Eddie's bedside to offer their services. I pick the Assembly of God on Imogene's advice. Her wobbly pseudo-soprano squeaks out Eddie's supposedly favorite hymn, *Nearer My God to Thee* as we sit in solemn silence in the pews. I suppress a giggle by putting my handkerchief over my face to wipe away my "tears."

ॐ

Uncle Eddie is big in my life for more than his size. Like Nancy M's father, "I never met another man who could hold a candle to him." His exploits are legend—reported in shocked but titillated tones. My son Ben, himself a recovering alcoholic, nails it in a letter written after his visit in July 1999, the year before Eddie dies.

Ben's story of trip to Mountain Home
July 8, 1999

It was a long journey to make for such a short visit. A four-hour flight to Dallas, a change of planes, 45 minutes to Little Rock, and then a four-hour drive through a lightning storm and pounding rain. But even more noticeable than the distance I traveled was the spiritual space I traversed when I walked into the room to visit this man. My great-uncle was in his final days in a nursing home, having lived a long life and now suffering from what surely was his last illness.

I had only spent time with Uncle Eddie sporadically over the years. My grandmother's brother, who lived as a fishing guide in rural Arkansas, was not a regular part of family gatherings or holidays. Stories of his escapades and infamy were, however, a regular topic in our family for as long as I could remember.

His only daughter, who he left with her mother at a young age, was often a guest in my mother's house. A beautiful woman with two young children and a handsome husband seemed to be as far removed from the stories of her father and his lifestyle as anyone could be. I didn't even see the resemblance to his story when she left that family and journeyed out on her own when the two boys were still in grade school, to search for a life more in line with her dreams, whatever they may have been.

Although it was clear that no one approved of the lifestyle that was portrayed in the stories about my uncle, they were still told with gusto and always a humorous ending. While it was clear his portrayal as an alcoholic was something seen as shameful, his antics and accomplishments seemed to me to be more legendary than scandalous. He was a free spirit, the life of the party, and the salesman who was a big part of the success of my grandfather's company. And, oh yes, there were a few minor difficulties that went along with his tendency towards strong drink.

I will never know what impact those stories (or the drinking atmosphere in which they were told), had on my own experiences with alcohol and drugs. The truth is, I hadn't ever given it much thought until my visit to Uncle Eddie's deathbed. As he shared his remembrances of the "good times," I found myself very easily identifying with the spirit I felt him describing.

"Ben, I only ever wanted two things out of life: fun and pleasure. As long as there was booze and a pretty woman, I was in my element."

One of his visitors commented on the fact that I seemed to have an ironic sense of humor and good nature. I pointed to my uncle and observed that I had come by it naturally, and even more so if you knew my grandfather: his brother-in-law, business partner and friend. To which my uncle replied, "Yes, but Andy was steadfast, not like you and me."

My uncle and I definitely shared a similar drinking history. Chasing life with a passion and zeal for the minute. Loving the exhilaration of never really knowing what the next second may bring. Living for the excitement of night after night of being the life of the party. But I had assumed that, like me, he had come to a place where the life we were living had come to a dead end. Where all the promises the "good life" had ever made had been shown as just one more lie. So now, when he identified me as a compatriot in appreciation for that former life, it felt more like an indictment than a convivial overture.

The other visitors, of whom there were many, to my uncle's room were mostly from his recently joined church, which happened to be of the same denomination that I attended. It seemed that he had thoroughly embraced the forgiveness that is a part of my belief. The piece that seemed to be missing was any realization of what the things were he might have needed forgiveness for.

The trip home was just as long as the one there. But it wasn't the journey, or even the realization of the closeness of his death, which made the trip so emotionally tiring. I think that it was the realization of how easily we can fool ourselves. As he was lying in that bed telling me how dumb all the help was in that nursing home, how far down he had come as a human being, I knew that his only living daughter was 400 miles away waiting for the news of his death so that she could cash in an insurance policy. There seemed to be no thought on his part about what impact his life might have had on the people he had left in his wake—only thoughts about the fun he had.

And the truly scary piece was that I knew that it could just as easily have been me.

34

The Last Act

Ben's words haunt me on my final visit to Eddie's bedside. I fly from Mexico alone.

Eddie can no longer walk or sit without his bed rolled up, but he never stops talking. He opines at length about how good his life has been. He drank a lot, sure, but who had that ever hurt? Why did everybody carry on about his drinking, just an enjoyable pastime? He warms to the subject and reruns the script with added flourishes at every telling. Between versions, he sips water through a straw I hold to his lips.

"I never did anything but enjoy myself when I was drunk. What was so wrong with that?"

I set his glass firmly on the bedside table and add water from the hospital carafe.

"You never beat your wife when you were sober," I say, looking him in the eye.

"Beat my wife? What are you talking about? Which wife?"

I sketch my memory of his assault on Thelma.

"What? Why, you were just a child when Sally was a baby. You are making that up. You couldn't remember that far back. I would never hit a woman."

He rings for a bedpan. I escape to the Carriage Inn.

When Eddie and Faye's house is sold at the end of his life, I collect on the $9,000 promissory note and split it with my sister.

ﺄﮫ

The memory Eddie says I made up:

I am 10.

My cousin Sally is two months old. Thelma and Eddie ask me to babysit. I am proud of my first job. Sally is asleep when I arrive, and scheduled to sleep through the night. Union is a small town; my mother and grandmother are minutes away. I am a sentry on duty more than a caretaker.

I munch all the Fritos Thelma left for me, wash them down with two Cokes, and nod off on the sofa reading the latest Nancy Drew mystery. I go to Sally's room and look in her crib. She lies on her stomach, motionless. I cuddle under one of Gram's afghans and doze off on the couch next to the crib. Thelma will wake me when they return, and Uncle Eddie will drive me home. They are meeting friends at the Colonial Tavern.

Slam—I jerk awake—was that the door?

Thelma and Eddie are shouting—loud, strange. Is it really them?

Closer now.

I catch, "You jealous bitch!"

" ... the nerve, right in front of me ... "

I bury my head under the afghan.

Thuds.

Furniture moving?

Stomps, floorboards squeak. I think they are down the hall from my door.

Thelma's voice: "Pat, Pat, Pat," louder each time, pleading.

I roll off the couch and open the door.

Thelma crouches in the corner, arms over her head, like a third-grader warding off a dodge ball.

My uncle towers over her, his eyes dark slits.

He sees me, glares, steps away from Thelma.

"He's ... beating me," she chokes.

Sally wails behind me.

Thelma murmurs, "The baby."

I turn and run back to Sally's crib, pick her up, glad to get out of there. She is beet red. I press her hot little body to me until her mother takes her from my arms.

Later that night, I am home in my own bed.

Raised voices from downstairs. I creep to the top of the stairs, my eavesdropping post.

The three adults recap the night's events. Gram berates the villain; her voice seethes with venom I have never heard from her. I can't believe she is condemning Uncle Eddie, her favorite.

"Imagine, calling the police," she goes on. "She ... called ... the ... police. And with Pat right there in the house."

She? She said "she"? I strain to catch more.

"If everybody called the police when her husband had a few too many ... "

It's Thelma. Gram is talking about Thelma.

She must not know Eddie was beating her. Should I go down and tell what I saw?

I hesitate, listen longer. No, no.

Thelma is a traitor because she called the police and told on Uncle Eddie.

ॐ

There were many lessons on denial in my childhood, but this incident influenced me more profoundly than most. Telling tales outside the family was the unforgivable sin. I could not reconcile my wonderful, warm Gram with a person who thought it was okay to beat your wife; keeping family secrects must be very, very important to override common humanity.

I must never tell. Until this memoir, I never have. Nor did any of the characters in the drama ever mention it in my presence again.

35

Confrontation

This time I do not ignore the bad things; I speak up. And provoke a bitter encounter with my mother.

My father is down to his final few months. He still feeds himself and gets to the bathroom on his own, but that is the limit of his energy. The cancer's progress means when he is hungry and able to eat, he needs nutritious foods that do not nauseate him. Snacks throughout the day, rather than a rigid breakfast-lunch-dinner schedule.

I want to hire a home health worker to prepare Dad's meals and do whatever else he needs.

We talk at the iconic maple dining room table, site of many of Mother's gourmet meals. Even without its three extra leaves, it barely fits into the dining area of their rented home, just blocks away from ours. Dad is asleep in the bedroom Mother rarely enters, except with a plate of food. My father spends his days reading magazines, watching sports on TV, and talking to visitors. Ready to go after a wonderful life, he tells us all.

Mother sits in her accustomed place at one end of the table, her iced tea in front of her. I sit on her left, my hands cupped over my teacup, relishing the steam warming my fingers.

I fish a brochure out of my briefcase. It is from the Family Service Agency, highlighting their home health aides. I recite my upbeat script: my friend Lillian founded Family Service and was director until she moved to Florida; two or three friends used their services and said the people they sent were competent. I struggle to suppress the false cheeriness in my voice; I so want this to be a no-big-deal chat, light, offhand. I slide the pamphlet across the table to Mother.

Mother lights a cigarette and pauses to blow the smoke out of one side of her mouth, a sure sign a pronouncement is on its way.

"What in the hell would they do here?" Mother shoves the leaflet back to me after a cursory glance at the cover. "Just more people for me to cook for."

I tuck the offending pamphlet out of sight.

"The idea would be for them to feed Dad, not for you to feed them," I begin.

Mother's eyes shoot sparks.

"I have been feeding your father for over 50 years, and I am not about to have some stranger come in here and take over my kitchen now."

I lose it.

"He can't wait until you get up for his breakfast. You don't want him fixing his own. He can't pour himself a bowl of cereal in your private kitchen. He is dying and you …"

"I know he's dying. And I can take care of him. No strangers are coming into this house."

She glances toward the kitchen, with its smell of chicken soup simmering. The fragrance is powerful testimony to Mother's competence. She expects me to say, "I know you still make the best pot of soup in the civilized world." But I close in.

"Mother, this is an impossible situation. You sit in that chair in front of the TV and pass out most nights, and can't get up in the morning. Dad can't wait for you to be sober enough … "

"There you go again. What's with this obsession of yours about drinking? Now you have convinced Ben he drinks too much. I don't know what's wrong with you. I am perfectly able to fix your father whatever he wants. He hardly eats anything anyway."

"What if he is hungry and you are not …"

Mother stubs out her Viceroy in her personal ashtray so hard that the ashes fly onto the tablecloth.

"Look at that," she points. "Look what you made me do."

I get up and bring a dishrag from the sink to sweep the ashes away.

"That won't work. Look, you're rubbing ashes into my white lace tablecloth. I'll take care of that. Sit down," she orders.

"Listen to me," she continues. "I am Andy's wife. I have legal authority. If you don't leave me alone, I am going to put him in a nursing home, and you won't be able to do a damned thing about it."

I leave, shaking with anger and frustration.

Mother never carries out her threat. Workers come in with her grudging approval. She insists on fixing their lunch.

It takes a year of therapy after my father's death before I stop hating her.

҉

It has taken longer to unravel my more complicated feelings.

Her model of wife and mother is embedded in my bones. I consciously rejected her role as stay-at-home, husband-knows-best wife, but spent years living her values, unaware how hooked I was. I see how trapped my mother was, in the same social boxes that held me captive.

My mother and grandmother made peace with the world they were born into. Men went out into the world and made money. Women's roles—child bearing and rearing, homemaking—were lauded in verse and prose, but the real power role was the moneymaker. There were exceptions, but the overall message, reiterated over and over again in film and song and story, was clear: Men Rule.

Mother and Gram thrived in their own ways, never by bucking the system. No revolutionary conversation crossed their lips in all my years of eavesdropping.

Virginia left high school, which she loved, at 15, and lied about her age to take a job at Eagle Stamp because her father was out of work. Virginia loved her job. When she married my father at 18, he insisted she quit work; people would think he could not support his wife. The times she returned to the working world, when they owned stores after Bourbeuse was sold, a certain spring returned to her step.

Gram never held a paying job. She went from her sister's home to marriage to my grandfather, and when that marriage failed, lived first with her two sons, then with my mother and our family.

She was a master with a crochet hook. When I noticed other people's crocheting, I realized what a fine craftswoman she was. Her sister, Aunt Hattie, and her daughter, Lillian, made extra money as seamstresses, but Gram's afghans, quilts and pickled beets were for home consumption only. She invented a practice golf ball for my Dad's use hacking balls around the yard: our German shepherd Pal's hair stuffed in a tightly crocheted ball. All lauded her "pants" for glasses. Likewise, crocheted slippers of her unique design. Friends and family waited in line for her needle work—all gratis.

For Mother and Gram, bringing home the bacon/paycheck was the man's job. When my father insisted his bride quit her job, he fit Veblen's theory of conspicuous leisure: an idle family member at home proclaims the family's wealth to the world. Two idle family members—even better.

Papa was the breadwinner; Mother's home was her domain. She got an allowance for the household budget, and Dad bailed her out when she got too far behind in the department store bills. Famous Barr must be paid on time, he said, since the banks who financed his businesses kept a sharp eye on their star borrower's credit record.

ફ

My mother was a captive of the same forces that engulfed me: a culture steeped in domination and inequality of more kinds than had yet been identified. My suspicion is she was more aware than I was. So much for sociological analysis. There was also my "other mother," the warm woman who came to me in a dream two years after her death.

ફ

It is a week after Yom Kippur, with its recalling of loved ones gone before. I awaken at five, a tickle in my throat and a dull faint pain in my brow. Oh, no, not another bug. Just getting over a cold. I rise, gargle and go back to sleep, to awaken to the clear, soothing presence of my mother.

The only clear message I received during the Days of Awe just past was to write her story. A story to honor her worth, a love I devalued, hurt by what I perceived as her rejection during Dad's final illness. I was vengeful. I was right and she was wrong, and I wanted retribution. Whenever I mentioned her, sometimes even to a stranger, I said she was an alcoholic, the thing she was most ashamed of. Spite, a final in-your-face gotcha.

This was different—a warm fuzzy nostalgia for my mother. No dream details, just her benign presence when I awakened.

A scene from real life floats up: my mother coming to the breakfast table on my wedding day with red eyes, admitting she'd cried all night.

A friend I told about this asked if my mother did not like my chosen husband. I knew it was nothing to do with Harry; she was fond of him. Nor was she worrying about the trauma of my first sexual experience. She knew I was not a virgin, although we'd never talked about it.

Her tears were for the end of an era. She, like me, was ignoring the Buddha, and clinging instead of detaching. Our shared human frailty.

Never again would I be her little girl. Instead of a bride, Virginia saw the swaddled baby she took to the doctor with the strange rash that he laughed to see in December: a baby in enough blankets to produce the prickly heat rash common in St. Louis summers. (Virginia had reason to worry: The winter of 1932 was so cold Niagara Falls froze over, and deaths from influenza or pneumonia were common.);

Or the crawler, helping herself to food from our German Shepherd's bowl, with Pal standing by with amazing restraint watching the interloper eat her food;

Or the four-year-old princess onstage in the dance recital, bringing each flower to life with a touch of her glitter-star wand, then sitting down on her throne and taking off her shoe to scratch her foot;

Or the determined-to-be-independent kindergartner, walking home from Mary Magdalene's alone, only saved from certain death by her mother's intercepting her before the lethal Kingshighway and Chippewa crossing;

Or the star student, winning the prize for Best Reader in every grade.

Gone forever were the mother-daughter trips to St. Louis on the bus, shopping at Famous Barr, lunches in its tearoom, where her Pat learned to use the finger bowl that followed dessert. No more running for the bus from the movie theater where Mother tried to fit in a movie at the end of the day's shopping.

All past. Pat the Daughter was moving on to Pat the Wife.

Her love for me was real; my dream confirmed my soul's root wisdom.

36

Eleven Years Later

Mother dies in St. Elizabeth's Hospital. She has been in the extended care wing for a month. The cause of death is chronic brain syndrome, the result of alcohol abuse. Ironically, she dies sober. Meta, Tom, Ben, Harry and I had an intervention for Mother four years before.

My sister was not in favor. In the little time she might have left, Toni reasoned, why take away the comfort of her evening scotch? Mother drunk did not look comfortable to me. Toni did not veto the plan, so we hired a recommended facilitator. Mother entered a rehab facility and never drank again. It made the last years of her life infinitely easier for me, and I hope for her, too. We could communicate; the crabby old recluse gave way to a kinder, milder Virginia, more like the warm mother of my earlier memories.

The funeral is scheduled a week after her death to allow time for family to travel to Lafayette and avoid November 1, All Saints' Day, when a funeral could not be held in Blessed Sacrament Church. That moves her funeral to November 2, Day of the Dead in Mexico.

I decide to sit Shiva for my mother. Shiva is the Jewish observance of a seven-day mourning period after burial. The bereaved family stays home, receives visitors, and is joined by fellow Jews every evening to recite Kaddish, the traditional prayer for the dead. A *minyan* is required to recite this ancient prayer—10 Jews, in orthodox circles, 10 males. I receive visitors and recite the Kaddish, an ancient Aramaic prayer for the dead, every day of the week between Mother's death and her burial. A Jewish friend assures me this is not real Shiva and is ridiculous. "What is an Irish Jew to do?" I ask her. If it comforts me and honors my mother, who cares about kosher? I say Kaddish every morning for a year alone, also un-kosher, after which I know the prayer by heart. So there.

My sister and I offer to fund the trip for any children or grandchildren that can come to the funeral. Many show up. The little ones bring their costumes and go trick-or-treating; giving up Halloween for her funeral would not honor their grandmother's spirit. Mother would applaud and likely meet them at the door with her legendary butter cookies cut into pumpkins and witch's hats.

Harry and I join the family at their motel the night before the funeral. I bring a tape player and lead the kids in the then-popular Macarena, an easy line dance. We commandeer a large empty room next to the lobby. First one, then another, and then another—two young men and a woman—join us, whirling and soaring as they dance. They are Paul Taylor dancers, staying at the same motel; the music and kids have lured them in. None of us realize it is the famous dance troupe until we see posters advertising their performance in Purdue's Elliot Hall of Music. I regret we never thanked them for their incomparable gift, but their exuberant twirls are an indelible keepsake. An unexpected, spontaneous gift of grace. My mother loved dancing before the drink befuddled her mind and slowed her body, and dance is a more reliable high for me than any drug.

Meta gives the eulogy at the funeral Mass, wearing a prominent Star of David around her neck. No surprise, since she elicited shocked gasps the night before from the Temple Israel congregation by inserting "She" for God's name in the candle blessing.

The grandchildren remove the pall from the coffin as it is wheeled out of the church. The smallest, Paul, can barely see over the top, but his sister helps him hold onto a corner.

Afterwards, I write to my sister,

> When I reread Meta's eulogy, it was sad to think that Mother could make her grandchildren feel so special, yet not her own children, especially you, the precious second child she tried so long to conceive. I said this to Meta, who replied that children are not the same as grandchildren. She pointed out the window where

Harry was playing catch with Bella, something he rarely did with his sons, never with his daughter.

I felt this poignancy at our gathering but could not bring myself to express it. The family rule muzzled me: Speak no evil—especially about a dead mother. Yet our mother was a bundle of contradictions—a super hostess who hosted until she was too drunk to get the food on the table, a warm grandmother who sometimes left her children in the cold. I hope you and I can begin telling the truth—our truth.

ॐ

I am orphaned. My closest blood connections, mother, father, grandmother, all "passed away." Til now, I found that expression a wimpy code for "dead." Now I get it. My family passed, left me, went off someplace. I empathize with my friend Donna's dismay that her wonderful husband had left her. Death is like that—final, irreversible, feeling unreasonably like desertion.

Many intimates are gone with the wind, like Tara. Who is left? My sister and I drew closer in our bereavement. But my most intimate connection—with my spouse—needs work. Yet even if Harry and I were to click like George and Gracie, it would not be enough.

Why are so many of my interactions so flat? I slide along on the surface. My legacy of ignoring the dark side or trying to fix it gets in the way. And Midwestern politeness. And everyone's frantic work schedule.

Where to look for close friends?

My religious community? We go to Temple every Friday night, but the congregational tone is more Catholic than Mormon, casual rather than tightly knit. A regular at Shabbat services complains that we do nothing but go to synagogue and then home.

"I wish I knew you and Harry better," he says, "but I don't even know where you live. You've never met my wife, because she doesn't come to services." He is right. I wish I knew him better, this brilliant mathematician Teddy Bear with the physique and social graces of a hippopotamus. I want more, too, but life rushes on, and neither Harry and I nor the Teddy Bear invite each other to our homes.

Interest groups? The folk dance group is fun, but we go our separate ways after dance night same as after synagogue. I find like-minded souls in my writers' group—new friendships building slowly.

Camping, yes. David and Joan share their family and outdoorsy skills with us after the Gilners cajole us into trying camping. Warm memories abound of weekends spent in Indiana and Michigan state parks, around campfires. Our trek to the Everglades, following D & J's trailered boat in our truck camper with two of our adult children. Joan and David are treasured friends forever after.

Movies, certainly. My movie buddy Ruthanna and I bond over films our husbands would find tedious. There is no truth to their charge that we would watch any movie ever made, but we often turn to each other as the screen dims and agree, "Good thing we didn't drag Harry and Jon to this one." One of the Purdue Famous Films series is our most serious challenge. The erudite program notes prime us to watch for the symbolic intercourse, and we spend a studious hour at *Baskin and Robbins* after the show trying to figure out which scene that was.

Ruthanna is a spiritual connection as well. Harry and I first meet Ruthanna and Jon at a weekend retreat at Waycross, an Episcopal retreat center in the rambling deep woods of Brown County, Indiana. Ruthanna`s wry wit can fell a stuffed shirt at 100 yards. Her Christian faith is deep and rich, without a smidgen of the saccharine piety we both find cloying. She attends the early service on Sunday to avoid those who consider Sunday worship a fashion event.

League of Women Voters? Yes: Winnie, Maxine, many others. Less intimates than comrades in arms. All serious study, pouring over position papers, sitting alert through boring public meetings for a good cause. No casual coffees or time wasted on our inner lives.

Neighbors? Donna, of course, my Green Meadows backyard connection.

Workplace? Ouch. Not since grad school and Wabash Center. Maybe I should have stayed on that path. Maybe I would now be happily retired from a satisfying career, enjoying genial friends made along the way.

Maybe I will think about that tomorrow.

ॐ

My forays into the business world were not fertile ground.

When I left Wabash Center, I taught in the public schools for a year. Not a fit. Hostess Twinkies are big in the teachers' lunchroom.

Where to, what next? Two of our children are in college, the third about to finish high school. More money would be welcome. The business world is the real world where money is made.

I pay a fee to an employment agency and become Debit Agent 86 at the local Prudential office. Debit agents carried "books," cumbersome paper records of cash payments, a hangover from Gram's day, when a debit agent knocked on the door of St. Louis flats and collected pennies every week for burial policies. These $1,000 or $2,000 policies, often on children's lives, were popular in those days of high child mortality and little family savings.

I earn commissions, the purest form of capitalism; instant reward for results achieved.

My children cheer Agent 86, Maxwell Smart's number in *Get Smart*. When he is jealous of handsome new agent 43, his wife reassures him, "Oh, Max, you're worth two 43s," a quote my kids now chant when I feel unappreciated.

My father cautions, tongue-in-cheek, that debit agents in his day often squandered their day's collections in the corner bar. Despite the tragic family consequences of alcoholism, drinking is a favorite topic for humor. "Tossing a few back, bending the elbow, in his cups" are playful, almost endearing terms—drunkenness humanizes the imbiber.

I do not drink up my collections and I sell enough insurance to keep my job. Selling is straightforward, hard work. Training sessions and motivational speakers all unveil the same secret: Selling is a numbers game. A rookie like me needs to make 10 calls to make one appointment, and five appointments to make one sale; a seasoned agent makes three calls to get an appointment and closes two out of three sales.

I come into a 20-man office as the first female agent. It is culture shock on both sides. The only women's john is on the clerical side of the office—behind a locked door to discourage robbers; the lesser-paid clerks, all women, take in the money. They buzz me in to pee.

The guys gripe at having to clean up their language. Their "rough" language, unfit for my delicate feminine ears, is milder than the vocabulary of my young-adult children. What shocks me is their constant racial slurs. All white folks in the office. The dark-skinned population in Lafayette is tiny—a few local blacks and a handful of African students. Anyone hearing the office banter would imagine we lived in Harlem.

I'd smirked when my parents complained in hushed voices about the "darky problem" in St. Louis. "You can't go downtown anymore. 'They' have taken over Forest Park. Some malls are too dangerous to visit." Florissant is a northern suburb far from the black population center. Mother thanks God that the one black family in their neighborhood is "not that kind," but heaven help the poor St. Louisans forced to live elsewhere. I put their obsession down to their age. But the Pru agents are not so old.

The young studly star salesman breezes in the morning after a basketball game that Purdue lost to Michigan State. An old-timer greets him, "Hey, Ned, what did you think of last night's game?"

"Just fine, if you want to see five n**gers running up and down the floor," Ned sneers, throwing his briefcase down on his desk. He glances over to where I sit, head down, entering collections into my ledger book.

"Now, Pat, I'll bet you'll think I'm prejudiced," he says, insinuating his was a neutral remark.

I laugh. How ridiculous.

Where did these bigots come from? And why didn't the office manager shut them up?

In 2014 their racial slurs wouldn't be tolerated in any office in Lafayette or elsewhere. In 1992, that brand of racism was shrugged off. Not by me. I took seriously the Catholic insistence that we were all God's children. Father Rost, the priest who followed Father Hubert, came to town while I was in the eighth grade. He invited the Negro children in town to Immaculate Conception school. Our school always had a handful of non-Catholics in attendance. Public schools were segregated then and the "Negro school" was a dingy room in a rented house. Father Rost married Harry and me, baptized our first child, and was a friend until his early death.

I am proud to be a tolerant person, a bit smug in my political correctness. Until Barack Obama's grandmother takes me back to Luella's Porch. During his first campaign, Obama reports that his grandmother told him she was wary of black men. A child of her times, as was I.

Luella was a coal-black, skinny, homely woman of indeterminate age who came to help with the cleaning and do the ironing two days a week after my sister was born. She had a peculiar body odor that was an endless theme of my grandmother and mother's speculations. "But she is so clean," they would mutter. "What can it be?" It was indeed an odd smell. Since then, two acquaintances, both white, have had similar problems, caused by a change in body chemistry and disappeared after appropriate medication.

Luella made me uncomfortable. She was always pleasant, and I was polite but uneasy around her. I knew that racial prejudice was evil and pervasive in the culture. I was enlightened, but I did not know how to act around Luella, whose dark skin made her one of the oppressed.

One day my mother wanted to get a message to Luella, probably wanted her to do the dishes after a dinner party. Luella had no phone, so I was dispatched to her house, which was within easy walking distance of ours.

I rang the bell, rocking my sturdy school shoes back and forth on the worn wooden floorboards of the porch. Her husband answered the door. This large, very black man loomed in the doorway, opening the screen door, inviting me to come in. Feelings of surprise, discomfort, awkwardness, then, terror overwhelmed me. My avowed belief in equality before the Lord, my chastising my uncle for using the "n" word—all evaporated. Being invited into the house of a large black male had thrown me into a panic.

I responded in a way that shamed me even as I was doing it. "Luella, Luella," I called as I stepped through the door, my tone begging her to save me from—I can't remember his name, which still embarrasses me 70 years later. He was the anonymous black man with the mythical huge penis and libido. All the racist mythology I did not know I'd swallowed came boiling up. I must have delivered the message, however stumblingly, and gotten back home, shocked and ashamed of my behavior.

è

When Obama spoke of his grandmother, who was close to my age. I saw 12-year-old Pat, quaking at the front door of Luella's house. Trapped by the undertow of feelings that permeated me—unasked, unseen, unknown. Harry learns to call them "witch messages" during his therapy. Hauling all of mine to the surface and baring them to the light is this memoir's mission.

The world of insurance sales expands into the broader arena of "financial planning" in the 70s. My facility with numbers and ability to see the big picture in investments serves me well in the new environment. I get myself credentialed as a CLU (Chartered Life Underwriter) and CFP (Certified Financial Planner).

In 1979 I open Herzog Financial Services and offer financial advice for a fee. The morning after my father's mortality sent me reeling, my HFS office is the haven to which I flee. Not such a safe haven for investment risk. Financial advising is a minefield. A straight arrow by nature, I jump through all the certification hoops and register as an investment adviser with the SEC, but I sell tax shelters—hot items in those days of 50 percent tax brackets. When the Reagan tax reform goes into effect in 1986, many go bust. My clients lose money on my investment recommendations. Nobody sues, but my self-image as the wise, benign, conservative investment advisor collapses along with the bankrupt shopping centers.

At this opportune moment, the Bright National Bank needs a trust officer. I close my solo practice and take the job. The bank's solid backing reassures me and my clients, many of whom follow me to the bank trust department.

Bright National Bank is my most inhospitable workplace, surpassing even the Lafayette Prudential office with its macho sales crew. I am not part of the "bank family" referred to in interoffice memos, more like the alien from the outer space of West Lafayette. I count it a badge of honor to be an outsider at BNB, with its bologna salad and Diet Cokes.

As vice president and trust officer, I sit on the bank's investment committee—a nonvoting member and the only woman, Democrat, or non-churchgoer. When our bank attorney refers to a female lawyer in Lafayette as "that girl," I object that she is in her fifties and has practiced law for 20 years. Eyebrows raise, but he does not do it again. I am asked to stop by the PayLess supermarket on the way to the early morning trust committee meetings and pick up their freshly fried donuts.

The bank takes over a failed thrift during my tenure. I am moved to the S&L president's office in nearby Delphi, assigned to drum up trust business in this county seat town. I search for congenial staff there, maybe somebody to share lunch, having bombed out at the main office where I had been stationed.

Moving to a new office is always a pain and this move is no exception. Having the largest office in the corporation's six branches is poor solace. All el-fake-o rural Indiana wannabe. Heavy grass cloth wallpaper that shouts, "Look at me, I cost a lot of money." An ornate Bible so large it takes two hands to lift is plopped in the middle of a glass-topped coffee table in front of the sofa; a sofa with two matching armchairs. A desk almost big enough for table tennis. Seeing the bank's trust officer behind it is supposed to impress the local attorneys with how seriously Bright takes its responsibilities. Works, too. Attorney J's eyes scan the room while he keeps up a line of patter designed to make him sound cool, while he cases the joint.

Whether it is the private john, the grass cloth wallpaper, or the "Vice-President and Trust Officer" nameplate, no bank employee approaches the trust officer's throne. Maybe because

I never visit the pop machine, or am a Jew where Jews are exotic as anteaters. Or the dustup over the smoking area.

The operations manager, Ellie, is a chain smoker. These are the days when non-smoking rules began to appear in restaurants and offices. Secondhand smoke is declared dangerous. First, Ellie designates her office as the smoking area. But since her office adjoins the lobby, that does not meet requirements for separation from the rest of the bank space. She next chooses the computer room, a tiny corner housing the bank's general-use computer. Unaware of this new turn, I walk into the computer room one day, choke on the smoke, and pound down the hall to Ellie's office.

I arrive breathless to her now smoke-free space, which still reeks of cigarettes. "Janine works in that computer room all day, Ellie. How can it be a smoking area?"

"No problem there," Ellie assures me, poison-tipped arrows in every syllable. "Janine's husband smokes; she says it doesn't bother her a bit."

"Really?" I sit down across from her, uninvited. "What if she gets lung cancer and dies? Will her husband not sue the bank because he smokes, too?"

Her scowl tells me this is over the top from Busybody Smart-Ass VP.

The next day the branch manager calls me into his office and asks me to take any future problems up with him. I smile and agree, conciliatory Nice Girl Me. Why make waves?

A cantankerous trust client shows me another way.

37

Ida

I stand on the wide front porch, three steps up from a walk bordered by crocuses pushing up through grimy snow. Main Street, Camden. Next door is a Pizza King that doubles as a beauty parlor; across the street, a Baptist Church listed on the Carroll County historic register. I twist an ornate metal bar on the door beneath its lace-curtained window. A *brrrring* sounds inside. Steps approach, the door creaks open, and I face Mrs. Santa Claus herself: roly-poly, round faced with smile wrinkles framing her eyes. Instead of a red-and-white fur suit, she wears the gingham bonnet and cape over modest home-sewn dress of the German Baptists.

"I thought you might be coming," she says in a neutral tone. "You must be the woman from the bank. I'm Sarah, pleased to meet you."

I nod and smile. "I've come to see Ida Lloyd," I say. "We have been appointed her guardian."

"Yes, I heard. She's been expecting you."

I step into a parlor-dining room crowded with sturdy aging furniture, its hard wood polished to a soft gleam. Sarah motions to a door on the left a few steps from where I stand easing off my galoshes. "Just leave them there," Sarah says, pointing to a rug next to the door. I plant my wet boots gently on a handmade rag rug like my grandmother sewed from our cast-off clothes, the frayed edges of its crocheted braids a witness to its long and useful life.

I knock gently on Ida's door.

"You'll have to make more noise that that. She's deaf."

Louder, my gloves off now. A gruff voice tells me to come in.

I open the door. A woman wrapped in a plaid flannel robe lounges on a bed next to the porch window where the sun beams through. Her tall thin frame fills the bed. She turns toward me, squints, pushes her pillow up against the headboard and sits up.

"Hello, Mrs. Lloyd, I am from the Bright National Bank. We—"

"I know all about your butting in," Ida snaps. "Mary, my next-door neighbor for 40 years, was doing just fine helping me. And I don't need any help to begin with. I can take care of myself, have for 90 years, and don't know why I should stop now."

"I can understand how you feel, but ... "

"Well, how would you feel if the judge told you that you couldn't take care of your own affairs? Such a fright. If my son's so-called lawyer hadn't been the judge's cousin, everything would have been different. I thought it was all settled; Mary could keep writing my checks for me—that's all I need, you know. I just can't see to write right, but there is nothing wrong with my brain. I know what you're after—my money—just going to charge me high prices for what I can do for myself for free.

"If it wasn't for my eyesight, I would stay in my own house, just down the street. As it is, here I am, having to pay Sarah to take care of me—not that she charges high—she at least is a God-fearing woman who won't take advantage. And then, all the bills from my house down the street. One thing I want to tell you right now, just get it straight right from the start: I am not paying no bills for that house. Gaylord insists it belongs to him; so let him pay for it. No way am I spending one more penny on that place."

A pause for a breath, a glare at Intruder Banker, then, "It's Gaylord's now, isn't that true?"

I nod and assume my even voice of reason. "Yes, the judge determined that you and your late husband signed the property over to him years ago, and ..."

Ida sits up straight and tall and explodes: "Judge? That judge is in the pay of that woman lawyer he's so stuck on. I never signed such a paper, and anybody that says I did is lying through his teeth. Gaylord's my only son. He'll get the property soon enough when I die; why would we ever sign it over to him way back then, with my husband still alive and all?"

Rational Trust Officer: "Well, there can be a tax advantage to deeding property to children, although in your case ... "

Ida's voice rises in disgust. "My case isn't something you know a blessed thing about, and I'll thank you to keep your nose out of my business. Just get Mary back to pay my bills and I will not need your help now or ever." She turns toward the window, case closed.

I shuffle through my briefcase looking for an official paper to hand her, think better of it, then try again. "I'm sorry, our hands are tied. The judge has appointed Bright National Bank as your guardian."

"Guardian, guardian, what do I need with a guardian?" She is on the attack again.

The confrontation jerks along; I feel like Ferdinand the bull wanting to get out of the bullring. I decide on a strategic retreat and announce I will be back to see if Ida needs anything another day.

As I turn to leave, Ida mobilizes. She swings her legs to the floor and stands leaning against the bed, towering a head above me. Ferdinand is not getting back to his flowerbed so easily.

"Wait just a doggone minute. Don't be running out of here so fast. There's something I want to know—how do I get money? Do I still have my account at the Camden State Bank?"

My mind races. There is no Camden State Bank, must be an earlier name for Salin Bank.

"I'll have to check on that," I shout, so that Ida is sure to hear.

"Well, check on it right now," she demands. "I can't be without money. How will I pay Sarah if she has to pick up something for me from the store or buy medicine?"

"She can always send the bills to the bank, Mrs. Lloyd."

Ida rolls her eyes; clearly I am a hopeless case.

"Send bills? She has to have her money. I don't want her to have to wait. She already had to loan me money to buy my hair spray last week. That's just a shame, a plain shame."

Easing out the door: "I'll talk to Sarah as I go out and … "

Ida switches to megaphone mode. "What about my account at the Camden State Bank? Do I have to move it to your bank? I've been with Camden since I moved to town, and I want to know where my money is."

I smile my Unflappable Trust Officer smile. "I'll see what I can do."

"When, in your own good time? I want to know right now."

Drat. I am on my way home to Lafayette and an appointment to touch up my hair color. Ida appears poised to tackle me before I can get away.

"How do I know you will ever come back? Call the bank right now."

Looks like I am stuck. This woman is a pit bull. Easier to do it now and get her off my back.

"Okay. I'll call right away, Mrs. Lloyd."

I ask to use the phone, and am shown to a round walnut table in the dining room on which sits a black rotary-style dialer as antique as the table. I scan the well-thumbed pages of the slim local phone book for several seconds before I realize Ida has me looking under the Cs, for Camden State Bank. A call verifies Ida's account at Salin Bank, and I arrange to sign permission for Ida to withdraw small sums for her needs.

Which needs, she later reveals, include a hairdresser imported from Edna Mills, a hamlet five miles away. Ida explains only an up-do works for her, and "the local stylist don't do up-do's worth a hoot. A sin to pay somebody to fix it when in one day's time, it looks the same as it did before. When Anamarie does it, it stays the whole week. I don't want to look a sight five minutes after I pay the woman."

&

Ida ticks off other failings of mine: Sent to buy her new bras, I get the kind that she can't fit her boobs into; asked to hand toilet paper through the door of a stall, I tear off a pitiful measly swath.

The hearing aid drama is a more substantial clash.

Ida calls me to her room and carefully unwraps a small white box, the kind that might hold a pair of venerable clip earrings packed in cotton squares. The cotton squares look a bit gray and crushed—no jewelry lies between them. Instead, there is a tiny molded plastic item I recognize as a hearing aid.

"This here is broken, and I need it for my 100th birthday party," Ida announces. "I want you to fix it."

I reach for the box. "I'll take it to be repaired right away."

Ida looks horrified.

"Take it? No, no, I want *you* to fix it. It's not hard; just get the little piece in the middle to fit back into the hole."

I fumble with the plastic for a minute and then say, "Sorry, I know nothing about hearing aids. I'll take it to … "

Ida interrupts, tightening her hold on the box. "If you take it, you will never get it back in time, and it will cost a fortune. Can't you just take care of it? I could do it myself if I could see well enough."

Several rounds of sparring later, I pry the little white box from her hands. My friend, audiologist Dr. Mary C, pronounces the apparatus long dead, no resurrection possible. It is at least 10 years old; the usual life of this device is five years.

Ida is outraged. She insists she bought it recently and paid a fortune for it. I must have taken it to the wrong place, because it was certainly worth fixing, and what will she do now to be able to hear her son when he comes for her birthday party? The Prodigal Son is now off Ida's shit list; Gaylord is the prime birthday party arranger.

I suggest a new hearing aid as the only solution. At first Ida will have none of it, but changes her mind and allows me to drive her 20 miles to Lafayette to see Dr. C. The day goes well; Ida is unexpectedly cooperative. She actually seems to enjoy the exam. Dr. C is accommodating, professional, perfect.

The moment of truth arrives: the ordering of a new appliance.

"How much will this cost?" queries Ida. I jump and say her insurance will pay for it—a lie, but whatever the price, I know it will be astronomical on Ida's value scale.

I am right. "I'll have to think about it," Ida demurs. "Six hundred dollars is a lot of money, no matter who pays for it!"

"You will have to come back for a fitting if you decide to order one," Dr. C reminds her, keeping her voice level. She has spent half a day on the care and comforting of Imperial Ida.

"Let's just go ahead with the fitting, Dr. C," I interject from my corner. "It's a long trip for a 100-year-old."

After I help Ida into the car, I run back to the office and tell Dr. C to order the hearing aid. It will never be ready for the party unless we order it now. I figure once Ida can hear her son, the $600 will be forgotten.

Untrue. I deliver the hearing aid just four days before party day and run into a buzz saw. Ida is livid that I tricked her into buying the hearing aid with her own money. And she knows exactly what I am up to.

"How much of that $600 did you get to keep?" she wants to know. "And how much did the bank make on this deal?

"That woman you took me to doesn't know what she is doing if she couldn't fix my old hearing aid. There was not a blessed thing wrong with it. I wouldn't doubt she sold it to someone else, and well she might, it had a lot of good years left in it. Highway robbery is what it is to take people's good things and charge them 10 prices for new ones. Here I am paying out my good money for something I don't need or want, and you getting rich at my expense. Highway robbery is what it is. I've asked everybody here what a hearing aid costs and they all say that $600 is a pretty penny."

I slink out. The party happens. After all the vitriol, Ida keeps the hearing aid, wears it to her 100th birthday party, and never mentions it to me again.

è&

What a woman—100 years old, deaf as a post and almost blind, and still running her world. What spunk. What's wrong with me? Why can't I say what I think and stop being the prissy trust officer? Demand my rights. Take no prisoners.

Harry and I sit around the campfire, sipping beer and relaxing after a day at Turkey Run State Park. I get up to poke the fire. The bright red coals on the bottom of the biggest log need to be chipped off so that the unburned wood underneath catches fire. My grandmother taught me well.

We sit in silence, staring at the hypnotic flames. We are in shorts. Harry turns to me, focuses on my tennis shoes, and mumbles that he does not like the way my legs look since I gained weight. I look at my thighs, spread against the canvas of the camp chair. Larger now, true.

Ida would have said, "Too damned bad. Get over it. I'm 60 years old and so is my body. Get a grip. I am not your property."

Not me. Never. Not then. Not even now.

I laugh Harry's comment off as a thoughtless offhand remark.

He is serious. I can see that. Now that he has let me know his wishes, he expects I will fix my legs. After all, I no longer eat sardines. After he told me he hates the smell from the open tin on the table, I am ashamed to admit I never opened another can of sardines when Harry was around.

બ

I wish I had done more than marvel at Ida's iron will. She knew what she wanted and what could keep her from getting it. When that was the representative of the Evil Bank, she demanded her rights and then some. She got more of my time with her constant clashes than any other trust client. Vinegar worked better on this fly than honey.

Meanwhile I was placating the bank heavies, pretending our family belonged on the cover of *The Saturday Evening Post*, and skipping sardines. Ida was hard where I was soft, clear where I was fuzzy. My "adaptation, adjustment, improvisation wiles for surviving, thriving and transcending the world as is" (Lauren Berlant, *The Female Complaint*) were all honey—sticky and sickly sweet.

Ida's "wiles for survival" took a different direction—a track I neither traveled nor imagined was open to me. How did this woman with little education from a backwoods part of the world learn to take up for herself—manage to evade the popular culture that should have silenced or at least softened her tone? Hers was my grandmother's generation, if anything a time when strong women were less likely to be tolerated. Yet she chose double-barreled diatribes over orthodox mealy-mouthed sweet talk. The Annie Oakley of Camden, Indiana. Maybe I could escape someday, somehow, too.

Mexico moved a step closer.

38

Retirement

Bright National Bank is on its way out. The bank remains independent only six years after I join its staff. The end is a story in itself: the president shopped the bank without the Board's knowledge, and the resulting offers to buy were so good the shareholders demanded a sale.

The Hoosier Herzog's Holiday Hello for December
1994
Dastardly Diaspora Continues
Hoosier Herzogs Down to Two

When our daughter Meta and her family moved to Albuquerque in June, we became the last of the Mohicans, or at least, the last of the Hoosier Herzogs. Tom, whose home in Ithaca, New York, was the farthest from Indiana just two years ago, is now the closest. Ben is now the record-holder, 2,400 miles away in Tacoma, Washington. It's enough to make us consider migrating ourselves—and we have!

Partnership Planning

We spent a lot of time in Albuquerque talking with Meta and Leo about the future, because Pat just learned her employer, Bright National Bank, was likely to be sold to a larger bank. A searching question from Leo prompted Pat's decision to leave the financial world and do something different. He asked, "If you could do whatever you wanted, what would you do?"

A lifelong closet writer, Pat is determined to come out. Her decision has Harry rethinking his life as well. Will we continue to live in Indiana? Will we finish *Harry's Story*? Yes, the final editing will be Pat's first writing assignment when she retires.

So, stay tuned—the Hoosier Herzogs are on the move. One thing both hunger for in our new lives is good conversation, we may be coming your way.

Retirement bestows this unimaginable gift: 40 hours or more a week liberated. At long last I will have "world enough and time." *Poets and Writers* quotes a famous author who says a writer must read the same amount of time as she writes. I am delighted: Prospectuses and financial news had crowded out my reading for pleasure. I check out the maximum six books at a time from the library, but fall asleep reading during the day; reading has been my sleeping potion for too long. I adjust. My children give me a retirement present, a gift certificate from my favorite local bookstore. Memorial bookplates are included:

This book is a gift in recognition of the move to the
wider world by
Patricia Browne Herzog
as she moves from years of toil in the worlds of
teaching, consulting and banking.
With great and unending love from her offspring,
Tom, Meta & Ben
and their families,
Lisa, Andy & Noah; Leo, Shona & Bella;
Eileen, Chardae, Elizabeth, Paul & Carrera

Only one bookplate is still on my shelf, in Thich Nhat Hanh's *Peace In Every Step*.

ॐ

I tackle the 1,001 household tasks stockpiled until my retirement. I sense I am on overload, taking in more than I can process. I am a Cuisinart filled with dry flour, with not enough juice to make a batter. I need to be juiced. Reb Zalman says Israel juices Jews. Why not get juiced in Israel?

Our first adventure after my retirement is a three-week Elderhostel in Israel. At our first lodging, the Maccabees Complex in Tel Aviv, an enormous table holds more varieties of cheeses than Kraft ever imagined, fresh fruits and vegetables in profusion—eggplant three ways! I never make it past this "dairy table," which I learn later is supposed to be for those not eating meat at that meal. I come home an involuntary vegetarian; my body, previously beset with digestive difficulties, signals this is what it needs.

We are introduced to ultra-orthodoxy. Ugly. On Saturday, our hostess, Judy from my grad school days, lends us her car to drive to Hebrew University, where the Reform community holds Shabbat services. She warns Harry not to wear a *kippah*, which might provoke rocks thrown at her car for driving on the Sabbath.

Near the Wailing Wall, a Black Hat shoves an elderly tourist almost to the ground when he takes out his camera. In the brouhaha that follows, the Black Hat speaks American English to the elderly victim's son. As a Catholic, I often found my cohorts' actions—like picketing abortion clinics— repellent. Now I see that all of my new co-religionists are not the congenial lefties of Temple Israel in Indiana.

The night Prime Minister Yitzhak Rabin was shot our group is at a concert blocks away. In the week that follows, the agony of mourning fills the air we breathe. The soul of Israel is exposed, bleeding and wounded.

Maybe I did get juiced in Israel.

ε∂

My writing progress is slow, less poetic than my dreams. Clichés pour from my keyboard in a torrent; quality prose trickles like a leaky faucet. Days slide into weeks, then months, and the enthusiasm that took off like a rocket when I retired collapses at my feet like a deflated balloon.

As advertised, Harry and I tackle *Harry's Story: Turn and Return* in earnest. Harry writes, I edit, he revises; I format the final text. A running buddy urged Harry to write the book. Martin is an engineering prof and a transplanted Israeli. He has never heard a story like ours, he tells Harry—joint conversion to Judaism by two active members of their respective Christian churches. He inspires Harry to write his story.

The memoir bares both solid bricks and chinks in our partnership. We work well together; our editing sessions are animated but without heat. Good practice. Organization, style, scene making, juggling what to include, what to leave out—all issues in my own writing.

There are differences; Harry names all the book's chapters before a word is written. Pat's Story is retitled and reorganized over and over as I dig deeper.

Digging deeper is not Harry's specialty. When I read his first draft of a key scene—the first time he recalls identifying himself as a Jew—it rings false to my editorial ears.

On his first day at Purdue, he and his frat house host walk down the street, and Harry says, "I am surprised to see so few Jewish students here." Harry insists this was just a casual remark, equivalent to mentioning the brisk September wind. I probe; he balks. That's what happened; is he supposed to lie?

We talk. He resists. I object. He caves. Maybe something more personal than the weather was on his mind, Harry allows, since his remark prompts his confession to the fraternity guy that his grandparents were Jewish. His guide suspects that disqualifies Harry for membership. Harry opts out, saying he would not be comfortable pressing the issue, and finds another place to live.

Harry's affair with the church secretary is off-limits even though it was one impetus for the religion switch. This is too small a town, we decide, to put that episode in print. Mary Lou will be easy to identify even with a name change. Instead we construct "Teenage Torment," a chapter that lays Harry's marital unease at the feet of our disagreements about child rearing, exacerbated by three acting-out teenagers.

When I review that chapter for my memoir, I realize the timing is off. Our children were 10, 13 and 15 at the time of the potential split, too young for all the driving episodes reported in the Teenage Torment section. Now I wish I had not colluded in the sham, another example of how hard it was for me to acknowledge a painful truth. Making our near split all the kids' fault lets me off the hook and denies any problem within our partnership. An opportunity for deeper dialog lost. What would have happened if we hadn't prettied up *Harry's Story*—gone deeper into why we became Jews? Maybe we could not have done it. Our lives depended on leaving Dark Shadows to a TV series, where we could flip the switch.

I edit, add photos, and format in Word. The book is in our hands in January, 1997, 18 months after I retire.

The Good Wife scores again.

ૐ

I begin to work alone. Our shared space feels cramped.

Our office, an unused first-floor bedroom, is a spacious corner room with high windows that let in ample north and east light and frame the sky and the tops of oak trees that wave in every breeze. Redheaded woodpeckers drill perfect round holes in our redwood siding; if only I could peck out perfectly turned phrases with my beak. The birds continue drilling until we cut down the dead tree that holds their nest. For a week angry woodpeckers organize raucous protests outside our window.

We schedule separate time blocks. I print an "At Work" sign for the door with a jaunty clip art worker figure in one corner. But Harry needs a printout of household expenses the exact moment I struggle with an awkward phrase, and I want to retrieve my Day-Timer just when Harry is deep in a budget spreadsheet.

Our desk is a reclaimed wooden door balanced on two metal file cabinets. I cover it with papers, books to read, notes on websites to check, first drafts heavy with markups. Harry feels invaded. It has been his private space since his retirement nine years earlier. I am an interloper—a messy interloper.

We negotiate. Harry and his Apple stay in the office. The Herzog Financial Services desktop PC and I move downstairs to a belowground cubbyhole, the previous homeowner's office. Its basement window well fills with autumn leaves, and a tiny animal that moves with the speed of light tumbles in. A vole, our neighbor informs me after her cat deposits an unlucky cousin on her kitchen floor.

I feel trapped underground like the hapless vole. I cannot suppress an apprehensive sniff when I enter: Surely there is a musty smell. My nose detects only the stale paper smell from my financial planning records in a corner, still packed in file boxes ready for sorting.

I am reluctant to admit to Harry this is not working. I am not the princess who complains about the pea under the mattress, more the yeoman-like worker ant. A high-wattage lamp and a transistor radio for music help. I settle in. Better to grit my teeth than blow Ever-Adaptable Super Woman's cover.

ॐ

I take two semesters of creative writing at Purdue. The classes meet in the afternoon, and I leave the house hours early—to work in the library, lounge in the coffee shop, and wander around the campus, soaking up the nourishing atmosphere of a university. Soon I am staying after class to edit my assignments or leaf through the latest magazines in the library periodicals room. I look forward to my time away from home as the best part of my day. I find separation from Harry disturbingly refreshing.

I speak to my therapist, Jeanne. How can I make my time at home more attractive, she quizzes. Do I need to talk to my husband about rearranging our lives, speaking up about the things that I find stifling in our marriage? A good plan; I will talk to Harry. The right moment is hard to find. Several times I begin the conversation, then lose heart and quit.

ॐ

Not the first time I lose my voice. Minor disturbances strike me mute.

At the party the night before Ben's wedding, I am at the podium leading the Shabbat blessings when friends arrive late. They stand at the door, waiting for me to acknowledge them. I choke, don't know how to do it, so I ignore them, until they finally take the closest empty seats.

A new couple arrives for a Sunday night supper in the great room of Good Shepherd church. I have met the wife, so when they are a few feet from us, I introduce Harry to her. She murmurs a greeting and turns to the sweater-and-cords-clad guy at her side with, "This is my husband, Chris." He booms out to the room at large, "Hi, Pat, Hi, Harry," and I realize he is blind. I am too tongue-tied to reply to his greeting.

Uncomfortable moments like interruptions or blind people unnerve me.

Some dogs can't be trained to hunt because they run away at the sound of a shot. Thus the expression, "That dog won't hunt." One such was a likeable bird dog named Homer that my uncle bought at a discount because he was gun shy. I feel like Homer, marked down for my deficiencies. It doesn't take a gun to scare me off.

❧

The 1996 "Hoosier Herzogs' Holiday Hello" is a timid stab at separation. I have always thought Harry's contributions reek of the Cheery Holiday Letters of derisive fame. Besides, I am now a writer. We mail two versions. My breezy introduction: "New for 1996, and still at the same low price, folks: Separate Pat and Harry Hello's. The partnership is alive and well, but adapting to allow two new voices to find their range, sometimes solo, sometimes as a dynamic duo."

&

My dreams are confused, anxious, full of struggles with tasks that are never accomplished. I visit my therapist weekly to try to make sense of my confusion.

Every visit I wait to see what she is wearing when she opens the door and motions me into her consulting room. Her long, flowing skirts might be the color of ripe plums, the pattern of her draped tops abstract African art. I never remember her wearing the same thing twice over the several years we met. She reminds me of the Arabian princess of the 1001 nights. That woman saved her life by weaving her stories; Jeanne saves mine by listening to mine.

After our usual opening chitchat, I report awakening from a recent dream acutely uneasy and unsure why. Jeanne meets my eyes, nods, then looked down at the pad on her ample lap. Sitting next to her tall matronly form calms me.

I tell my dream.

> We are sitting around the table my parents bought for our new home on East State Street in Union, Missouri, after the birth of my sister, the same table the State Street Gang gathered around for jovial evenings of bridge, food and purloined cigarettes. The dream "we" is my family—my parents, sister and grandmother, husband and children, grandchildren, all or some of each. There is jovial laughter, loud talking, and then a little girl I do not know begins to cry. She is clearly miserable, hot tears run down her face soundlessly. We all try to comfort her. She continues to cry silently, and shakes her head at our questions, 'Does anything hurt? Are you hungry?'

> Somehow I know that her sadness is because she is not really one of our family—she is adopted. Something keeps me from saying this; it would be rude to bring it up. She leaves the room and I follow her to the bathroom. She is sitting on the toilet. I ask, "Is it because you are adopted?" She nods, relieved that someone understands.

Jeanne leans forward in her chair, listening closely. I fill the silence with a rush of explanation, "I have been puzzling over it, and I believe the girl is Sally, my cousin, from whom I am estranged. It means I must call her, reassure her she is still part of the family."

Jeanne questions me about Sally. I tell her she is my favorite cousin, my Uncle Eddie and Aunt Thelma's only child, ten years younger than me, whom I loved as a child. As an adult, she is plagued with drug and alcohol problems.

A silence. Jeanne comments that dream characters often represent the dreamer. Can I imagine myself as the child?

My hands sweat. I squirm in my chair. I want to run out of the room. Instead I burst into tears. Jeanne hands me the box of Kleenex at the ready on the table by her side.

Our session ends early.

As soon as Jeanne spoke, I knew I was the child. I felt her tears on my cheeks; her misery in isolation weighed me down. I am not family. I do not belong—at Prudential or at the bank. And now I am not at home in my own house.

39

The Roamers

Carole King sang it. I felt it. My family is "so far away. Why doesn't anybody stay in one place anymore?"

Both Harry and I spend less time at home in the years that follow. Having no jobs frees us to roam as we please. I pine for my children and grandchildren. My journals and dreams are filled with references to getting away, new homes. How can I be near them all—or at least one of them? When Harry and I moved to Indiana our families were disappointed. We tried to visit as often as we could to keep connected. More than I now think was wise. Now I feel deserted by my children. My head says they must make their own lives; my heart longs for their nearness.

Now that I am retired I can turn my energy to my children and grandchildren.

My daydreams descend to fantasy. I could help Tom with his research at Cornell. My graduate school experience trained me to do library work; why not assemble data for him as I had for my major professor? Ithaca is an attractive place; we could rent a little apartment near campus. I could do my own writing along with Tom's library searches. This bizarre idea never goes beyond my head; if I had told a friend, she might have helped me see I was careening off to outer-spaciness.

Never mind. My children were launched; I could play Super Savta (Hebrew for "grandmother") with more grace. Who could object to a fond grandmother coddling her grandchildren, especially given my skills with small children, my master's in child development?

I plan a series of grandchildren visits. We entertain four in an airport hotel for a Chicago weekend—the Aquarium, the Museum of Science and Industry. They want the beach; the hotel swimming pool is not Lake Michigan. We find the Lincoln Park Beach, then the zoo nearby. We organize camping trips to Michigan state parks on the lake.

I invite six grandchildren to a West Lafayette summer reunion. Harry balks. Too many kids in the house; they will drive him crazy. "You can go to a motel for the weekend," I say. "You mean I do not have a veto?" He does not. They all come. He stays home.

When the children visit solo, we make lists of what to do. This is one of Elizabeth's, age 8. Those activities we manage to fit in are lined through.

"Sing songs at Mulberry Lutheran Home (where my mother is living)
Go to park
Lunch in restaurant

~~Play at Shona's house~~

~~Rest~~

~~Buy dress~~

Fire outside

~~Walk in woods~~

Library

~~Play at *Saba* and *Savta*'s~~

~~Havdalah~~

Elizabeth was still making lists and choosing priorities for a weekend in San Miguel as a teenager studying Spanish in nearby Morelia. This time there is both a calendar and an activities list, and every activity on the list is checked as accomplished.

sábado

3	Pick up cookies for party
5:30	Savta to concert
7	Christmas concert and party after

domingo

8:30	*Marco colga piñata* (Mark hangs piñata)
9	Breakfast with Joan and Lynea
10:30	*pastorela* at St. Paul's

lunes

Lucy and familia

3–5   manicure and pedicure

other
Santa Clara for ice cream
Meet Lucina
Meet Ceci
Cards/dominoes
Botanical gardens

€

Harry has one cold after another in the harsh Indiana winter and is eager to find a winter retreat. Joan and David, our camping comrades, spend winters on Green Turtle Key, a tiny island in the Bahamas. We visit. Palms, warm sand, coral, spectacular blue water of the Caribbean. Gorgeous, relaxing, simpatico, but no Internet, no newspapers, one telephone on the island. The ocean, the beach, catching fish and cooking the fish fill our days. Reading, crossword puzzles or card games after dark—no movies, TV, concerts, plays. Two weeks is great, but enough. I feel cut off from my world, and the prices are more expensive than mainland retreats. Like Florida.

Destin, Florida is the answer, another couple assures us. We rent a condo in the same complex as theirs; two TVs, washer and dryer and a dishwasher, but not a single bookcase or decent reading light in the whole pastel Florida-cutesy apartment. The residents' highest priority is scouting the restaurants' Early Bird Specials. We move on.

Las Cruces, New Mexico is decent. It might have made the cut if we had not continued up the road to Albuquerque, where our daughter and her family live.

તર

Beneath our happy family Cone of Silence, the children's marriages disintegrate. The formal shot of our family taken at the Browne Group Reunion, to honor Mother while she was still alert, shows four smiling couples, Harry and I and our three children and their spouses, with our three grandchildren in the first row. A few years later all of our children were divorced. The last marriage standing, Harry's and mine, will end soon.

The Christmas Ben's first marriage ends, his wife takes three-year-old Elizabeth to her parents' home in Ohio for Christmas. This leaves toddler Paul alone with his dad. Super Savta alert. I fly to the rescue, literally, just like Mighty Mouse, "I come to save the day." Harry is busy with some meeting or another, and I take the plane to Tacoma alone. Harry joins me midway through a two-week visit.

તર

I write about my journey for our writers' group chapbook. A freelance writer in Lafayette, whom I admire for her grit and success, has formed the WCWG, Women's Creative Writing Group. I join posthaste. We meet in the Wells Community Center, the abandoned library where my children and I found *Millions of Cats*. Members do writing exercises, critique each other's work, attend workshops, organize readings, and publish two chapbooks.

My story reveals more than the cheery anecdote it reports:

I am en route to Tacoma, Washington to babysit my toddler grandson, Paul. In Detroit, the departures board says "delayed" for my flight. My plane will not leave for another three hours. Elation startles me. An airport delay is the stuff of constantly overheard complaints: "I was stuck in O'Hare for six hours; couldn't get out of Atlanta until noon; weather, they kept saying, but you know they never tell you the truth." Why am I thrilled?

There are emergency rations in my carry-on: an apple, a Ziplock bag of dried apricots, plus my two staples— Cin-A-Burst gum and a Payday candy bar, just in case they are not readily available. But this is no emergency, and I look forward to the array of airport food choices.

I wander, scan menu boards and try to decide; a crumbly-rich carrot bran muffin from Starbucks; tofu stir-fry at the Chinese; veggie pizza? No, the winner is a KFC Chicken Original Recipe wing, with its satisfying greasiness. I grazed well before the yuppies made it fashionable.

Savory tidbits to read, too—several old *New Yorkers* to browse and discard.

My fanny pack holds one each of a variety of pen types: ballpoint, highlighter, felt tip, in at least three colors, one unquestionably green. And a little blank notebook tucked in the middle.

I hike up and down the crowded aisles from one end of the airport to another, pulling my carry-on, drinking in the milieu, eavesdropping on the mini-dramas around me, seeking out the odd corner to exercise discreetly. This is what I love about public transportation, especially planes. Long spaces of lazy time. And no caretaking. Except of myself.

A display rack is shoved out into the traffic where two aisles cross. Sleep sets hang limply on oversized hangers—long shapeless T-shirts with a pair of knee socks pinned to their shoulders. A mock-ferocious dinosaur roars from the front of the shirt; his dinosaur legs stretch up the front of the socks, culminating in three lethal looking claws. Are dinosaurs three-toed like sloths? I pass by a few times before I stop.

"SPECIAL, 50% off. I pull out my trusty Visa. For the grandchildren. Paul will get a kick out of Savta the dinosaur putting him to bed.

Forget Paul. My dinosaur sox are a symbol of freedom.

ॐ

Paul and I hit it off. I trip and take a perfect pratfall on a slippery dock next to a restaurant on Puget Sound, and Paul finds this so funny, soon we are both falling down laughing: a perfect Savta escapade.

One rainy, mild day, I manage to lock us out of the house. And then can't start the VW beetle. Ben comes home from work to rescue us, and we are off to the Prospect Point Zoo and a shark show. We take a plastic shark home, make salt-and-flour clay and roll it into shark shapes. Paul's little arms quiver with excitement using the rolling pin.

Ben is pensive; he can't stop talking about Sarah and the death of the marriage. He is deeply hurt but hopeful for his future.

Seeing his pain and believing the babysit so successful, I suggest a temporary move to Tacoma to help Ben get settled in his new single state. Like Ithaca, it is an appealing place; we could find me a little apartment close enough to babysit, but private enough to have our own lives. I could take a job in a bank—at that time, banks are eager to get into financial planning. I have all my licenses and a résumé that includes bank trust officer.

Ben puts a quick end to the conversation. He needs to start his own life, with no help from me, and does not want his parents in Tacoma.

Later that year, Harry and I visit Meta in Albuquerque. A writers' workshop at Ghost Ranch, north of Santa Fe, draws me to New Mexico. Ghost Ranch is a special place, and my time there is stellar. Hale-Bopp is visiting, and the comet is spectacular in the dark skies over the ranch. The library is open 24 hours with hot water and the makings of coffee, tea or chocolate on hand. I can track Hale-Bopp and have a warm cuppa at any hour. My fellow work shoppers wow me. I bring my first and only short story; some of them are published authors. All overwhelm me with their writing skills.

Why not Albuquerque? The winter climate is milder than Indiana's.

Perfect. The congenial owner of Adobe and Roses, the B&B where we stay in the North Valley, owns a casita down the road, an open, writer-friendly space. Let's rent it, I say. Let's move here. Harry is taken aback, but willing to try it. The idea of living close to our daughter, who had just moved from Indiana, appeals to both of us.

The day before we fly back to Lafayette, Meta's husband asks for an audience. He and Meta come to Adobe and Roses. Leo spends what seems like half a day, probably an hour, haranguing me with what a disaster it would be for his family for us to move to Albuquerque. It is not acceptable for me to live nearby. Harry maybe, but not me. He says it brutally enough that on the way home, I decide never to speak to him again.

Albuquerque is out, Tacoma is out, and Ithaca was never a serious option.

Super Savta has fallen flat. My grandchildren are plane rides and chasms of understanding away. On the ride home across endless Texas miles of interstate, we are flagged down for a road construction site. As we wait, I watch a tanned guy with a *Don't Mess with Texas* cap pulled down over his eyes guide his giant machine to tamp down a newly laid road surface. The gravelly mix makes a hard scrunch sound as it flattens under the heavy roller. Just like oiling the streets in Union. I am as forlorn as my mother, stuck in an unfriendly place, beset by unfriendly steamrollers. The weight of rejection flattens me like the cartoon Road Runner run over by a bus.

Harry sympathizes, but his talk moves quickly to a new plan; he is euphoric about a friend's recommendation for a winter retreat that sounds perfect: San Miguel de Allende.

40

San Miguel

In time the Rockies may crumble,

Gibraltar may tumble,

They're only made of clay.

But our love is here to stay.

    —Ira and George Gershwin, *Our Love Is Here to Stay*

The cracks in Pat and Harry's Gibraltar widen in San Miguel de Allende, a colonial town in the heart of Mexico: its *cuna de independencia*, cradle of Independence.

Rentals are scarce in 1998; landlords demand a three-month minimum stay. Harry rents an apartment for January, February and March for $1,000 a month. Over my kicking and screaming. Mexico for three frigging months? Where the grimy runny-nosed children and the raggedy street beggars will shame a well-off *gringa* like me? Mexico? Where everyone who goes there gets bellyaches, or worse? Three months of no writers' group? No therapist? No Purdue library? No meditation group? No women's circle?

Harry pleads. Just this once. If I'm miserable, we'll come home early. Okay, I pout, but this is a one-shot deal. If he insists on Mexico next winter, I will visit him when and if I feel like it.

∾✦

The Mexico City airport teems. Fellow travelers range from swish señoritas made up for the TV camera to harried families lugging mounds of cartons held together with duct tape. Porters angle for customers shouting incomprehensible phrases. We walk through the sliding doors into the international arrival gate, where unruly welcomers behind a barrier wave arms and signs:

JOSEPH GONZALEZ,
Hotel Camino Real,
Conferencia del Sagrado Corazón.

I use my four words of Spanish to ask for the bus to San Miguel. A porter motions to a kiosk, says we need a cab to another station; can't get there from here. According to our landlady there's a bus from the airport, so this doesn't compute. With luck and the grace of *El Sagrado Corazón*, we share a cab with a business type bound for a city near San Miguel. He teaches us how to pronounce Querétaro, where we can get a cab to our destination.

Four hours later we drag our four suitcases into our apartment on Barranca, flop down on the twin beds and put our feet up. Made it.

We are too curious to stay inside long. While there is still daylight, we walk down the steep hill on Calle Correo to the *jardín,* the central square. A cathedral-size pink stone church, *La Parroquia,* dominates the square, where trimmed laurel trees shade tourists and locals sitting on iron benches.

We revive over a leisurely meal of Kung Pao chicken for Harry and broiled red snapper for me at El Pegaso, a block from the jardín. Back up the hill, we locate a neighborhood *tienda* for essentials like milk, sugar and coffee for breakfast, along with tortillas fresh from a mechanical press at the *tortillería* next door. What? They do not shape them by hand like in the movies?

I unwind, gulp in the ambiance with the mountain air, and fall in love.

ã

How could a change of place make such a difference?

San Miguel is a shock: the tropical sun, agreeably warm in January at 6,500 feet above sea level; the saturated colors— intense rose-pink, cobalt blue, warm gold, deep indigo; the costumed mariachis on the square; the *"Elote!"* chant from the pushcart vendor of roasted corn, ready to slather with mayonnaise and sprinkle with chili; the assorted clang of church bells at all hours and in every *colonia* (neighborhood), the before-dawn fireworks—even the nightly barking dogs charm me.

El Pegaso is soon Harry's favorite restaurant of all time. I'd fretted about how a vegetarian would survive three months of Taco Bell. El Pegaso is as far from Taco Bell as San Miguel is from West Lafayette. Dozens of restaurants pamper tourists' stomachs with bottled water and purified vegetables.

I thought the food would be fiery; Albuquerque's cuisine is *más picante*. We eat *comida* in the middle of the day like good Mexicans. We make friends with *enchiladas suizas*, *chiles en nogada*, and *sopas*—the *sabrosa* (tasty) soups that introduce every meal: *consomé de pollo*, rich with rice, vegetables and chicken chunks; cold avocado, cucumber, and carrot soup and *sopa azteca*, a tomato broth garnished with chopped chilies, onions and taco chips. San Miguel food enhances my digestion and steals my soul.

We scan *Atención San Miguel*, the English-language weekly newspaper, and uncover treasure after treasure in our New World. A Jewish community meets for Torah study every Shabbat morning. There is daily practice in a meditation center perched on the fourth floor of a colonial building just off the *jardín*, where the view itself is a meditation. Fellow diners greet us newcomers. We soon have congenial partners for meals and the rich menu of concerts, English-language plays, lectures and tours to nearby attractions. We hear chamber music at St. Paul's, mariachis in the jardín, jazz at Tío Lucas.

These people can talk. And think. We meet not a single Newt Gingrich fan. We warm to all things Latin; when the pope visits Cuba, he is on our doorstep. Everyone is on vacation, with "world enough and time" for the good stuff.

We walk. Our U.S. life revolves around our two cars. Here we pass close enough to fellow humans on the narrow sidewalks to smell them, especially the Mexican men, who never leave the house cologne-free. We inhale vignettes of street life along with the fresh, dry air. I buy Mexican embroidered blouses and handmade street jewelry and soon look like an authentic American tourist.

I email glowing reports back to the States.

El Independiente, a bilingual, biweekly newspaper publishes two of my paeans. One title is prophetic: "A Wandering Jew Takes Root in San Miguel." I meet Sareda, *El Independiente*'s editor, and Lucina, the Spanish-language editor. Lucina is a treasured friend still, as was Sareda until her death. In her final years I smuggled her U.S.-prescribed morphine across the border a couple of times. Lucina and Sareda introduce me to International PEN, and seduce me with the range and quality of our conversations.

Lucina and Elizabeth, another PEN member, introduce me to an exercise class they share. Magda, the instructor, is a glowing, open hearted Mexican preschool teacher, who leads us from 7-8 AM Monday through Friday in her own brand of aerobic dancing. She teaches in the evening after school also with the same verve. Her energy and style keep me coming back year after year at 7 AM. My reward is often breakfast with my PEN buddies in whatever café is open when we at 8:15 AM.

Not all the folks back home understand my enthusiasm.

It is the dry season.

I write, "I had wondered what a maid was going to do six days a week in this little apartment. Now I see. Even though Juana diligently swipes a rag across the tops of the furniture daily, there is a thick layer of dust on every surface an hour after she leaves for the day."

My friend's email reply puzzles me:

"So I assume you are coming home early?"

She misunderstands—the dust in San Miguel is blessed by the Virgin of Guadalupe.

ஒ

Harry does not thrive.

He'd injured his knee before leaving, likely during his customary noon run at the Purdue track. A doc at West Lafayette's Urgent Care diagnosed a pulled muscle that would heal quickly. It does not. His knee hurts more all the time. In late January he awakens in such pain that we race by ambulance to San José Hospital, in Querétaro. Harry has surgery for a torn meniscus and is back in San Miguel recuperating in a few days. We borrow floats to facilitate his water exercises from Joan Nagle, a fellow meditator and aqua-aerobics instructor. (We later buy a house together.)

All seems to be going well until Harry announces on February 4th that he is lonely and bored, and wants to go home.

I write in my journal:

I am angry and disappointed and very blue. Harry wants to go home. I love this place. Have just gotten comfortable, know where everything is, the absolute smorgasbord of things to do, see. And I have just begun my writing projects; have hopes of sharing them with Rachel.

What makes me so sad? Part of it is loss. I am in Al-anon again, meditating in the gorgeous Centro de Meditación every morning, etc., etc., etc. And now, like the King of Siam, I find: "It's a puzzlement." If I leave here, I leave sun and leisure and no cars and a setting that nourishes me mightily. Of course, I must leave anyway in a month, so this is just shortening a temporary stay. There is no way Harry would ever move here; I can see that. I have to wait for him to die before I can live in San Miguel. And yet, is that true? Am I again using him for a scapegoat? Playing the codependent? Taking his troubles on as my own?

But how not to? How to escape the tie that binds? Divorce Harry because he is disabled? Could I live with that? Leave Harry in Lafayette when I returned to San Miguel? Hmmmmmmm.....

Could he manage on his own? I made a solemn vow to stick with him in sickness and in health. He broke his. Does that make the whole thing null and void?

Not for me.

What is my obligation?

Harry is a functioning adult. Can he find his own way without me at his side?

I did feel an upsurge of affection and attachment when he was in surgery in Querétaro. I don't really want to be free of him. I just don't want to be responsible for him. For his care and feeding. Here, it is hard. There is so much I want to do on my own. Eating in restaurants and going to concerts interests Harry; living here entices me.

༄

My powerful attraction to San Miguel unnerves me. I had been to enough 12-step meetings to recognize the geographic solution, the drunk's refuge: "If I move to Topeka, I can stop drinking."

All the frantic journaling should have alerted me to something big going on. It is still focused on Harry, what to do about him, how I feel about him. My complaints, ambivalence and talk about freedom seem confined to my writing. Why are dinosaur socks a symbol of freedom? From what—Harry? I share none of this with my husband. No wonder he is blindsided when I walk away.

༄

Months ago we invited my sister, Toni, and her husband to visit us in Mexico. With Harry wavering, my hopes hang on their arrival. I call my sister and beg them to come. Maybe they can cheer Harry up enough to get him through his funk. Ken and Toni arrive within the week; I almost kiss their feet.

Having another guy around lifts my husband's spirits; by the end of their visit there is no more talk of going home early.

ૐ

The dreaded day comes. On the bus ride back to Mexico City my San Miguel high slips away, fading like the bright colors of tissue-paper banners strung in the tropical sun. When we walk into Benito Juárez International Airport for the trip back to Indiana, a McDonald's slaps me in the face. I weep. Is it over? If I come back, will the dogs just be barking dogs? Why am I going back—to what? I snuffle through a pack of purse-size tissues before we board, but by Houston my pocket calendar holds a "to do" list ready for landing.

I am back in harness before I know I've taken the bit.

41

On the Road

The year before, Harry had pleaded for three months in Mexico. Now I want more. Harry resists. Fine, I do not mind being on my own. Does not sound good to Harry. He hates being alone.

We are stuck.

Our daughter suggests a mediator who had helped her and her husband thrash out a contract for shared work. We make an appointment for our planned visit to her Albuquerque home.

Perhaps because we are stopped at an emotional barrier, we flaunt our physical freedom. That spring we set out on a mammoth drive-around typical of our post-retirement trips: St. Louis for a bar mitzvah, on to Albuquerque and granddaughter Bella's birthday, then to my sister's in Lubbock.

St. Louis to Albuquerque is the long leg: 1,000-plus miles of boring Interstate 44. We break the trip halfway, on the outskirts of Oklahoma City.

Next day, we stop for lunch at one of the dusty little exits in the Texas Panhandle. I take the wheel. A half hour later I run my thumb over my ring finger—bare. No wedding ring; and this was the third one for my one and only marriage. I'd lost the first two. Harry said he'd bought enough rings when I lost the second. I commissioned a local jeweler to design a third—silver with a small opal, my birthstone. It suited me; when I wore it I checked my finger often, determined to die wearing this one.

We reverse course back to the mom-and-pop restaurant where we'd eaten. We avoid fast food on the road, opt instead for local color. This one's color was dingy Texas grey. It is now past prime lunchtime. The lone customer swivels on his counter stool when we open the door. When he sees Interloper Me looking at him, he turns quickly back to his coffee. Shades of Shorty's.

The round woman at the cash register listens to my story; her sidewise glance warns me she thinks I am accusing her of stealing my ring. I make clear I think I lost it. She rests her hands on the apron covering her stomach shelf in sympathy. No, nothing found.

She steps into the kitchen. *Nada* from the rest of the workers.

Had they emptied the trash?

They had not. She motions to a jumbo plastic container in the corner.

"You can …" she begins. I have already lifted the swinging cover and am deep in plastic plates, wadded napkins, cigarette butts and slightly drippy paper cups.

I work fast; I see Apron Lady does not approve.

I paw through the trashcan twice.

I see Harry out of the corner of my eye, poised near the door, detached from the sordid scene.

I am embarrassed, flustered, annoyed with myself. I've lost a third ring, one I really care about, delayed our long drive for this wild goose chase. What is wrong with me?

It is a long, tense ride to our Super 8.

42

Mediation

We find the office after a few wrong turns, and park in a gravel lot next to the building—a bungalow converted to an office. The mediator greets us from behind a desk in the reception room. She is a warm, welcoming, professional social-worker type with bouncy brownish hair falling to her shoulders. Her simple shirtwaist's full skirt swirls as she walks us to a square room where three chairs face each other in a triangle.

We sit. Mediator has a clipboard on her lap; from which she checks our basic data—names, addresses, referred by?

She collects our "assignments"—a brief statement from each of us on our agreements, differences, and what we expect from the session. I take mine from my purse, Harry, from his shirt pocket. She scrutinizes each before adding it to her clipboard.

She reads aloud the Topics for Mediation Session, upon which we have both agreed:

Common ground/goals

Want to stay in partnership

Want to grow within partnership

Items for negotiation

Allotment of time between Indiana and Mexico, underlying which is:

Living separately for periods of longer than ???

She straightens in her chair, a "down-to-business" move, divides her gaze evenly between us, then looks directly into my eyes, as she reads my paper, glancing down in brief spurts. A Teleprompter performance without a Teleprompter.

She asks me to read my wants, since we were asked not to share them with each other before the meeting.

My Wants

Separation: I have noted over the past few years, particularly since leaving my job at the bank, that I can be much more productive, satisfied, have a feeling of well-being, fully functioning, when I am either alone or in an impersonal atmosphere: the library at Purdue, the garden, the ravine, a lounge or coffee shop, where others may be present, but I am not expected to interact with them except perfunctorily.

In our household: A separate room for working/studying has been helpful, also not being responsible for meal planning or being together for all meals.

Resigning from responsibility for providing food; reorganization of the household is in progress, also helpful.

Withdrawing from constant contact, even casual, is helpful for me to focus.

My Wants are time and space away, whether in Mexico or not.

Would like to try being in another location altogether. How to balance the time, how to work this out, unclear.

(Two upcoming tests: Weekend with Union Queens, Weekend at Ball State for Womyn's Music Festival)

Would like to rent Mexican apartment for year;

Have separate workspace wherever we live (both rentals at this stage);

Try time apart, perhaps longer than weekends;

Within together time, separate more than now.

The mediator asks me to expand.

I say I want more than three months a year in San Miguel. I drone on, determined to keep my cool, no tears.

Harry's turn.

His list stresses his comfort with Lafayette, Purdue, the Jewish community. He is an enthusiastic Chamber of Commerce shill.

The mediator's voice caresses him. She can see how much he loves his Indiana home.

But—puzzled frown and a glance at her clipboard—he does not want to be alone there?

Harry nods, shifts in his chair and blinks rapidly, a signal of anxiety I know well.

Are there any Indiana activities he enjoys without Pat?

"Oh, yes." Now he's relieved. He ticks off the list: his men's group, noon jogs at the Purdue track, Temple Israel's board, Purdue basketball. He pauses, gives her a look that implies the list goes on and on.

"And Pat does not join you in these activities?"

"No." His voice is tentative. This sounds like a trap; he tries to figure out where this woman is going. Sounds like the trick question on the exam.

"Then why is it so important for her to be in Lafayette all the time?"

Harry scans the room out of the corner of his eye—avoiding my eyes or the mediator's.

Harry rarely says anything significant while making eye contact. There are times when I get up and move to where his eyes are when this habit annoys me. Sensitive conversations are tough when my partner will not look me in the eye.

Harry scurries down a promising path—his work on the cemetery records. Explanation of the complicated spreadsheet he's made to locate the old graves. "Pat is great with spreadsheets," he says. "I need her support." His volume rises; he is speaking *ex cathedra* now, like the pope when he defines Infallible Doctrine. "And support ... support is how I view marriage."

What is this? I never worked on the grave plotting. Has he forgotten I am in the room?

He trails off. The mediator concentrates on her clipboard for a beat, leans towards Harry, no more than a quarter bubble off plumb.

"Let's try something, just to clarify. Let's imagine that, God forbid, Pat were to die suddenly. What would you do?"

Harry's face lights up. The dreaded final has hit the subject of his all night cram. He clears his throat and focuses on a spot over the mediator's right shoulder.

"That's clear enough," he begins, his tone didactic now. We are at a seminar. "First of all, our Jewish tradition specifies a mourning period. I would observe that period, a year, I think, no, eleven months. Then, I would find another wife."

I hear no more.

ॐ

We sign an agreement. We will rent an apartment year-round in San Miguel. Harry will spend January, February, March there; Pat, two months more without Harry—a month before he arrives and a month after he leaves; to be renegotiated after a year's trial.

We must have paid the mediator's fee, left her office; I can't remember. I speak little on the 20-minute drive back to Adobe and Roses in the North Valley. Once in our room, I erupt.

His prescribed Jewish mourning period reduces me to a cipher. Another woman can fill my place in a heartbeat, after a respectable period.

I am a replaceable part. Rent-A-Wife.

My anger baffles Harry. There has been some mistake. He quickly assures me I don't understand; his response was a compliment. He likes being married to me so much, he would marry again as soon as possible. He meant to show how much he values our partnership.

I give up and go for a walk on the irrigation ditch path.

৯৯

I am abandoned, stung.

I picture Harry marking off the months in his Purdue pocket calendar until he can begin dating.

I'd fretted Harry was more interested in my braininess than my unique Self. Consoled myself that after his affair, he had opted for me: Pat the one and only.

Now I see myself as the more convenient, reliable choice.

I feel cheated. Forty-six years of generosity—time, talent and treasure poured into our marital cup.

Luke 6:38 comes back to me, the Bible verse I'd trusted earlier.

> Good measure, pressed down, shaken together and running over will they pour into your lap. For whatever measure you use with other people, they will use in their dealings with you.

Where is my running over cup, the good measure pouring into my lap?

è▲

My daughter gets the full force of my fury at lunch the next day. Meta is my only confidant, since I still honor the taboo on speaking about personal problems outside the family.

I am ready to end the marriage.

But I do not. Harry and I fly back to Indiana together. A week later I email Meta that Harry and I are *bashert*—Hebrew for "fated." We will work out our differences.

I design calling cards with our contact information in Indiana and Mexico, proclaiming:

The P & H Partnership

Established 25 April 1953

Pat and Harry Herzog

The intact partnership was a rock of my faith: unvoiced, unexamined, but immoveable.

We stumble on. The marriage never recovers.

43

Mediation Reprise

I feel like an old workhorse blinking at the light after shaking off her blinders.

Harry had it right.

Rather than being angry with him for undervaluing my uniqueness, I should have thanked him for telling the truth. He described our marriage as it was: Handmaiden Pat at the ready, filling the role of a proper wife. Harry neither noticed nor demanded my virtuous "sacrifices." This was my fantasy; I bought into the family tradition of wife/mother/employee giving 110 percent and demanding nothing but discreet adoration.

And the infamous question? What would he do if I died?

Right on again, Harry.

Marriage is a partnership, not a suicide pact.

Bashert? Two souls destined for each other, like in Mexico, the *media naranja*: Every woman is half an orange until she finds the predestined other half of her orange? Dale Evans and Roy Rogers riding off into the sunset together? Bullshit, dangerous bullshit, swallowed whole. Sugar-coated with Christian compassion or Jewish blarney—my personal crazy-making mix.

Harry knew. We'd vowed "Til death do us part," not to throw ourselves on the funeral pyre or swallow poison like Romeo when he thinks Juliet is dead. The claptrap I thought long cleansed from my liberated woman's head still fogged my vision. I still saw myself as Savior to Poor Harry, who is unable to live without my support—Harry's definition of marriage.

❧

How would I have answered the mediator's question?

I would greet Harry's death with relief. Now I could I have broccoli soup for breakfast, dance all night in the *jardín*, rent a bachelorette pad in San Miguel. Why would I ever want another spouse—enough already of marriage!

❧

Flashback to Bright National Bank: A co-worker invites me to join a golf class. "No," I demur, "just another thing I would do without Harry," thinking of folk dancing, my women's circle, meditation, writers' group, Jackie Sorenson's aerobic dance.

"I'll learn golf after he dies."

She does a double take, not sure whether to take me seriously. When she sees this is exactly what I mean, she looks away in embarrassment.

ริ๛

The marriage was over before we crossed the mediator's threshold. It took me another three years of twists and turns to hear what my "document" proclaimed.

She who is deaf, let her hear.

Sooner or later.

44

Youssef

The fault line that opened at the mediation session widens when I return to San Miguel that fall without Harry, as per the mediation agreement. My salvation will be writing my story, I decide. Excerpts from those writings bare my state of mind during those crucial months. Discontent drips from my pen:

September 20, 1998

The fields around the Bajío airport are green from the summer rains. Yellow flowers dot the ground around the runway, welcoming me to the land of Santa Clara milkshakes and mesquite honey. As per our mediation agreement, Harry will join me in early December.

I arrive hungry for San Miguel, my friends, my space. This time I would write, write, write.

Two months on my own. A gift. A blessing. A curse. A time to grow. A time to vegetate. A time to count my blessings and forget both the pleasures and the pains of Indiana and my marriage.

Long afternoons flow by, reading and letter writing in the third-floor studio, with frequent breaks to stroll the roof outside the studio door, where San Miguel swirls out below me like a Mexican dancer's full circle skirt. This is the peace of the Purdue Union ladies' lounge, Ghost Ranch or my cabin at the Bourbeuse Resort.

Alone, free to eat and move and sleep and waken and dress and exercise when and where I please, unfettered by the silken cords of partnership. A nibble of street mariachi here, a full-course banquet of a string quartet there. More to nourish me than I could ever dream.

November

Harry will be with me soon. I am in mourning already.

Living with Harry shouldn't have to exclude these moments; I must insist on them. Harry would never object. Yet I can't imagine how we will live together in this apartment, and I will continue to be so free. My years as the linchpin, the role I learned from my tribe and my time, paralyze me.

Unproductive talk. If I want to live alone, I can. End a partnership of more than 47 years? Not lightly. I have been married almost 70 percent of my life. Tom, Meta and Ben bind us forever. Children no more, their times of dependency long past, my job as nurturer dried up like my breasts. Does my role in their lives depend on being married to their father?

There is something else: In my gut, I do not trust Harry. I see how he shuts out any old friend who becomes burdensome—X, Y, and poor R, who had the bad taste to die in a car crash while he was in therapy with her. He is so sorry for Z, he tells me, tied down taking care of his invalid wife. It chills me. I do not want this person with me during my final days. I am afraid that once I lose my competence, I will be taken care of but not cherished. I do not want to be the albatross around Harry's neck.

My mother. As she lost it and began to ignore stains on her dress and pick up butter with her fingers, Harry withdrew. I think he found her troubling, vaguely disgusting. He avoided being in the same room with her. When our friend Joan developed cancer and ran through the gamut of surgery, radiation and chemo, Harry's visits grew brief and strained. Joan told me she understood: "Harry just can't handle serious illness."

Happily for me, in San Miguel Harry does not have the Jewish Federation, the cemetery committee, or Purdue alumni meetings: activities I find stultifying, the people involved worse than boring. After an evening with them I feel leeched of authenticity and verve. Can I tell Harry this without attacking his core?

I'll find a way. I am asking for respect; I must give it.

Trying to steer a course through these shoals is not easy. But if we are to have any life together, I must honor Harry as a person, and get over it. A line from *South Pacific* says it all: "It's a waste of time to worry about things that he is not; Be thankful for the things he's got."

Which are?

- ✓ Joy in our family, our children and grandchildren
- ✓ Respect for my competence, a woman who can pull her own weight
- ✓ Pride in my intellectual prowess, my ability to edit his writing
- ✓ Agreement about money; our ability to negotiate budgets without rancor
- ✓ Trust in my fidelity to him
- ✓ Realization I will "take care of him" whenever necessary
- ✓ Worshipping and meditating together, our at-home-ness in Judaism
- ✓ Love of music, going to performances of kinds of music we both like
- ✓ Traveling together
- ✓ Good food, cooking, sharing meals with friends
- ✓ Similar standards of cleanliness and neatness in our abode
- ✓ Commitment to *tikun olam* (repairing the world); joint work for various causes
- ✓ Kindness to each other

Oops. Where did I read that when a wife begins making lists of good things about her husband, she may be trying to find reasons to stay together?

May 5, 1999

With Harry I feel stale, not connected, and guilty that I am touchy, quick to bristle at small things—like his slitting open my mail for me. Maybe I am not touchy. I sense an attempt to control, to fold me into his system. Not consciously. I'd be shocked if Harry had any idea why he did it. I doubt it is to make my life easier, as he insists. Like many of the little courtesies bestowed by Harry, they uphold The System, which has no place for my Wild Woman Self, who might opt for her own system, or none at all.

Why should anyone of good faith and open mind be offended when a husband hurries around the car to open her door? And yet, somehow it diminishes me. Partners don't treat each other like invalids.

At the Clarion Motel in Ithaca

Harry is having breakfast—the Continental buffet style of modern budget motels. He turns the wheel to fill his bowl with Cheerios from their giant plastic container, then comes over to the table where I sit with my tea and asks, "Where is the milk?"

I smile but say nothing, hearing a five-year-old talking to his mother. Harry looks around and finds the milk. Then I feel guilty. Doesn't Harry deserve someone who will appreciate him more? Who doesn't sneer at his not being able to find the milk? Can't I engage Harry and the rest of the world and honor every Spark I meet? I do it with children all the time, wouldn't dream of putting down a child's ignorance. Go where he is in mind and heart and honor his Spark.

May 28

I can't wait for Harry to experience Ghost Ranch. As we near, winding through spectacular mountain vistas, I point out Chimney Rock, subject of several Georgia O'Keefe paintings. I am so excited I almost miss the turnoff, then pull in and park in the high-prairie bowl that shelters the main buildings. The well of energy and spirit of the place floods back. We hike in the creek bed that reminds me of the Blackhawk ravine I treasured. I lead Harry to my beloved library, the field where I watched Hale-Bopp cruise across the sky. Nothing clicks; Harry does not want to stay long. We drive back to Adobe and Roses, see a forgettable movie, eat at Wendy's afterward, a Harry favorite.

September, Back in Mexico

In this state of mind, no surprise that another man captures my attention.

Youssef is a regular at the meditation center where I sit most mornings. A few inches taller than me, slight, full curly beard, gentle sculptured face like one of the wise men in the Christmas crèche. Appropriate in Mexico, where *los Tres Reyes* bring the children's gifts on January 6, the Feast of the Epiphany, when the Three Kings arrived in the Scripture story with gifts of myrrh, frankincense and gold for the baby Jesus.

Another snowbird, a Canadian. His parents are Lebanese immigrants, Maronite Catholics. We can both chant the Latin Mass, a bizarre connection for two people who met at a Buddhist center. Harry later dubs him "that Lebanese Canadian Arab."

October 2000

The next fall, in my first months in Mexico without Harry, my spirits perk up.

Youssef and I join a group of meditator friends to hear visiting Cuban musicians. El Gato is a low-ceilinged, funky bar down three steps from the sidewalk on a side street in El Centro. A smoke-filled speakeasy from a Prohibition-era movie, but liquor is legal and nobody smokes. The trio belts out Cuban rhythms in a corner, and the dance floor fills around the packed wooden tables with bench seats.

We dance. Youssef can dance. The music, the night, the warm male body all come together in a sensual rush. A month later I am still reeling.

November 2, *Día de los Muertos*, Day of the Dead

I finally do it, send Youssef an email saying how much I wanted to spend the night with him after dancing together. We have both been gingerly skirting the romantic attachment. Like Jimmy Carter, I am adulterous in my heart.

One of the surprises is my lack of guilt. After 47 years of exclusive sex with Harry, I thought I was committed to chastity. I'd never been seriously tempted by another human being. I have fantasized freely about new lovers, but the romance always begins when I am a widow.

When my friend Zuzu remarks she'd never leave an attractive guy like Harry alone for two months, my heart leaps. Maybe Harry will find somebody else while I'm in San Miguel. Mary Lou is available, so far as I know. A neat solution, win-win for both of us.

But if that's what I want, why wait for Mary Lou to free me? And why does Mary Lou keep coming to mind? Do I think Harry owes me one? Do I want revenge?

No, I really and truly want Harry content. Maybe someone else would make him happier than I have. Like Woody Allen on death, "Death doesn't scare me, I just don't want to be around when it's happening." Harry is a sweet guy; I just don't want him around all the time.

I think about returning to Indiana and its pleasures, pains and dead zones. More than anything else, the day-to-day life there is bland. Bland? Changing religions, careers, dealing with death, three children's life crises, my husband's infidelity, his long slow recovery from the scars of his early life. Bland? Only compared to San Miguel.

Nothing bland, dead or flat in San Miguel. I am high from the most exciting evening of dancing in my life, feeling keenly the tearful, regretful sense of loss now that Youssef is returning to Canada.

I was the initiator of most of our time together—dinner in my apartment, a movie, *tashlich* (casting our sins, in the form of bread, on the water to prepare for the Jewish New Year), the farewell dinner, music and dancing.

Nothing was quite kosher. There is always a tape playing in the background: Married women do not invite men into their houses when their husbands are absent. There is a twinge at a movie when Syd comes over to say hello and I introduce him to Youssef. Syd's glance reminds me how quickly word spreads in San Miguel. An eyebrow-raiser to be seen with a guy when my husband is 1,500 miles away.

November 7

It is time to join Harry in Indiana and return with him to San Miguel. I fly to Indianapolis on November 7, 2000, the first Tuesday after the first Monday of November in a Leap Year: presidential Election Day in the USA.

My plane lands just in time for us to get to Joan and David's to watch the election returns together. As the early returns scroll across the TV, Bush and Gore are running neck and neck, but Gore is predicted to win. Harry complains of abdominal pain. It worsens; David drives us to the ER, where the diagnosis is an inflamed gall bladder; surgery is scheduled for the next morning.

Harry spends several days in St. Elizabeth's, where I visit him daily. A nurse pulls me aside the second day and suggests I speak to my husband. When she brings his towel and bowl in the morning, he says he will wait for his wife to help him bathe. He needs to practice taking care of himself, she scolds.

The mediation scene flashes back. Harry wants me by his side at all times. This is his second hospitalization, after the first in Mexico with his bum knee. Is it the beginning? Will a string of illnesses follow?

My callousness embarrasses me. Is my concern that Harry will not be there for me in my final days a reflection of my reluctance to be there for him? Where is my loyalty, the virtue I value so highly?

December

Harry is able to travel again by early December, and we fly back to Mexico together. I broach the subject of my discontent. It is time for a Serious Talk.

I have an honest talk with Harry about friendships that are mine, not ours. Mention Youssef. Harry confesses feeling threatened by that particular friendship. I convey my need for such friends, that while I am not searching for a new husband or trying to end our partnership, for me it has to be a partnership in which I am able to do the things I most want to do.

Harry understands. We are making progress; this is the beginning of a new "us." Maybe those cards touting the Pat and Harry Partnership were prophetic rather than pathetic.

Two Days Later

Only two days later, all the buoyancy and hope for the future is gone in a blink.

I am elated when Harry says he wants to talk again after our satisfying conversation the day before. Previous meanderings about finding myself have often seemed borderline self-indulgent to Harry, and I feel I sound lame in the telling.

Harry sits down squarely in the middle of the massive poured-cement couch, made comfy by square custom pillows. I position my favorite *equipali* barrel chair a few feet away to face him directly.

He wants to talk about sex, he says. After rambling discussions of its importance to him and what it means in a marriage, he clears his throat and raises the volume.

"I don't want you having sex with that man," he says—it's the pope again.

I am stunned into uncustomary silence.

Harry's tone is like previous rule settings, "No tents in this house, no more musical instruments."

"I heard you rave on about what a wonderful time you had dancing with him, and I just want you to know, it is not to go any further," he proclaims.

As my grandmother would have said, that got my back up. This is a scare-a-teenager-about-drugs lecture, not a conversation.

My impulse is to run out the door to Youssef's place. Where I had not yet set foot.

I say little, nod in reply. A visceral repulsion shuts my customarily wide-open Irish mouth.

A line has been crossed—in the same way I imagine Harry sees "having sex with that man" as a crucial boundary. No one can tell me what to do with my body.

Within days I am in Youssef's bed.

After the fateful deed, I whisper to Youssef that I am a terrible conspirator and will probably tell my husband.

"What will he do?" Youssef asks.

My words erupt spontaneously. "He will walk."

Harry will not tolerate adultery. Somehow, someplace, I know this is a sure path to freedom. No more gentle signals like dinosaur sox. It's the rainbow sign.

God gave Noah the rainbow sign: No more water, the fire this time (Negro spiritual.)

Later December

Why had I immediately told Harry, Meta and many others what a wonderful time I'd had dancing with Youssef? To defuse it, say it's perfectly innocent fun, that I can have it all? Now I understand the "Don't ask, don't tell" policy on which not only the military but most marriages operate. It was a bitter realization for me, without an easy resolution. Messy, sticky, exactly what I don't do well. Like sex, which I've managed to avoid doing with a full sense of engagement for a long, long time.

I feel weepy, unnerved, not valued.

Pretty weird to feel not valued because my husband doesn't want me to have sex with another man. What's this all about? About my fantasy of acting out my quest for my authentic self, intimacy, connection. Whatever fancy name I've been calling it, it's clear that in Harry's world, it spells adultery, at least with a man. I guess I'm lucky to have almost all female friends.

Dreary old, conventional old, blabbermouth me. Had to tell everyone how much I liked dancing with Youssef, so that it would be instantly sanitized into an okay friendship that had nothing to do with my partnership with Harry. Right! And I went rushing home afterwards in a taxi because I was sleepy. Right!

So is this the soap opera scene where Meryl Streep has her hand on the door handle and takes several frames *not* to jump out of the car in *The Bridges of Madison County?* That movie shamelessly exploits all of us who stood by our man and let life pass us by. But if I really think that, am I staying with Harry as my Catholic wifely duty? Were Youssef to drop dead tomorrow, along with any potentially attractive males I am fated to meet in the rest of my life, would that change what I am wanting, what I am needing in my life?

ቇ

Revisiting this rush of purple prose, I blush. I see myself as Meryl Streep with her hand on the pickup truck door, milking the scene. A drama queen preparing not for my virtuous return home as Good Wife and Mother like Streep, but for my joyous split in the Albuquerque airport. My role as Searcher for Truth dominates the script. It's a real part of the story, or I would have deleted all those old computer files instead of including them.

But where are the close-ups of Pat's role, or wide-angle lens shots that took in more of the scene? More comforting to focus on Harry.

I sound stuck in interminable journaling and dream recording, not quite sure how to handle Harry or marriage or my life. Lots of hand wringing. Why did it take me so long to do something—thrash out my complaints with Harry or leave the marriage? But then I had been practicing denial and self-censorship over a lifetime.

I was beginning to uncover more than I wanted to know about myself and I was loath to follow those leads. Digging deeper might be painful. Like Scarlett O'Hara, I would think about that tomorrow.

If there is "world enough and time."

45

Rush to Sunport

I report my infidelity to Harry within days. He begins daily sessions with a psychiatrist and after a week, asks me to join him. We go together and discuss our marriage. Harry says the sessions make him aware of how much I mean to him.

We continue the dialog in our apartment over lunch. Harry speaks about adultery, his moral values, what Judaism teaches, and on and on. A sense of profound rejection overwhelms me. I hear a theology professor in a lecture hall, not a man speaking to the wife across the lunch table. Harry makes more eye contact with the chicken sandwich on his plate than with me.

I flee to the roof for private tears, then return to confront Harry, now rinsing our lunch dishes in the sink. More talk, some opening, then we stop to go to book group—a mistake.

That night, we engage in another painful, tender, open talk about our marriage, our lives, ourselves. Then to bed, and, in Harry's words, "the best sex in our marriage."

૨૨

A light bulb along the way:

FFSS: Fucking Follows Soul Stuff

It's the sex, stupid (à la Bill Clinton's winning campaign strategy: It's the economy, stupid).

To my newly sensitized nose, my dreams of the past seven years reek of sex. Should have smelled the Einstein's cinnamon bagels in the trail of breadcrumbs leading to the witch's house in the woods.

Sex intricately entangled with soul. My dogged search for Self, for connection, is full of references to being juiced, awakening, describing sensuality of every kind except sex.

Poetry, meditation, discussions about the spiritual path—any talking that went deeper (penetration again) was a turn-on, unacknowledged, unbidden, but definitely there. How could I have missed it?

De hecho (in fact), it would have taken a giant leap over the wall for me to recognize the sexuality. I had that all under control: in theory, in every way I could chronicle with comfort. No clue as to how stunted my own responses were after so many years of accommodation. The sex in the dreams was symbolic, I insisted. The sensuality did not include, point to, imply, sexuality. My well-trained brain would never acknowledge the possibility of my seeking another partner while I was married. Masturbation was okay, both physical and mental—with books, films, fantasies. Adultery was out of the question.

But my brain wasn't firmly in charge. And so I went dancing with Youssef.

Dancing? Omigod, part of my life since I was four years old.

Dancing class and recitals at four

Square dancing in high school

Dancing as sex with boyfriends

Folk dancing

Moving to Jackie Sorenson's choreography for 30 years

Dancing on the beach at Green Turtle Key

Dancing with kids at Wabash Center, grandchildren

Solo dancing at parties, bar/bat mitzvahs

Leading the Macarena with the Paul Taylor dancers on Mother's funeral weekend

Never with Harry, well, almost never. From those first chaste fox trots at the New Year's dance the day after we met to the rare coaxed folk dances, never with soul, never with abandon. Abandon is a no-no in Harry's repertoire—or in my narrow reading of Harry's repertoire.

&

In this state of high tension we arrive at our daughter's house in Albuquerque for a long-promised babysitting gig with granddaughters Shona and Bella. This not our usual Babysitting Scene. Their parents separated months before after bitter fights, and tension still hangs heavy in the house. This trip there is no list, like five-year-old Elizabeth's battered 3x5 card. Bella and Shona respond to my suggestions—zoo? river walk? movie? with "Maybe tomorrow."

Their mother is earning her yoga teacher's certification in Ojai, California; their dad is in town. He calls several times, wanting to talk to one of them. Shona will not speak to him; Bella is kinder. Leo asks me to intercede for him; can't I see that Shona needs help to deal with this rejection of her father?

I reply I am more worried that Bella's generosity blinds her to reality. I don't mention my worry that Good Bella might turn out like Good Pat.

Harry's and my conversations continue, muted by not wanting to burden our granddaughters with our trauma. We fail; Shona later expresses anger to her mother that we split up while we were in their home.

∂❧

We talk and talk and talk.

Harry is adamant: I must give up the boyfriend and San Miguel if I want to stay married. He points out that adultery is banned both in the Jewish faith and in the Buddhist teachings that Youssef follows.

I have two options: return to Indiana, work with my trusted analyst there to find a way to stay married and live a

San Miguel-style life in Indiana, with more independence and solo time. The other, we divorce and I move to San Miguel.

I hesitate; my resentment of Harry's veto of more Youssef seems flimsy grounds to break up a 48-year marriage. The world agrees with Harry; I do, too, in my reasonable moments. The boyfriend is not an alternative spouse. My refusal to end the relationship is like my insistence on a Catholic wedding—damned if Delphine or her son can dictate my path. Harry's outrage at my adultery makes me feel like chattel: a totally unreasonable response from the therapist's, Harry's and the conventional point of view.

As for my discontent, I've been waffling about the causes of my restlessness since my father's death many years earlier. Is the geographic solution the easy way out? A way to escape working on my problems?

ॐ

Harry calls the Gilners for counsel. He speaks extensively to Maxine, in her marriage counselor role. After one long phone conversation with her, he comes to the kitchen where I am chopping vegetables for a stir-fry. He is buoyant, happier than I have seen him since this crisis began.

"Pat, I just learned something really important from Maxine." He slides onto one of the counter stools across from me.

The winning lottery ticket? I almost ask. Instead I register polite interest as I switch from carrot chopping to celery. My gut distrusts Maxine's pat solutions. She has enlightened me about correct child-rearing techniques too many times.

"She knows of a case like ours, a friend, maybe you remember Shirley, the wife of Frank's colleague?"

I remember the case well, but I play dumb.

Harry pauses, allows time to jog my memory. "Well, doesn't matter. With your, uh, unusual behavior, Maxine thinks it's possible there is something … something physical. Which means you must promise me to make an appointment with a doctor just as soon as you get off the plane in Lafayette."

I turn away to rinse my hands in the sink, not wanting Harry to see my reaction.

"So you think this could be something serious?" I dry my hands, keep my voice neutral.

He does not want to elaborate, but finally says, "Well, it *could* be a brain tumor, not that that is the only possibility."

"So you think I might have a brain tumor?" trying to keep my voice flat.

"Well, your symptoms, total change of personality, doing things you never did before … " he stops as he sees my face. Reading my sober stare as fear for my life, he adds, "Of course, these things are treatable, even if …" He launches a clinical discussion of the marvelous new research on the brain.

"I see," I murmur, and hurry down the hall to the bathroom and lock the door.

❧

Harry is thrilled at the prospect of my brain tumor. This solves everything. I am sick, not unhappy. Shirley, the woman Maxine referred to, died a few months after diagnosis. Surely Maxine told him the end of that story.

Of course she did. But that's okay because, after the customary mourning period, he can look for another wife. Lucky Harry, he can start right now. This is it for Good Wife Pat.

❧

Days later, at Albuquerque Sunport:

We part at the burrito stand entrance, me to my gate, Harry back to the car. His voice trembles, "I don't know when I'll see you again." I feign a sad look. I see I am set up in this scenario as the fabled Hard-Hearted Hannah, the Vamp of Savannah. Ella Fitzgerald sings in my ear as I struggle to look sympathetic.

> *They call her Hard-Hearted Hannah,*
> *The vamp of Savannah,*
> *The meanest gal in town;*
> *Leather is tough, but Hannah's heart is tougher,*
> *She's a gal who loves to see men suffer!*

I walk away exhilarated—a champagne high, a Lake Michigan high, a Mayim, Mayim high-step high. I meander to Indiana by my cheap and circuitous route, feeling powerfully alive and grateful to be on my own.

࿇

Grateful, joyous, flying high, no words can describe my euphoric state in my new freedom. San Miguel is even brighter than I remembered it. I rent a smaller apartment, my first solo nest since my brief fling at the single life in Columbia, Missouri almost 50 years before.

I spell out a plan for my new life: Spend less on living space, more on travel, study, who knows what. Pay only for the space I need. One bedroom with a suitable workspace. Order my space for serious work—reduce clutter, have tools conveniently and aesthetically arranged. Arrange my time around my work. Delight in where I am and who and what I find there. Eat, sing, dance, play, exercise, cook, talk, read, and on and on and on, but never nest again.

I will copy the cardinals outside my home office window on Seventh Street in Lafayette—better models than humans. They build a nest for offspring, then sleep and eat à la carte ever after. As "in the present moment" as it gets.

Go, cardinals!

46

The Trouble with Pat

Liberated Woman bustles about her new apartment, fussing with her pictures, starting new stories, when all hell breaks loose. An email arrives from my angry daughter, crushed at my betrayal of confidence. She has discovered I read her private diary while on our visit before Sunport.

❧

Harry and I moved to Meta's bedroom on that visit because Shona was ill. Meta gave us the upstairs guest room, but when Shona developed a fever and vomiting, I wanted to be on the same floor with her so that I could hear her in the night.

Meta had not cleared her room, as she would have if we were scheduled to sleep in her bed.

My eyes zeroed in on the well-thumbed spiral notebook on Meta's bedside table. It took a day and a half for me to pick it up. I wouldn't read it—just look to see what it was. The first page was a lament about "my mother." The words burned my eyes, all written in Meta's distinctive script. The cursed notebook went to the back of the bookshelf.

Not for long.

That evening—with the dog walked, the granddaughters settled in their beds, and Harry dozing over *The New York Times* in his rocker—I grabbed the notebook from where I'd stashed it and headed for the bathroom. Behind a locked door, I crouched on the closed toilet seat and bent over the forbidden document like an addict eager for her fix.

My heart pounded, guilt stuck like a fishbone in my throat, but I read on. Every word on every page, then back to memorize the harshest passages.

Disgusted with myself, I crammed the book behind the top row of books in the office bookshelf. No, it must be where I found it, on Meta's bedside table. Harry was already in bed when I skulked in with the guilty read and slipped into bed.

"What's wrong?" he said. I must have betrayed my shaken state.

When I was able to talk, I said, "I … I read Meta's diary, and I am so, so ashamed."

৯৯

Soon another email lands in my Yahoo inbox—a landmine waiting for me to trip it, this one from my older son, Tom.

Calmly, impassively, Tom lays out his case. No whining, no rant that I can discount as an isolated fit of temper. He balances his cry of pain with generosity of spirit:

It would be false for me to say that I had an unhappy childhood, or that there were no positive qualities to your parenting. In certain respects I feel privileged to be in our family tree, and I remain grateful for the many positive things you did do.

Tom is concerned about his youngest son, whose problems he fears are rooted in "the Browne-Herzog curse."

Dad described the Herzog curse in *Harry's Story*. He was raised by an abusive father, and passed this on by terrorizing myself and Meta, and perhaps also Ben. The Browne curse is unexplained, but I experience it as a form of narcissism that caused Mom to fail to effectively attach and empathize during my childhood.

My purpose is to end the Browne-Herzog curse by raising healthy children, and I don't think it is possible to eradicate something until it is named.

There must be some mistake. Is Tom on drugs? What can he be talking about? My treasured, pampered first-born? Memories of a happy little guy flicker through my mind: reciting *The Cat in the Hat* as I turn the pages; shooting suction cup arrows at the target painted on our sliding glass patio doors at his Indian-themed seventh birthday party; grinning victoriously on top of the biggest snow fort in the neighborhood, his and his neighborhood buddies' prize creation.

Narcissism? Doesn't that mean a person who only thinks of herself? My children are central to my life. How could they experience me as distant, cold? I feel exposed, my guts laid open for all to see, an overripe watermelon split with one brutal blow of the butcher knife.

๛

Meta recommends a book, Elan Golomb, *Trapped in the Mirror, Adult Children of Narcissists in Their Struggle for Self.*

I scan the characteristics of narcissism and gulp as I see myself reflected;

An inflated sense of self-importance.

Doesn't Mother Earth see herself as the center of the universe? Exhibitionism. I love to perform, whether it is leading a line dance or reading Dr. Seuss.

But a narcissist? The mother who has devoted so much time and energy to her children?

Hadn't I repeated a zillion times, "Don't hesitate to critique my [cooking, insurance selling, computer skills, report writing, speeches]. As long as you don't criticize my child rearing, I'm thick-skinned. Raising my children is what I consider my true contribution to the world, and my most cherished skill."

No question mothering was my Holy Grail, but I thought I'd located the chalice. Everything under control. Or not.

Some of my writing records doubts.

Like "Mother's Day," a short piece I wrote in 1996.

"Why I Hate Mother's Day"

Tom says he resented my making fun of Mother's Day when he was a little boy. He wanted to have a mother he could give Mother's Day presents to like the rest of the kids.

Being a mother secretly scares me. It brightens my life and exposes me as a fake. I want to be this interesting friend that appeals to my children with her wit, depth of understanding and insightful words. I envision my children turning to me, telling me their innermost struggles, marveling at my sage counsel and telling their friends what an amazing person their mother is. No wonder I don't like Mother's Day. How could a perky Hallmark verse compete with being taken into my offspring's heart?

I don't want a card from Tom and Ben and Meta. I don't want flowers. I don't want them to remember that I love the smell of carnations, or Joy perfume, or dangly earrings, or turtles, or bell hooks' books. I want them to want to be my buddies—ugh—surely not that cozy; I want them to bask in the glow of the best mother in the whole world.

I hunger for intimacy and my children are ready-made intimates, tied to me by a physical bond that they can never sever. But I want it both ways. I want to keep the biologic bond, the flesh of my flesh thing, but at the same time have Tom, Meta and Ben—and their spouses, for good measure—just happen to want to be my friend because they find me such an interesting woman.

I want them to marvel that no one would ever think of me as 63. Their friends to remark what a scintillating woman their mother is: charming, warm, loving, bright, with-it, so good with children, so giving of herself. Imagine, she comes to sit with Andy and Noah for a whole week. Imagine, she writes chapter books for Elizabeth. Imagine, she sends carefully chosen presents for all four children on a birthday, even Eileen's children, whom she's only just met.

Imagine, imagine, imagine.

Mother's Day. Can't I let my children off the hook? Cut the apron strings? Grow up? Be gracious about a card or phone call?

But I feel so lonely for them.

Is it all ego, this loneliness, that I should badmouth Mother's Day?

My mother's love for her mother did not meet my standards. And yet, she insisted that Gram's picture be by her bed in the Mulberry Lutheran Home.

Harry and I took Mother to Mass on her last Christmas Day. Setting into the special wheelchair aisle in Blessed Sacrament Church, after braving the 10 yards from the car to the door in blowing snow and bitter cold, she struggled to get out the longest sentence she uttered in that last year of her life: "Wait till Gram hears how you took me out in this weather," she said, mildly chiding us, but clearly looking forward to telling this story to her mother, long dead.

Maybe I should settle for a card.

47

Diving Deeper

Maybe I need to look deeper at my mothering. My betrayal of my daughter's trust was a devastating blow to my integrity. How could I have done such a thing? But a narcissist? How does that fit?

Wait ... my mentor Thomas Moore talks about narcissism. I pore over his writings for comfort. Moore helps; I begin to get it.

The popular take on Narcissus is that the beautiful youth who dived into the pool was done in by his vanity. All his friends told him how handsome he was, and when he saw his reflection in the pool, he was so enamored of his gorgeousness he tried to embrace himself. Instead, he fell into the pool and drowned. Selfish lout.

Not Moore's take.

Narcissus did indeed think himself the hottest stallion in the forest. However, when he looked deep into that pool, what he saw reflected was his Self, in all its splendor and potential for growth. He was overcome with longing for the more satisfying beauty he saw, and gladly died to reach it. As we must all die to vanity/superficiality to be reborn fully human and flower into maturity. The bright yellow daffodil (Narcissus reborn) thrusts out of the thawing soil every spring to remind us of the myth.

Better. Clearer. Oh. Yes.

Of course I had to be a perfect mother, on the surface—all those birthday cakes and Big Lump games. Not bad things in themselves; I suspect my children recall the birthday parties with a smile. But the Real Thing is something else—the connection of my beautiful Self to theirs. Sadly I was so far from diving into the pool and finding my own identity, I had no clue about my children's inner lives.

My hunger for Meta's diary betrayed my thirst for reaching her on a deeper level, where I had not been able to connect. My narcissism—it must mean something that it hurts to write the word—kept me from forming a deep mother-daughter bond.

ૐ

Hints come back to me: no grand dramas, just mini-scenes that unsettle.

Meta recently reunited with her best friend from Klondike Elementary, Kate, now a published novelist. Kate recounts that she knew Meta would be her best friend when she climbed on the bus the first day of kindergarten wearing bright red lipstick.

Meta explains: Like her brother before her, she knew she would board the big yellow school bus at our mailbox on State Road 26 W. With minutes to go before bus time, she worried that her lips would get chapped during the long morning away from home. She scurried into our bedroom and rifled through my cosmetics drawer. Lipstick. That would do it. She hurriedly painted her lips from the prettiest looking case, just as Tom yelled that the bus was coming down the road.

A charming story that no longer charms. Why did Meta have to search for lip gloss on her own? I knew nothing about the incident until 50 years later. Not a mother she could run to for help. Not unless it was for planning a Valentine's Day room party. Not an empathetic mom who would inquire what her daughter needed on this first day of school. A cheerleader mom, not a warm lap to crawl into.

ह♣

Lake Michigan. Tom and Meta retell another story often. I laugh—a cute anecdote from their childhood.

The four of us spend a day in Warren Dunes State Park, picnicking on the Lake Michigan beach. Ben is yet unborn, so the children are four and two. Lunchtime; Harry and I lug the picnic basket and cooler up a hill to a spot under the shade of a tree. I unpack the breaded pork chop sandwiches. The two children are within sight in the lake, floating on a plastic mattress.

Harry is doling out the paper plates as Tom and Meta run up to the spot we've staked out. "We almost drowned," Tom spouts, breathless. "The float turned over, and we were over our heads. Meta kept grabbing me around the neck to get her head out of the water, and I couldn't breathe. If a man hadn't come over and helped, we'd be dead."

I smile, say how nice of the man. They are exaggerating, I am sure. We would have noticed were they in any trouble.

"No, no, really, Mom. We almost drowned," Tom insists. I give them both a hug and say I am glad they did not. They can tell I think this is a tall tale.

There is a sour edge to Tom and Meta's retelling; they are still irritated because we didn't believe they almost drowned. As I never took seriously how frightened their father's anger made them.

❧

Ben disliked school from the start. He wanted to stay home from kindergarten much of the time. When his teacher voiced concern, I attributed his discomfort at school to all the fun we had at home. Whatever was wrong—and now I believe there was a great deal wrong—I never questioned Ben or tried to puzzle it out. Whether it led to his early drug use and addiction, I will never know. My talent was for entertaining preschoolers, not dealing with their darker feelings.

Another narcissism symptom: a tendency to over-idealize or devalue people based largely on a narrow focus.

Ben marries a second time; he has joint custody of the two children from his first marriage, Elizabeth and Paul. The two spend alternate weeks with Ben and with their mother. His new wife has two daughters, Chardae and Carrera. Chardae and Elizabeth are both are in second grade. Carrera is three years old; Paul is four.

Ben invites me to visit: "I know you will want to meet your new granddaughters."

I do. I arrive for a visit eager to meet the new "blended family," as they describe themselves.

Ben's new wife is beautiful, lively, welcoming. Eileen takes me with her to run errands, have coffee, and to canvass the thrift stores where she is a super savvy shopper.

The children's bedrooms are on the lower level of the house, along with their toys and paraphernalia. We go down almost as soon as I arrive to get acquainted and play games. I sense that Chardae is bullying my beloved Elizabeth, and is unkind to her sister, Carrera, who is an impulsive, a-bit-out-of-control preschooler. With my eagle eye and Super Savta's protective cape spread over Elizabeth and Paul, I bristle and find more and more evidence for my theory.

I am alarmed that the children are on their own downstairs, with both parents upstairs most of the time. I ask Elizabeth if this is typical and she says her father and Eileen need time to "work things out."

I keep my concerns to myself; I don't want to begin the relationship by criticizing the new couple. But I begin assembling a dossier to judge them secretly by my high falutin' standards.

ह

My unnerving perception of the new family hardens over the next few days. The upper floor of the house is clearly the parents' domain. The children visit for meals, departures, arrivals, and family TV time. The lower level is an ever-changing collage of toys and clothes and stuff. Wet towels carpet the bathroom—one or more discarded after each of the four daily showers.

Each child fills a role.

Paul slips quietly into the background with a book or his Etch-A-Sketch. Some of the exuberance of the two-year-old enchanted with the gecko at the zoo when we were last together shines through, especially when he taps his toy drum, the instrument that will become his passion.

Carrera charges through the day at laser speed, touching down for an occasional TV show or Polly Pocket session. Her lightning strikes leave occasional scars: broken toys, punched siblings, defaced drawings. She is always in danger, Chardae reminds the fiery little redhead, of getting into Big Trouble, which I deduce means a spanking.

Elizabeth is no longer the sparkly Elizabeth of my memory, the Dorothy who transformed a previous home into the Land of Oz for her fifth birthday. Dorothy's (Elizabeth's) guests were Tin Men or Cowardly Lions or Wicked Witches of the West and followed the yellow brick road painted on butcher paper to an Emerald City feast. She is subdued now in my eyes.

Chardae leads the troops with aplomb. Her voice reverberates like "Attention Kmart Shoppers": giving directions, making corrections, prodding ever onward.

Together she and Elizabeth make posters, gather costumes for their productions, and sing and dance when they aren't changing clothes or doing each other's hair. Their many cooperative projects don't reassure me. Impartial observance is not my style.

るゝ

I am uneasy, already grading the new household. I plan the final exam.

Would Chardae and Elizabeth like a second-graders-only expedition? They would. With their parents' blessing, we schedule a "farewell to Savta" shopping/movie adventure.

Chardae and Elizabeth choose the movie, Eileen maps our route, and we are off in one of the family cars.

My tilt light blinks when Chardae asks if we can stop to buy candy. I do not think we need candy and say so. "I brought my own money," she assures me. Reluctantly, I pull into the closest shopping center. All three of us troop into the Rite Aid. Chardae selects Tootsie Rolls and Reese's peanut butter cups, pays for them, and stashes the bag in her purse. Her grade: rude, nutritionally bankrupt, and selfish.

We head for Borders to choose their gifts: Elizabeth has already decided on a book, which she locates posthaste and drops into a lounge chair to read.

Chardae wanders the stacks. I tag along, suggesting books she might like, all of which she spurns. My hand is poised over *Winnie the Pooh* when an excited Chardae whirls up the aisle, holding a bubble-wrapped Barbie's Pink Three-Story Dream Townhouse.

"Don't you already have three Barbie dolls at home?" I ask, appalled that Borders sells such merchandise.

"Is it too much?" she asks, plaintively.

"No, I don't care if you spend $23, but would you really use another Barbie accessory?" Was she trying to top Elizabeth $12 book? I picture the 45 plastic pieces of Barbie's Dream Townhouse strewn over the family room floor.

With Chardae's deflated look, any remaining lightheartedness fades. We slog to a truce over another non-book choice, and head for the movie. Our film is playing right across from Borders. I steer across the busy intersection, park the car, and buy the tickets.

As I struggle to hold onto the tickets, get the change into my billfold and shove it into my purse, the girls rush ahead and line up at the multiplex snack bar—enemy territory. A grandmother who pays rip-off prices for bad food at movies aids the forces of consumerism-greed-mammon.

When our turn comes, Chardae eyes the giant M&M's beneath the glass counter.

"Let's share some popcorn," I say, a concession to the special occasion.

The attendant interjects a sprightly "We have a special today: a jumbo popcorn and three super-size cokes for $20, a savings of ..."

I cut him off at the knees.

"I am not buying Coca-Cola." I pause, then realize the two seven-year-olds standing on either side of me may be thirsty. "Do you have bottled water?"

An uncomfortable silence.

"Well, maybe you two could share a Coke," I surrender weakly.

Elizabeth flips her hair back. "We don't need anything to drink," she says. I see Miser Grandma is embarrassing her.

Chardae's disapproving glare bores into my side.

"Good." I hand over a $20 bill. "Just a jumbo popcorn, please."

Did we see *James and the Giant Peach*? Maybe. I was stewing too much to notice—for a movie junkie like me, a sign of serious malfunction.

ॐ

I fly back to Indiana the next day, fuming, ticking off Ben's new family's shortcomings. Ben and Eileen failed my litmus test, constructed with my Purdue master's in child development and my self-anointed Priestess in Parenting. Their child rearing bordered on Neanderthal. Spanking children is a throwback to the Victorian age. Hitler's evil bent was fueled by his parents' beatings.

Was this part of their evangelical Christian beliefs? I accept this new religious affiliation, but if it includes child abuse like spanking, or child neglect—exiling the children to a distant part of the house—well. And Chardae, that little dictator, can't they see how she is crushing Elizabeth?

I hold this doctrine with fundamentalist certainty, and promulgate it to everyone who will listen.

ॐ

The Tacoma recollection shocks me and sends me reeling with self-discovery. I was a snob. Passed judgment on everything I saw. Insisted on the new children being Proper Grandchildren with cultural correctness and tastes only for nutritious food. No allowance made for the difficulty of fitting two families together. No compassion for my son or his wife. No human warmth or contact with these two young girls, struggling to adjust to a new man in the house and a new role for their mother. I was a textbook example of "devaluing people based largely on a narrow focus." I missed my chance to bring two lovely young girls into the Savta fold. They have forgiven me; I have tried to make amends, but I mourn for an opportunity that will never come again.

48

Winter Bloom

The moving finger writes, and having writ, moves on.
Nor all thy piety nor wit, can call it back to cancel half
a line
Nor all thy tears wash out a word of it.

—The Rubáiyát of Omar Khayyám

It is not until Meta's diary, Tom's email and Al-anon's fifth
step, a "searching and fearless moral inventory," that the truth
drilled through my protective enamel to the decay around the
nerve. What my role lacked, my children were trying to tell
me, was a present, living, breathing woman in the part. I
rushed through my previous life like an understudy waiting for
my chance to go onstage. Life was in the future. No wonder I
could not connect to husband or children; the Real Patricia
had yet to stand up. I needed to dive into the pool and drown
that surface imposter to be born again as a living, pulsing
human.

But that was not the end. Sunport was not the end. Nor
Meta's Diary. Nor Tom's Bomb. Nor my Tacoma
misadventure.

As Aunt Louise used to say when I bemoaned a missed opportunity, "Honey, you ain't dead yet!"

ɺ⚫

This memoir is not another fearless inventory, a chance to confess my sins and get absolution from sympathetic readers. What moved me to write is what happened next: How did I dig myself out of that hole?

Mine was the world of the Veiled Prophet, with his message that women and dark skins must stay in their place. I felt the conflict between my admiration for my father and empathy for my mother who shared my restrictions as a woman. I absorbed the code of speak no evil, whether of ghostly grandfathers or wife beatings; married to save my husband from his mean mother and chilling childhood; took my Happy Homemaker's role so seriously I could be unnerved by a couple of cronies at Shorty's diner or my mother-in-law's command-performance lunch. I became a Cookie-Baking Automaton rather than a Warm-Lap Mom.

The last chapter in Thomas Moore's re-creation of the Narcissus myth is worth telling, the scene where Narcissus "realizes that absorption in oneself that is soulless and loveless is deeply unsatisfying, and looks elsewhere for gratification." My elsewhere is my soulful and loving Self, the Patricia that can form genuine emotional connections.

Which is why I embrace the peers who warmed my soul from the Famous Barr playroom through Green Meadows and San Miguel, and why I treasure the intellectual camaraderie that began in Mary Magdalene kindergarten, expanded with the University of Chicago and Purdue grad school and enriches me now at PEN forums, San Miguel literary conferences and classes on Jewish mysticism.

Agnes taught me with a single look that being a Good Wife is not a full-time assignment. From my mother I learned that alcoholism, like most problems, would not go away because I ignored it.

Deep experiences lifted my gaze above my navel to the small "c" catholic world view of Immaculate Conception, the warmth of buddies like Donna and Ruthanna who demanded no performance in exchange for their friendship, the insights from meditation, both practical (watch Purdue basketball with your mother) and ethereal (undeniable connection with God).

I am no longer the Hard-Hearted Hannah that walked away from my husband at Sunport, nor yet the gorgeous, soft blossom I am dying to become. Death is 30 years closer than it was the afternoon I glimpsed my cold corpse reflected in my father's eyes. Closer, but kindlier than on that dark day in 1983. My body is long past its springtime, but I greet spring with a warmer heart.

Opening, receiving, listening, showing vulnerability—all still challenge me. There are moments when Super Pat rides again. I am sure if C uses the exercise I demonstrate, her back pain will disappear, and if E responds to her boyfriend's latest peccadillo as I counsel, their relationship will blossom.

Then I catch my breath and see myself bouncing on The Cat's ball:

> The Pat in the Hat
>
> Look at me, Look at me, Look at me now!
>
> I can scramble the eggs while I grind coffee beans;
>
> I can grind coffee beans while I scan PBS;
>
> I can scan PBS while I write my next speech;
>
> I can write the League speech while I bake birthday cakes;
>
> I can bake birthday cakes while I calm the mad spouse;
>
> I can calm the mad spouse while I soothe the sick kid;
>
> I can do all these tricks while I bounce on the ball.
>
> It is fun to have fun but you have to know how.
>
> That is what The Pat said, then she fell on her head.

I stop after the coffee beans. Usually.

The family and friends who walked with me in my story gained humanity in my eyes as I mined the past. I know them better now. A warmer mantle extends over the whole cast, including Grandma Herzog, the pseudo-villain of the piece. I have arrived where the villain/hero dichotomy melds into

Oneness with all its warts and beauty marks and drones and shooting stars.

As a searcher on the congenial path of Judaism, I find nourishment in meditation, 12-step work, the teachings of the Buddha and the priceless gift of the Sabbath.

While I have said little about my physical activity in this memoir, I am convinced keeping active has contributed to my spiritual growth. My early morning aerobics, dancing, yoga, and weight training have moved me towards emotional as well as physical health, *por lo menos* (at the least). I am now addicted; a few days without my regular exercise routine and I am achy and grouchy.

As the spring of 2014 flows into summer, I count the Omer, the 50 days between Passover and Shavuot. Every day I meditate and chant on a daily theme from Rabbi Yonassan Gershom, *49 Gates of Light: Kabbalistic Meditations for Counting the Omer.*

Yesterday, the 11th day of the Omer, a quote from Pirkei Avot, 2:18 electrified me:

> If you could change the world, what would you do? Today, take one step toward putting your vision into

action, keeping in mind that it is not for you to complete the work, but neither are you free to quit.

I will take my first step when I know what it is, and I will not quit.

ॐ

For all my blessings, lessons learned, and the challenges that birthed the learning, I give thanks. *Baruch HaShem, Allah Akbar, namaste*, and gracias a Jesús, hijo de la Virgen de Guadalupe.

Acknowledgments

During its 15 years in progress, this book was made possible by the advice, handholding, editing and support of Meta Hirschl, Lucina Kathmann, Mary Pennington, Colleen Runge, Elizabeth Starčević, Linda Work, and Sandra Young; members of the Women's Creative Writing Group, Kristin Matz, Kathy Mayer, Nancy Patchen and Nancy Triplett; my teachers Eva Hunter and Patricia Henley; meticulous editor Jane Onstott; my amazingly intuitive writing coach, Judyth Hill; and all whose friendship and insights nudged me along. Thank you!

The wisdom of countless meditation teachers, spiritual writers, retreat leaders and 12-step comrades helped warm my heart, as did family and friends who stayed with me through my icier moments.

Muchísimas gracias a todos.

Made in the USA
Charleston, SC
31 August 2014